queersexlife

# queer
# sex
# life

*Autobiographical Notes*

*on Sexuality, Gender and*

*Identity*

TERRY GOLDIE

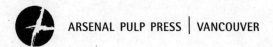 ARSENAL PULP PRESS | VANCOUVER

queersexlife
Copyright © 2008 by Terry Goldie

ARSENAL PULP PRESS
Suite 200, 341 Water Street
Vancouver, BC
Canada  V6B 1B8
*arsenalpulp.com*

The publisher gratefully acknowledges the support of the Canada Council for the
Arts and the British Columbia Arts Council for its publishing program, and the
Government of Canada through the Book Publishing Industry Development Program
and the Government of British Columbia through the Book Publishing Tax Credit
Program for its publishing activities.

Book design by Shyla Seller
Editing by Robert Ballantyne and Brian Lam
Cover photograph: Joe Ovelman—"Snow Queen (7)" copyright Joe Ovelman,
courtesy Conner Contemporary Art, Washington, DC.

Printed and bound in Canada

Library and Archives Canada Cataloguing in Publication:

Goldie, Terry
    Queersexlife : autobiographical notes on sexuality, gender & identity / Terry
Goldie.

Includes bibliographical references and index.
ISBN 978-1-55152-236-4

    1. Homosexuality.  2. Gender identity.  3. Gays—Identity.  4. Sex (Psychology).
5. Goldie, Terry.  6. Gays—Canada—Biography.  I. Title.

HQ75.8.G65A3 2008              306.76'6              C2008-901856-7

I had thought of dedicating this to my various lovers, but then I thought that some might not appreciate it. So instead I dedicate it to someone who has never been a lover but always a friend—and a wonderful colleague: Michael Hurley.

# Contents

## Acknowledgments

Parts of "Dragging Feminism?" appeared in "Dragging Out the Queen," *Revealing Male Bodies*, edited by Nancy Tuana et al (Indiana: Indiana University Press, 2002), 125-145.

Thanks to Robert Ballantyne, always a committed and supportive editor; to Brian Lam for many forms of assistance, not least with my prose; to David Coodin for checking the quotations; to Stephanie Hart and Jeff Lloyd for library searches; to Beatrix Thomasi and Pamela Lewis for the drag photographs, and to Deanne Williams, first reader of the manuscript.

And to skinny white girl. Always to skinny white girl.

# Introduction

I don't think I'm trying to create a neologism with the title of this book, but rather a melding of three words to represent how those things have jammed together in my experience. The last two parts do not need much explanation: this is my view of sex from the vantage point of my life, my life according to its sexual experience. On the other hand, I think "queer" needs some elucidation.

Gentle reader, you might be sick of explanations of the term "queer." While almost anyone who is a part of the panoply of sexual diversities will be happy that sexual freedom has advanced considerably in the last forty years, some of us might be less pleased that "queer" has developed with it, along with endless discussions of its meaning. Like participants in other twentieth-century liberation movements, homosexual activists embraced labels that had previously been used to attack them, from the Radical Faeries to Dykes on Bikes; the most ubiquitous example today is "queer." Two prominent contemporary usages by the homosexual community are in "Queer Nation," the sexual radical in opposition to social norms, and in queer theory, an intellectual position that acclaims the ultimate instability of all received assumptions about gender and sexuality. As I note in the chapter on bisexuality, Jonathan Dollimore worries that this can turn into "facile postmodernism."[1] (14)

A quick perusal of the Oxford English Dictionary suggests the base of the word. The earliest example comes from 1508: "Heir cumis our awin queir Clerk." In other words, "queer" as strange or slightly off. Then from 1561, "A Quire bird is one that came lately out of prison." 1740 provides "Instead of returning the good Guinea again, they used to give a Queer One."[2] The earliest usage that specifies a homosexual meaning is from 1922, noted as coming from the delightfully named The Practical Value of Scientific Study of Juvenile Delinquents (Children's Bureau, US Depart-

---

1. For more extended discussions of the term "queer," look at Chapters Five and Nine:
2. The 1508 reference is from William Dunbar, The flyting of Dunbar and Kennedie; 1561, from John Awdelay, The fraternitye of vacabondes; and 1740, from Ordinary of Newgate, his Account III 15/1.

ment of Labor): "A young man, easily ascertainable to be unusually fine in other characteristics, is probably 'queer' in sex tendency."

I am uncomfortable applying to myself the recent meanings of queer. I don't consider myself in opposition to society, but rather I am afraid that I am in most ways insufferably bourgeois. On the other hand, perhaps my identity in some ways flirts with the "facile postmodern." I don't like this thought, but whenever I assert an identity I always think of it as a relative category rather than an absolute. Thus I am "gay" not because this is the essence of my being, but because I view myself as more homosexual than those who are not "gay." On the other hand, the earlier dictionary meanings of "queer" strike me as perfectly suitable to who I think I am. I know that I have always been considered by others to be a rather different person, some kind of "queir Clerk." While I have luckily never been imprisoned, various people have suggested that I have come from some alien place and thus am a "Quire bird." Both gay and straight have suggested that I am somehow counterfeit, deceiving the world in claiming to be part of either group. I cherish the day when two women asserted, hours apart, that "You have always looked like a fag," and "You aren't really gay, you know." Neither seemed to think I was the "good Guinea," although the latter believed I was not the good Guinea because I claimed not to be the good Guinea. And as I note below, my greatest interest in this book is my own "sex tendency."

This of course raises the question of why should my "greatest interest" be of interest to you? The answer is primarily to provide a specific focus to the discussion. K.M. Colby says of the autobiographical 'I':

> 'I' can thus refer to an observed or an observer. (Naturally, an observer cannot observe itself but must be taken for granted by transcendental argument.) Introspection of what is referred to as 'I' is a process of retrospection, i.e., inspection of something which has already been produced by a preceding cycle of mental activity. It can be reacted to in the next cycle like any other content of awareness.
> (Stoller 233)

Colby's argument is a bit opaque, primarily because the process is as well. The observer cannot be the observed. Thus the "transcendental argument" is that someone must be doing the observing in order for observation to happen, but in order to avoid a perpetual *mise en abîme*, the observer must be "taken for granted." Even if there is a chain of observers, the final one must be accepted without dissection. If the observer and the observed are the same person then the separation is accomplished by retrospection. The observer and the observed are not "the same" because the observer observes who the observed was in the past, although that past might be seconds before. My argument here is that even if this is the case, retrospection approximates combining the observed and the observer, in a fashion particularly suitable when the observer is attempting an analysis of the sexual experiences of the observed.

As in that reference to Colby, much of this book is an evaluation and assessment of the analyses of others. Partly this is a continuation of the usual academic process; this book is a "review of the literature." Thus while the reason for the book and the commentary that shapes it are the product of my experiences, the substance, what I am tempted to call the "meat" of the book, is the work of scholars from a variety of fields, first and foremost sexology but also psychology, sociology, anthropology, medicine, history, geography, philosophy, and other disciplines. My process is one that I have found useful throughout my life, both professionally and personally. I consider a problem and then look for some text that reflects on something similar. Then I respond to that reflection and attempt to come up with at least partially enlightening conclusions.

In many cases I have found insights from unlikely sources. Thus Bruno Latour, in *Pandora's Hope: Essays on the Reality of Science Studies*, states that "The actor does not yet have an essence. It is defined only as a list of effects—or performances—in a laboratory. Only later does one deduce from these performances a competence, that is, a substance that explains why the actor behaves as it does." (308) In other words, the actor is only a series of actions until the observer sums up these actions with explanations that create a person who has done these actions. I find this a compelling summary of my own process of becoming. I have seen actions, my actions, over the years, and my continuing introspection or, according to Colby, retrospection, has led to the conclusions that I present in this study. This is Latour's "substance."

The autobiography, especially the coming out story, is the generic gay narrative. A recent book, *First Person Queer: Who we are (so far)*, presents no less than forty brief examples (Labonté and Schimel). But as the subtitle of the present volume suggests, this is not an "autobiography" but rather "autobiographical notes." I am under no delusion that my life is sufficiently unusual to justify an autobiography, although I cannot deny that I have at times been a figure of note. In his memoir, *Dr. Delicious*, Robert Lecker states, "if only I had dressed more like Terry Goldie, a CanLit specialist who routinely showed up at conferences wearing thong-like bikini briefs and sandals" (166). The sandals are true, but the "bikini briefs" are not. Still, I seem to have been sufficiently remarkable to Dr. Lecker to be part of his autobiographical lament.

More to the point of the present book, while I make no claims to be a sartorial model, even in the chapter on drag, I will claim that my perspective on sexual matters might be of interest because of the various ways it is framed, as a public statement of certain sexual points of view. Ruth Behar encapsulates her ideal anthropologist in an observer who is emotionally marked: *The Vulnerable Observer*. She agrees that autobiography in academic work must be justified: "Skeptics might reasonably ask: At a moment when the autobiographical voice is so highly commodified—most visibly in the talk shows of Oprah and Geraldo Rivera—shouldn't scholars write against the grain of this personalizing of culture, rather than reproduce it?" (25) Her answer is that the attempt to share the inside of the self observing enhances rather than detracts from scholarship.

Frank Browning, in *A Queer Geography: Journeys Toward a Sexual Self*, sees a particular value in the perspective employed by gay journalists: "By observing (and coming out is a public self-observance) the queerness of ourselves, we inevitably change how and what we observe in the world as well." (140) Jerome Bruner, in his essay "The Autobiographical

Process," suggests why "public self-observance" is important in autobiography:

> ... one's reflections on both one's self and one's world
> cannot be one's own alone: you and your version
> of your world must be public, recognizable enough
> to be negotiable in the 'conversation of lives.' So
> emerges the classic criterion of what constitutes 'good'
> autobiography—that it be communicable through its
> representativeness." (43)

That representativeness is important if the text is to be "negotiable," but still more if it is to be named, to be "recognizable" as fitting a certain niche, in this case that of "gay." Browning justifies why Michel Foucault avoided such naming:

> His mistrust of calling himself 'gay,' I think, was not fear
> of personal embarrassment or lost prestige, but that by
> adopting a category of sexual identification, he would have
> sacrificed his own ruthless quest for knowledge for the
> security of a new regime of normalcy. To be normal was
> to be dead. (161)

I hesitate to disagree with any praise of Foucault, especially of his "quest for knowledge." Like thousands of others, the present book would not exist if not for how Foucault has changed writing and thinking. However, I certainly hope Foucault's avoidance of the label had a more reasonable impetus than some pseudo-radical assumption that "to be normal was to be dead." Presumably every aspect of Foucault's life was sufficiently documented—or at least the object of enough flagrant rumours—that he was in little danger of being considered "normal." In any case, many of the Foucauldian concepts, most particularly his version of genealogy, are about reconfiguring the norm in order to understand it a different way. My suspicion is that rather than avoiding the normal, Foucault was avoiding exactly the representativeness that Browning praises above. To be "gay" is a complex life—as is any other—but for most people, both gay and straight, those complexities are contained within a package conceived a certain way by each observer. I'm sure that he found that just being labeled "Foucault" was insufficiently expansive, much less to accept being trapped within the category of "gay."

Another thinker who is no doubt too absent by name in this book but ever present in thought is Sigmund Freud. While Freud is constantly asserted to be sexist and often represented as homophobic, his ideas on sex permeate anything written on the subject. One of my students once gave an anti-Freud presentation in which she made a number of *ad hominem* statements about Freud's biography in order to buttress her dismissal of his ideas. When I pointed out to her that all of her interpretations were based on theories created by psychoanalysis, she thought I was being unfair. If you can't attack Freud without being Freudian, what hope is there? As so many have observed, it is easy to dismiss Freud's claims of scientific rigour and objectivity, but almost impossible to escape the grasp his ideas have over every concept we have on sexual psychology, very much including our views of homosexuality.

To assess the complexities of "the homosexual" with precise scientific objectivity is beyond me, and I think probably beyond anyone. Throughout this study there are references to many who have tried, with various degrees of success. Someone who has been for me an inspiration, a trial, and even at times a source of laughter is the late John Money. He has come to fascinate me sufficiently that I am now beginning a book devoted to his work, its amazing successes and thundering—even cataclysmic—failures, all in pursuit of *scientia sexualis*. He has become a prime example of blind scientism in sexology. Thus his attempt to depict clear descriptions in *Gay, Straight and In-Between: The Sexology of Erotic Orientation* is arguably even more plagued than others:

> Many social science writers and sex therapists differentiate
> object choice, gender identity, and gender role. This
> enables them to say, for example, that a man is masculine
> in his gender identity and gender role, but homosexual
> in orientation and object choice. The alternative is to say

> he has a masculine G-I/R [Gender Identity/Role] except
> for the sexuoerotic imagery and ideation of his romantic
> life, love life, and sex life in dreams and fantasies, and
> in their translation into actual practices (and vice versa
> for a lesbian). This alternative formulation circumvents
> the scientific fallacy inherent in the term object choice,
> namely that heterosexuality and homosexuality have their
> origin in voluntary choice and are therefore already fully
> explained by fiat, without the superfluous addition of
> more research—which constitutes the fallacy of scientific
> nihilism. (85)

One need not be a scientific nihilist to decide this is not a satisfactory explanation.

Most of these theorists are seeking explanations that are not just satisfactory but general, applicable to a category such as "gay" or "homosexuality." As the title suggests, Edward Stein's *The Mismeasure of Desire: The Science, Theory, and Ethics of Sexual Orientation* is less convinced than Money that scientific positivism can provide answers, but that does not mean I find easy agreement with his assessments: "The general point is that just because there are different social structures surrounding some human phenomenon in the past and the present does not necessarily mean that the two phenomena are different. Consider the example of pregnancy." (96) I am sure there are deep reasons why pregnancy is so often the example of full truth but perhaps it is not the best analogy for male homosexuality. If homosexuality means only some sort of sexual activity between males then the term might apply in different spaces at different times, but it always means more. Two manifestations may be argued to be the same "phenomena," although this is not because the manifestations are the same but because the observer views them as such. This is only one reason why the present study seldom posits general answers about identity, but rather examines actions and suggests the implications of those actions.

The autobiographical elements of this study are admittedly navel-gazing—or perhaps self-microscopy. I have chosen to act in certain ways and I am interested in attempting to discover why I have so acted. I have made choices and wish to understand those choices. Thus one of the most basic truisms about sexual orientation seems to me worth questioning. This is one "fact" that Stein presents as a given: "Sexual orientations are *immutable*, that is, beyond a certain point in a person's development, a person's sexual orientation cannot be changed. Immutability is a distinct claim from determinism." (291) In other words, while Stein is cynical about the various hypotheses as to what determines sexual orientation, he has no doubt it is an unchanging truth of personhood. The momentary mutations in this immutability, that one drunken night when a heterosexual acted homosexually or a homosexual heterosexually, can be fully incorporated merely by stretching the boundaries of bisexuality. Of course, sufficient stretching of bisexuality would erase sexual orientation and make its immutability a moot point. Instead, in reflecting on my own life I see much more that is mutable. There are sexual opportunities that I would never pursue, many others that I have not pursued, and some I have pursued and found unsuitable. I have yet to see any of these, however, as so foreordained by something called "sexual orientation" as to be outside the space of mutability. My sexual world has been a mutable sphere, and parts of this book explore this mutability.

Mutability and contradiction. One of the first readers of this manuscript stated that the most evident theme is contradiction of what one might assume to be the case. This can be seen in each chapter. Thus the homosexual child is not sexual, the penis belongs to the other not the self, there is no bisexual, anal sex is for the self not the other, the dinge queen is not a racist, the drag queen is emphatically a male, stranger sex is a pursuit of love, and coming out of the closet is never a full truth. Even the chapter on *The Crying Game* produces the ultimate object as subject. I am not making a claim such as Walt Whitman's:

You say I contradict myself. So I contradict myself

I am large. I contain multitudes. ("Song of Myself")

I do not have the grandeur to contain contradictions. Rather my experience has been that contradictions are the primary truth of my sexuality. Thus to explore the complexity of one "gay" experience is often to explore the elements that seem hardly "gay" at all.

Gary Dowsett's *Practicing Desire: Homosexual Sex in the Era of AIDS*, a sociological study of a number of Australian men, offers the following assessment of one of his cases:

> Harriet exemplifies the active construction of the self
> within a discursive framing of a homosexual desire.
> Yet the frame is very pliable and without its contents
> it threatens to collapse. To some extent being gay, that
> is, clarifying a sexual identity, is a discursive practice
> providing sufficient direction to enable men to cluster
> with like others; it is a collective resolution of individual
> desire. It becomes the vantage point from which the rest
> are assessed. But Harriet's example calls for a different
> conceptualization of sexual identity. To stretch the concept
> to include a preoperative transsexual prostitute, a dragon
> [drag queen], a gay man with a sluttish sexual appetite,
> these experiences of transgressive male sexual interests
> renders the term unwieldy. The term 'sexual subjectivity'
> offers a larger conceptual space to encompass the
> ingredients Harriet illustrated. (107-108)

Thus, like Harriet, all of Dowsett's cases, including those who consider themselves "gay," demonstrate the impossibility of "gay" as a sexological description. As Dowsett asserts:

> Being gay emerges in these case studies as a different
> kind of struggle, at one level more cultural than personal,
> more social than sexual, related to an ongoing reordering
> and resurfacing within larger discursive frameworks and
> in practices; it is of an order different from that of the
> pursuit of homosexual sex itself. (142)

With the possible exception of the chapter on the closet, and even including the chapter on *The Crying Game*, this book is less about "being gay" than about the meaning of that pursuit.

In *A Critique of Postcolonial Reason*, Gayatri Chakravorty Spivak reflects on her position as an "Indian." Many observers, including those who are Indian themselves, have seen her either negatively or positively as a representative—or anti-representative—of the expatriate Indian. She herself provides a more complex explanation for using Indian examples:

> I turn to Indian material because, in the absence of
> advanced disciplinary training, that accident of birth and
> education had provided me with a *sense* of the historical
> canvas, a hold on some of the pertinent languages that are
> useful tools for a *bricoleur*—especially when she is armed
> with the Marxist skepticism of 'concrete experience' as the
> final arbiter and with a critique of disciplinary formations.
> (209)

I can claim "advanced disciplinary training" in neither sex nor sexology. I share Spivak's doubts as to "concrete experience" as a final arbiter, although most gay autobiographies seem to assert just that. I consider this book to be the work of a *bricoleur*, and the various chapters, from penis worship to stranger sex, are reflections of the "pertinent languages" in which I have had conversations.

Spivak rejects the label either of herself as an expert Indian or of her experience or anecdotes as perfectly exemplary. In the same way, I cannot see myself as representing "gay" in a fashion that either suits most gay readers or even that will help non-gay readers understand what it means to be gay. Instead I explore a variety of experiences of sexuality from one perspective, my own. I am less interested in what it means to be "gay," "homosexual," or even "bisexual" than in my own role in various experiences, from coming out to anal sex. Browning states of young people: "More and more they ask of themselves and of their mates not 'who am I?' but 'How should I act?'" (221) Rather than exploring ethical issues, this book tries to answer the question: "How have I acted and what does that mean?"

To some extent I am responding to the attitude Calvin Thomas considers at the beginning of his book, *Male Matters: Masculinity, Anxiety, and the Male Body on the Line*:

> The issue, in other words, becomes not writing about
> the body but *writing itself as a bodily function*. Thus the book
> concerns an unease about the male body as a material
> site of linguistic production, a corporeal tension between
> (gendered) identity and (self-) representation. This
> tension, particularly as it is exacerbated by the visibility
> of writing, troubles the construction of normative,
> hegemonic masculinity; it disturbs what Kaja Silverman
> calls 'the dominant fiction'—the 'ideological belief
> [through which] a society's "reality" is constituted and
> sustained, and [through which] a subject lays claim to a
> normative identity' (*Male Subjectivity* 15). My argument is that
> males accede to the dominant fiction and identify with
> normative masculinity and its fictions of dominance by
> learning how to assuage this anxiety; the mechanisms of
> assuagement are ideologically embedded in cultural modes
> of representational containment that govern and restrict
> the visibility of male bodies and male bodily productions.
> (3)

This book refuses once again the "taken for granted," that "dominant fiction" of an unconsidered masculine point of view, a writing without a body. Instead, it emanates from a male body sexualized in different ways and examines how this non-normative masculinity works.

Jeffrey Weeks' *Sexuality and its Discontents: Meanings, Myths & Modern Sexualities* lurks behind much of this book. His comment on how to understand the body is particularly relevant: "the body can no longer be seen as a biological given which emits its own meaning. It must be understood instead as an ensemble of potentialities which are given meaning only in society." (122-123) Still more important to me is a later comment on how that meaning can be understood:

> We are left with the body and its potentialities for
> pleasure. This is a particularly ambiguous phrase which
> states an ambition without specifying its means of
> attainment. I intend to take it as a metaphor for the
> subjectivisation of erotic pleasure, for the willingness to
> explore possibilities which may run counter to received
> definitions but which nevertheless, in context, with full
> awareness of the needs and limits of the situation, can be
> affirmed. (245)

This book is an exploration of that subjectivisation of erotic pleasure, quite specifically in the chapter on anal sex, situationally in the chapter on stranger sex, potentially in the chapter on the homosexual child, and responsively in the chapter on coming out.

I constantly return to myself not as a being but as a doing. This book is less about "me" and more about the way I perceive what I have done, in the light of a variety of studies and analyses by sexologists, sociologists, psychologists, and various other scholars and commentators. My focus on personal actions and experiences is thus that slippery being of cultural studies, the subject position. Slavoj Žižek, in *The Sublime Object of Ideology*, describes Fichte's view of the subject:

> the subject 'posits', sublates-mediates, transforms the
> given positivity of objects: he transforms it into a
> manifestation of his own creativity; but this positing
> remains forever bound to its presuppositions—to the
> positively given objectivity upon which it performs its
> negative activity. (224-225)

While I cannot claim anything such as a general truth in my comments in that I am bound by my presuppositions, I would argue that there is a "given positivity of objects," in this case a number of experiences, which provides the material of this book. The objects are the justification, and the subject position is the explanation for how these objects are seen.

As all reading this will note, one of the chapters is not like the others. The chapter on *The Crying Game* was the genesis of this book. As a professor of English who has written a number of books on various texts, I was interested in a text-based study that used autobiography in an explicit fashion. When the opportunity arose to give a plenary lecture to scholars from various aspects of literary studies, it seemed a good occasion to try this out. Thus the *Crying Game* chapter is a reading of the film that uses my personal experience as a lens, as an analogy, at times as a homology. As a result of this process, I decided to do a book on sexuality, using an approximation of the same method.

In both cases, I was stimulated by what I saw as a significant absence in scholarly studies. In discussing the *Crying Game*, I explore the tendency for the critic to slip by the nuance of his or her own subject position. It seems easy to label yourself as "gay" or "lesbian" and assume this is sufficient explanation, but in my own experience as a reader, this is not enough. Michael King has written a brief biography of John Money, which concludes as follows:

> Inevitably, there was curiosity, in the United States and in New Zealand, about sexuality and lifestyle choices made by the man who had built a highly visible career studying and writing about the sexuality of others. Of that dimension of his own life, Money, who was briefly married in the early 1950s, had this to say:
>
>> "By trial and error, I discovered the unstressfulness of self-sufficiency in both living and working.... I have never worked in total isolation but always with assistants and colleagues. Nor have I lived sexually abstinent, but in a give-and-take of sexual visitations and friendly companionships with compatible partners, some women, some men, some briefly, some with continuity ending only in death." (43-44)

This brief quotation seems to be the only explanation in print of his own sexuality, from a man who has published thousands of pages on the sexuality of other people. I don't believe it is only my prurient curiosity that wants to know more about the experience of the observer and analyst.

While many of the comments are brief, I appreciate the various times that Spivak has used her situation and experiences in order to elucidate the position from which she writes. When, in *The Critique*, she refers to herself as a "postcolonial informant," I have a strong sense of how that space is shaped. I am still more impressed with the extensive use of autobiographical fragments by Eve Kosofsky Sedgwick. Her "White Glasses," on how she learned to read as a gay man, continues to be an inspiration for me, as do her various examinations of what it means to be a "fat woman." To my knowledge, there are few books in which a theorist has explored his own sexual subject positions this way. The prime example is probably Patrick Califia, but the one who has always appealed most to me is Samuel Delaney. While his *Times Square Red, Times Square Blue* uses a very different methodology than I do, his fearless practice is always a model for me.

The more common approach is that presented by theorists such as Judith Butler. In *Excitable Speech: A Politics of the Performative*, Judith Butler refers to the importance of "the injurious word ... that not only names a social subject, but constructs that subject in the naming, and constructs that subject through a violating interpellation." (49) But what is the word that has constructed her as a subject? Is it just "lesbian," or is it something else? Could it be something about her sexual practice? I have often noted that for me the equivalent to Fredric Jameson's "always historicize" has been "always homosexualize." In other words, I tend to reconfigure each observation, each thought, according to homosexuality. As I reflected on this process, however, I realized that it is seldom so simple. As well, I often "bisexualize," I sometimes "de-closetize," and there are even times, times that seem far removed from the topic, that I "penis-observize."

While I usually find the theories of Gilles Deleuze to be too free-floating to be useful, his analysis of "Bergson's Conception of Difference" includes an assessment of the subject that seems particularly appropriate to the present study:

> It is tendencies that are dually opposed to each other
> [s'opposent deux à deux], that differ in nature. It is the tendency
> that is the subject. A being [être] is not the subject but the
> expression of the tendency, and furthermore, a being
> is only the expression of a tendency in so far as this is
> contrasted with another tendency. It is in this way that
> intuition presents itself as a method of difference or
> division: that of dividing the mixture into two tendencies.
> This method is something other than a spatial analysis,
> more than a description of experience and less (in
> appearance) than a transcendental analysis. It certainly
> raises itself to the conditions of the given, but these
> conditions are tendency-subjects, they are themselves
> given in a certain way, they are lived. Moreover, they are
> at the same time the pure and the lived, the living and the
> lived, the absolute and the lived. (46)

Thus, the following chapters describe the lived not as a transcendental self, but as the experiences of just such a tendency-subject. Rather than emanations contained within the dominant normative depicted by Thomas, they are vectors, often ones that contradict each other.

There are various ways that I represent subject positions here that many may find shameful. This is not just the obvious, the homophobia of "God made Adam and Eve, not Adam and Steve" and such. It is also the shame in various gay cultures associated with bisexuality, with being anal passive, with stranger sex. George Chauncey notes that in the 1930s the criminalizing of homosexuality was specifically associated with shame:

> Numerous articles warned that in breaking with

social convention to the extent necessary to engage in
homosexual behavior, a man had demonstrated the refusal
to adjust to social norms that was the hallmark of the
psychopath, and he could easily degenerate further. (359)

Thus, another part of the agenda here is to use self-revelation of aspects
of sexuality traditionally hidden as shameful. This is one more area in
which that term "queer" fits as a title, in its embrace of the pejorative.
This book provides an insider's view of topics rarely explored in academic
studies and, when explored, are usually without any acknowledgment
of inside knowledge. Yet this is not to suggest that "shame" is in some
sense a motivation. Rosamund Dalziell, in *Shameful Autobiographies: Shame in
Contemporary Australian Autobiographies and Culture*, provides this assessment:

When the process of confronting shame and loss and of
reviewing a life is represented in a text intended for the
gaze of a benign reader, the autobiographer's narrating
self is no longer isolated, having aligned him/herself
with the other in regarding the shamed and abandoned
narrated self. (263)

If I were writing an actual autobiography, this could be an interpretation.
I would be writing from the couch, an analysand providing a narrative
of shame as I storytell my way to psychic health. However, not only am
I not writing an autobiography, I actually have not felt this shame from
which I must recover. I have known that I must hide aspects of my life
from parents, other relatives, even from partners; this has not been from
fear of shame but rather from anxiety at how their assumption of shame
might make them treat me. At the age of fifty-seven I feel sufficiently
immune from such repercussions that I can allow my shamelessness to
be used in this exploration.

In this case, "shamelessness" is all about sexual desire. In *The Emergence of Sexuality: Historical Epistemology and the Formation of Concepts*, Arnold Davidson states:

Although Foucault is not everywhere consistent in his

terminology, I would claim that we should draw the
conclusion from his discussions, here [History of Sex vol. 1]
and elsewhere, that while *ars erotica* is organized around the
framework of body-pleasure-intensification, *scientia sexualis*
is organized around the axis of subject-desire-truth. It is as
if one could say that the imposition of true discourses on
the subject of sexuality leads to the centrality of a theory
of sexual desire, while the discourse of pleasure and the
search for its intensification are exterior to a science of
sexual desire. (211)

In my original concept of this book I had intended to title it "theoretical
thoughts," but I then decided that "theory" is too value-laden and open-
ended to be useful in this context. However, throughout this book
there lurk Foucauldian and Freudian theories of sexual desire. The list
of "Works Cited" is primarily composed of books on such theories.
Many of them make rather large claims towards "truth." In this case, I
claim no "truth" beyond my own subjectivity. However, the exploration
throughout follows that axis of subject-desire-truth. And the discourse
of pleasure is at least anterior to this "science."

Ah yes, pleasure. Is anyone having any fun here? I make a number
of references to Douglas Sadownick's *Sex Between Men: An Intimate History of
the Sex Lives of Gay Men Postwar to Present*. Anyone who has read it will know
that he and I do not have similar approaches to processing information.
Still, as one often finds when reading the text of someone "other," there
are many moments when his version of the truth is all too applicable to
my own practice: "Rational thinking, which some gay men have per-
fected as a tool for living almost second to sex, is no help when it comes
to understanding sex." (5) Ouch. This book is intentionally, incessantly
rational. I have taken what often seems one of the most irrational aspects
of human life, sexual desire, and applied to it as much reason as I can
bring to bear. My hope for this process is that more than forty years of
sexual desire and more than thirty years of being a professional intellectual will add up to some interesting analysis. To a certain extent I agree

once more with Sadownick:

> ... homosexual libido (one's vital energies) is the
> motivating energy that informs this book and informs, at
> least from my perspective, gay life. It is largely an error in
> judgment (and one from which I suffered) that sees sex as
> the defining principle of this libido. I would argue instead
> that sex is an effect of libido, or the extroverted end result
> of it. (12)

Still, queersexlife is not so much about "my life"—or even "gay life"—as
it is about one sex life. There are many aspects of my "libido," at least
in the Jungian sense, which have little to do with the present volume.
Thus, while most of my sexual activity has had nothing to do with
reproduction and my introspection of my retrospection can find no
drive to reproduce, I seem to have been born to be a parent. Much
of my life has been spent avoiding sexual activity that could interfere
with that parenting, including a three-year period of what I would
call "involuntary celibacy." Yet I lament none of this. And thus while
I formally dedicate this book to my colleague and friend Michael
Hurley, there is also some subliminal dedication to my children and
grandchildren, people who I presume will never read this and probably
have little interest in it, except as one more example of the strange things
their father—and grandfather—does with his time. Still, I include them
here as a recognition that, as Jung suggested, there are more instinctual
drives than sex.

## 2. Life (Re)Writing: Identifying or Identity Defying

> "Who knows the secrets of the human heart?"
> —*The Crying Game*

*Thirteen ways of looking at Dil and Me* [3]

### 1. Life re: writing

The opening credits of *The Crying Game* offer a long slow pan, viewing a small funfair through the darkness under a bridge. They remain my favourite part of the film. When I first saw it, I enjoyed the way it sets an atmosphere, but on repeated viewing I have come to love the perhaps less than subtle symbolism: "bridge," "carnival," "shadow." Another noteworthy element is the soundtrack, which includes Percy Sledge singing "When a Man Loves a Woman." Like the image, that title, and the lines of the song, offers many significant connections. One of the most important ones is that I bought the LP in 1966.

The first image here is my mother, in approximately 1918. The story I was told is that she is playing Peter Pan in a school production in Weyburn, Saskatchewan. But perhaps the central thing in her mind was that her father had just died in the trenches in France. Or perhaps not. I have no record of her thoughts then or even her thoughts about the photograph. I am performing the usual critical function of interpreting her text, in a way that exceeds that which the text might

---

3. Some of the associations in this article are obvious, some oblique. I have offered references for those that seem to belong under the usual heading of "works cited," but for the most part other intertexts are left without notes or reference. To begin, however, I offer Wallace Stevens's poem "Thirteen Ways of Looking at a Blackbird" as a remnant of my thirty years teaching English in universities.

verify. But why should you care about my mother or me? If we live in an era when the author is dead, why is the critic so much alive? In most forms of literary criticism in the twentieth century, the critic was visible only in his text, and only through his text. This text did an interesting double slippage: "Here, Shakespeare reveals...." While the author's persona somehow became his text, the critic was nowhere to be seen, a detached scientific dissector who simply stated what Shakespeare reveals. But in this analysis I—excuse me, sir, can I use 'I' in this essay?—am doing an attached experiment.

This is a modern issue: when Coleridge writes about his reading, there is no doubt he sees it to be important that his personal subjectivity controls his criticism. In the twentieth century, one more "rise of science" led literary analysis towards a veil of objectivity. Recent attempts to lift that veil reflect a turn in ethnography. Earlier the native informant was a barely named figure in the ethnographer's great journey of discovery. The informant was very different from the equivalent in literary criticism, the famous author taking up shelves in the library. With the ethnographer's acceptance of the ethical imperative to give the informant recognition came the need to admit the ethnographer's own subjectivity. Sometimes this produced studies in which the ostensible culture under examination enters only after pages of guilty gazing at the ethnographer's navel.

There are many recent examples of the literary academic similarly obsessed with umbilical remnants. One of the more famous—or infamous—is Jane Gallop. Leaving aside the parts that might be called gossip offered by Gallop, her supporters, and her opponents, her basic argument for her methodology is presented in the introduction to *Thinking Through the Body*:

> In collecting my essays for this retrospective volume,
> I found myself adding autobiographical bits, not only,
> I hope, because I tend toward exhibitionism but,
> more important, because at times I think through
> autobiography: that is to say, the chain of associations that

I am pursuing in my reading passes through things that
happened to me. (4)

My argument here is similar. My thoughts on The Crying Game have
developed through my autobiography, and my "chain of associations" in
this article connects to my experiences.

Literary criticism that in some way works through autobiography
disappoints in various ways. One is through references such as that to
"When a Man Loves a Woman." The critic brings up his or her version of
Proust's madeleine and then wanders off into literary criticism. Another
is detailed and irrelevant personal history, such as about my grandfather.
A third is the photograph of my mother as a psychological reference for
me: how a mother-obsessed reader operates. I am offering a reading by
a gay man, and mother-obsession certainly fits the stereotype. Given that
my mother here appears as a cross-dresser, there is all kinds of potential.
Perhaps cross-dressing is genetic and transmitted through the mother's
DNA rather than her nylons. But that can lead away from criticism to a
fourth version: the autobiographical criticism that says "What matters
here isn't my reading of the text but me, and I happen to mention the
text every now and then." I call this the Miss Piggy disappointment.

Still, as Jerome Bruner notes in his essay "The Autobiographical Process," the autobiography offers a particular asset for the reader in that it
provides an overt version of what Bruner calls "stance": "the autobiographer's posture toward the world, toward self, toward fate and the possible, and also toward interpretation itself." (45) Thus, while I recognize
the danger of Miss Piggy's obsession with "moi," I am here asserting
the importance of stance, that tried-and-true emblem of contemporary
discourse: the subject position. The assertion of this type of autobiography in literary criticism is usually quite brief and general. The most
common one is just "I am a woman." This likely explains or justifies a
feminist reading, but it could also support other readings that seem to
reflect the experience of being a woman. Yet contemporary feminists do
not want to conflate all women within some concept of Woman. They
differentiate through elements such as race and ethnicity, and at times

age or experiences such as having given birth or sexual orientation. As I noted in the introduction, however, many famous texts by gay and lesbian scholars do no more than identify their authors as homosexual. Does that define a subject position?

## 2. Identity Text?

The Crying Game was enormously successful, especially given that the producers first thought of it as a small independent film, something for the cinéaste, or at least the intellectual. One reason was the quite intricate plot, which I shall attempt to summarize as quickly as possible. Fergus, played by Stephen Rea, committed IRA volunteer, bonds with his hostage Jody, a black British soldier, performed by Forest Whitaker. A British attack results in Jody dying and Fergus on the run in England. Fergus looks up Jody's black girlfriend, Dil (Jaye Davidson), and they fall in love, but when Dil reveals she has a penis Fergus is not happy. Fergus's old IRA girlfriend, Jude (Miranda Richardson), comes looking for him for both personal and professional reasons. The pursuant IRA action leads to a few more deaths, most notably Jude's, shot by Dil. The film ends with Fergus serving time for the killing of Jude, and being visited regularly by Dil.

In spite of all these entanglements, however, the film became an international mainstream success. There could have been many reasons for this triumph, such as the harsh villainy of the IRA, the film noir portrayal by Richardson, or the very Channel Four representation of the London demi-monde in the Metro Bar, where Dil sings. Still, the explanation usually given is Jaye Davidson's performance as Dil. Most have agreed that it is extraordinarily difficult to perceive that Davidson is a male: all published commentary said that no one who had seen the film should reveal the secret. This would be akin to the naming of the murderer in an Agatha Christie novel. Post-film conversations seemed invariably devoted to "Did you know?" Gay males and heterosexual women appeared to have a particular investment in claiming to have seen Dil's hidden maleness very early in the film.

The film was generally divorced from the identity audiences one might have expected. The absence of an Irish audience might not be surprising given that the IRA are represented as blindly dogmatic, to the extent of seeming inhuman. Still, the black British characters might have drawn racial interest, and Dil herself would seem likely to draw the same devotees as other drag or transsexual movies, but this generally has not happened. Some have claimed it is a "gay movie," but I have never heard anyone who is gay make this claim. The identities in the film are cultures to be observed by mainstream outsiders rather than points of empathic entry for other insiders.

## 3. Who is Watching?

Laura Mulvey's essay "Visual Pleasure and Narrative Cinema" succinctly defines a central problem in film theory, the relationship between the viewer and the characters in a film. She considers only a Lacanian interpretation of heterosexual gender, but within that space she contributes an apt depiction of how cinema works, as in the following:

> There are three different looks associated with cinema:
> that of the camera as it records the pro-filmic event, that
> of the audience as it watches the final product, and that of
> the characters at each other within the screen illusion. (17)

Mulvey's primary interest is the second one, and particularly a gendered version: what is now well-known as the male gaze, in which the audience shares the space of the central male character and observes the female observed by this male.

Although Mulvey does not use the term, she is especially concerned with what has been called suture, the way the apparent relationship between camera and character controls the audience perception. Thus when look one, the camera, offers to look two, the audience, a view that clearly represents the male protagonist, a possible look three, then the suture is with that character. In traditional terms, the audience shares the position of subject with him, and thus views other characters as objects. One might expect a film to offer multiple empathies, as an Aristotelian might argue theatre does. In the theatre, an audience member can choose to watch a minor character on the edge of the stage, but in the cinema, the camera offers the audience something already seen: the viewer's perception is already implied.

Mulvey is not critiquing a text, like various early feminists who attacked the way male authors represented women in novels, but rather a process. Lacan claims that a woman telling a joke must take on a male persona for the joke to function. Mulvey presents the same situation for the female viewer of the classic film, in which she must share the eyes of the hero and use his eyes to view the female object of his gaze. As a number of recent analysts have suggested, this becomes still more complicated for the homosexual viewer of the heterosexual film. He or she might be the appropriate gender, but if the love object is wrong, how can he or she share the gaze?

Most of my personal responses are similar in form to those of any other "sophisticated" viewer. I travel on a continuum, between disdainful, distant analysis, and an enmeshed involvement. At the latter end, when my heart is racing and the tears flowing, can I claim to sit on my own shoulder and examine this emotional process? Once when lecturing on *The Crying Game*, I told my class that this is my favourite film but that I was "not a black British transwoman." As one of my students replied, "That's it: take away the easy answer." No. The easy answer is that I am a white male heterosexual IRA volunteer.

## 4. Fergus is Watching

When *The Crying Game* opens, Jody and Jude walk through the fun fair; at the edge of the scene lurks a man who will prove to be Fergus. As the camera follows them, it swings around to share Fergus's perspective, looking through the crowd and across the games. From this point, the camera focuses either on Fergus's eyes or through them: the defining moments show what Fergus sees. This can be quite emphatic, as when he gives us the images of Jody struggling to eat and talk through his hood—object without eyes—or being killed by the British troop transport.

The narrative is similarly tied to the protagonist. Fergus thinks he knows who he is, a dedicated IRA volunteer. His bonding with Jody disrupts this self-containment, however, and his escape to England is a typical journey of self-discovery. When he falls for Dil and, as Dil says, "gives her a look," we—male and female, gay and straight—join his eyes and his heart. Whether or not we in the audience are surprised that Dil is a biological male, we know that Fergus is amazed, and we must be amazed with him.

Then the film splits in a rather strange way. The central narrative continues with Fergus, especially as defined by the camera exemplified by the Metro bar. When Fergus first enters, it seems a normal neighbourhood pub. With each subsequent visit, however, it changes subtly. The second time, there are a few in the crowd of ambiguous sexual orientation. After Fergus has learned Dil's secret the bar becomes obvious, with at least one cross-dresser with a five-o'clock shadow. Then Jude returns, restarting the IRA plot.

On the edge, however, Dil provides an object lesson in subjectivity, the limit to Mulvey's claim as to the power of the gaze. In the bar she obsessively refers to herself in the third person, with Col the bartender always there to reinterpret. When the IRA plot requires Fergus to disguise Dil in Jody's old clothes, Dil seems to lose all sense of self. She doesn't become male or even androgynous, but rather, just an empty vessel. She is nothing to look at in both the figurative and the literal sense, and is reinvested only after she kills Jude. The plot suggests that she eliminates Jude to protect Fergus, but as she shoots, Dil recalls Jody: "She used those tits and that cute little arse to get him." Dil then asks Fergus, "Tell me what she wore."

In the opening scene Jude was garbed as a working-class slut with bits of body pouring out everywhere. On return she is a femme fatale, in a brilliant forties ensemble with a lovely little peplum jacket, her tits and arse contained yet very much to the fore. But the under-dressed

Dil realizes that Jude is playing a part, one that suits her biology. Her appearance suggests a perversion that has been called "homovestism." In this, unlike transvestism, the female seeks to replace a lack of power not through male dress but through an extraordinarily female guise, a version of power-dressing that over-emphasizes the figure. Many of Madonna's personas seem to follow this route: a radiation of such extreme femaleness that it produces a power equal to a male. Thus when I suggested that the murder "reinvests" Dil, I mean this quite specifically. She must erase this woman in woman's clothing before she can once more put on her proper women's clothing, as she does for the final scene when she visits Fergus in prison.

I suggest this is an object lesson because it is the object who provides the lesson. The narrative should be telling us that the subject, Fergus, must grow through experience until he understands. At one level this is what happens—it seems that what he must come to understand is that Dil is a woman. And not just that: he must learn that clothes make the woman, that surfaces are profound. Dil only breathes when she is living a cliché and apparently this is a valid source of breath. While the logical choice is to be Fergus, the subject, the eyes of the camera, Dil, the object that exists only through being seen by the camera, seems to have the greater understanding.

## 5. Identifying the Critic

The question of identity is temporal, in many ways. The first readers of Virginia Woolf's *A Room of One's Own* must have been impressed just to see a woman claiming the right to read as a woman. The same is true of the various early gay critics who were seen to be analyzing homosexual texts from the point of view of homosexuals. But just as "woman" became too broad, so now does homosexual. Yet at least at present, this is generally less often an addition that modifies an existing identity, as in the African-American woman, a change from the person who might have been satisfied within the category of African-American, than a shift from one position to another. Thus Leslie Feinberg moves from lesbian to the transgender category, which is now expanding in a number of directions.

One example is Jay Prosser's *Second Skins: The Body Narratives of Transsexuality*. He begins with an almost generic autobiographical move: "I spent the bulk of the first month of my transsexual transition from female to male teaching an undergraduate course on the contemporary American novel." (1) After the first few pages, however, Prosser moves into a distant "objective" analysis, but like all critics, with choices that seem subjective. He seldom mentions the difference between male to female and female to male narratives. Is this because there are no differences? Or because his transsexual position makes him think them insignificant? Or is it his position as a male? At the end, Prosser returns, very briefly, to the personal: "I blow my cover, and embody my narrative with this photograph." (234)

There are many reasons for a photograph. As Prosser suggests, it makes the body of the author a presence. Thus *Second Skins* has a male transsexual not just as a narrative at the beginning of the book, but also as a physical image at the end. Prosser is what he claims to be. The mind of the book emanates from this body in the photograph making the book even more autobiographical in the sense claimed by Sidonie Smith in "Identity's Body": "discursive capillaries circulate one's 'flesh and blood' through the textual body of self-writing, wrapped up as it is in the anatomy of origins and genealogies." (267) So much more when the flesh is visible. Still, the photograph provides no answers to my questions above. Instead it at once increases the autobiographical presence and blurs the borders of the autobiographical critic. Prosser has given few hints as to what attitudes make him see these narratives the way he does. The reader looks at this photograph and, as with all photographs, constructs resonant dimensions for the image and for the attitudes that this image is likely to have.

Thus the first photograph of me in drag (see page 168). I originally used it when I delivered "Dragging Out the Queen" as a colloquium paper. I refer to this simple drag shot here to resonate for the reader in association with Dil's various "glamour" appearances in the film. It is my equivalent of Prosser's photograph, although it does not make me into the same category as Dil. I am not black, not transsexual, not British, not a hairdresser. All such distinctions are potentially very important. I first saw the film with a boyfriend who is Maori. He observed that the only obviously racialized people in the film, Jody and Dil, were the primary sexual objects. He found that this completely prevented him from identification. A number of my transsexual friends have rejected Dil as in any sense representative of their experiences. Thus, my role here offers only one version of subjectivity that claims a positive relation to the film. Many other subjectivities do not.

I believe, however, that this photograph explains my role at least somewhat more than just a name, such as "gay" or even "cross-dresser." Visual images allow a different type of expansion than do verbal descriptions, especially those that are in essence denotative. The word "gay" is "of essence" in a way in which the photograph of a gay man is not, no matter how stereotypical the latter. I presume that the image of the critic writing this piece is both revealing and informative. Exactly how it informs is up to the subject position of the reader. I include it because I make the autobiographical claim of some kind of identification with Dil.

## 6. Love Photos

There are two central photographic elements in *The Crying Game*. As Fergus and Jody become close, they share various intimacies. Instead of being opposites—the British soldier and the IRA guard—they are the same: two low-ranking military men, caught in decisions made by their superiors and trying to assert their humanity in spite of their impotence. In such a gesture, Jody shows Fergus a photograph of his love, a beautiful young black woman. Fergus's comments are typical, that any man would find Dil desirable. Her photograph is woman as man's possession and woman as medium of exchange between men. It stimulates Fergus's desire, which briefly stimulates Jody's jealousy. The photograph assures that Dil is only object.

She might be opposed to a woman in action. The only one in the film is Jude and a large part of her action is transformation. After Jody was trapped by her blowzy tart, she reverts to an Irish stereotype in a rather messy Aran sweater, doing little except to supply tea and sandwiches. And then there is the femme fatale. In each guise she is very different from the Dil of the photograph, who radiates an innocent sensuality. Race could be a question, but as the soldierly bond between Fergus and Jody replaces race with comradeship, so the discussion of Dil's photograph shows that Fergus is able to appreciate perfect womanhood regardless of race.

The second photographic moment is at Dil's. Jody is now dead and exists only as photograph. While in Jody's wallet, Dil was a live woman reduced to object, an appropriate sexist categorization; now, on Dil's wall, Jody is a dead man elevated to hero, once more a gendered image. Even the contexts are gendered. The man's wallet keeps the currency of his manhood, whether a wife or children. Dil's various Jody pictures are tellingly arranged around her mirror, so she sees herself as object with Jody as object. The shrine of her favourite heartthrob maintains her girlishness on into womanhood. When Fergus first encounters the photo wall, he is rather taken aback. He came to see Dil at least partly out of guilt. Jody had wanted him to see Dil if he died, but now Fergus must face his role in the death of Dil's heroic man. And to add further insult, he is attracted to Jody's beautiful woman.

Photographs are a contradiction in film. They are in fact moving images, appearing as the film moves through the projector, but are also usually part of a narrative action, as Fergus holds Jody's wallet or peers at Dil's wall. And yet, as in the above, they are also a contradiction to the action of the story: the image of the absent girlfriend, the image of the dead boyfriend. When Fergus interacts with Jody, his subjectivity is always limited by the subjectivity of the other. The object between them is perceived for the viewer by Fergus, but his quizzical glance is always concerned as to how the object is perceived by Jody.

I am thus emphasizing two subjects, Jody and Fergus, with one object, Dil. There are of course many possible identities for them— soldiers, English, Irish, black, white—but in this case I am claiming that they are performing as heterosexual men. As I have noted elsewhere:

> It is a commonplace to recall Bishop Berkeley's observation
> that to exist is to be perceived. This has been extended
> in many ways, often in claims not about the object
> which is perceived but rather about the subject which is
> perceiving. Thus one possible interpretation is that I exist
> as a subject because I perceive and you exist as a subject
> because I perceive you perceiving. For the majority view
> of the minority culture, a third stage might be added:
> "You are you because I perceive you perceiving as you."
> Or for the minority individual viewing one of his or
> her cohort, it might be phrased: "You are one with me
> because I perceive you perceiving in my way." This is a
> secondary element of definitions of identity, such as race,
> after "facts" such as skin colour, genealogy, etc. It is more
> about the active subjectivity of the individual, whether
> that subjectivity is viewed from without or from within. It
> is more akin to the position of minority religion, defined
> by the individual's own claim to belong, an assertion of
> faith. (Goldie, *Pink Snow*, 4)

This is a constantly unstable interaction. The photograph here allows Fergus's subjectivity full flower, as the camera watches his eyes watching the objects, Dil or Jody. Still, as in my comment above, while Fergus is watching, who is the Fergus who is watching, what prompts his desire, and how is that desire connected to me as a viewer?

### 7. Identifying

Diana Fuss's very helpful book, *Identification Papers*, begins with quotations from Freud and Lacan, which depict identification as a method to reproduce a love object within to replace that missing without, much like *The Crying Game*'s photographs. Fuss takes it further:

> Identification is a process that keeps identity at a distance,
> that prevents identity from ever approximating the status
> of an ontological given, even as it makes possible the
> formation of an illusion of identity as immediate, secure,
> and totalizable. It is one of the central claims of this book
> that it is precisely identity that becomes problematic in
> and through the work of identification. (2)

This is an interesting comment on autobiographical criticism. In most examples it is the assurance of identity that compels the autobiography. If I don't believe in an ontological given called "African-American," why should I care if this is the identity of the critic? But Fuss's version of identification can create a circle that justifies the importance of such labels from a somewhat different direction. The assertion by the critic that she is African-American need not be a totalizable identity but can be an identification in much the same way Fuss describes. The critic yearns for the category of African-American and therefore constitutes it through desire as herself. This is perhaps not less satisfying than an unproblematized identity, but rather more.

The usual Marxist conundrum about representation plays nicely here. In a political context, it matters whether the speaker is representing as in speaking as the culture, or representing as in speaking for the culture. So the African-American critic speaks as the culture: this is how an African-American reads this text, and for the culture: this suggests the African-American position on this text. The last is an admittedly quibbling phrase. Henry Louis Gates' critique of Zora Neale Hurston is not the view of all African-Americans *ex cathedra*. But perhaps that identification can work both to justify and to explain. Thus Gates at once lacks and also inhabits this African-American identity as representation. The fluidity becomes still more extreme—and less defining—for categories such as the gay critic, but the operation is still as Fuss describes. Her system of identification is a productive narcissism and when the critic engages in identification while performing criticism, the text is caught within the process of desire.

The introduction to my book Pink Snow, from which I quoted above, attempts to go some distance to explain how I see the gay critic's relationship to a text or, in other words, my relationship to a text. In a more explicitly autobiographical context, however, what does "gay" mean? I am identifying, as a viewer, with Dil. Having had many conversations with people who saw the film, I found that few "gay men" identified with Dil. Thus, how am I privileging my own reading through a word such as "gay"? Instead, I am suggesting that "gay" is a beginning identification that might assist a reader of this article in the same way as the photograph mentioned earlier. No subject position can ever be defined in toto, but I am offering a few elements that I perceive as central to my reading. I could be wrong.

### 8. Is Jimmy Scottish?

The identity questions of The Crying Game go well beyond whether Dil is a woman. They commence at the beginning with a visceral tension as the blonde Jude and the black Jody hold hands at a rural Irish fun fair. Fergus tries very hard to see Jody as a "legitimate target," just another English soldier, but his blackness becomes too much of an interruption. Even when they engage in the traditional ritual competition of whose national sport is better, simple identity is impossible. Fergus inevitably accepts hurley as the playing field embodiment of the Irish nation, but to Jody cricket represents the poverty of Antigua rather than being a gentlemanly English sport.

Jody tells Fergus a story that follows a pattern common in many traditional tales. As the frog gives the scorpion a ride across the river, the scorpion stings the frog. The frog is amazed at such a suicidal action, but the scorpion says, "It's in my nature." The manner of filming Jody's story—the light, the focus, the pace—demonstrates its importance, and it is retold by Fergus to Dil in the final scene of the film. It is first ironic: Jody believes all the Irish are this way and Fergus believes all the English are that way. They are clearly wrong. Yet the parable is also accurate: Jody knows that it is Fergus's nature to be kind in spite of his Irishness.

The first scene of Fergus in England is revealing of many parts of identity. The cricket match in the beautiful sun is viewed from the narrow gap in the brick wall that Fergus is dismantling. He has become the proverbial Irish navy, and his boss calls him "Pat," like "George" for blacks in the American south or "Jackie" for Aboriginals in Australia, the improper proper name for a nameless ethnic identity. When he first meets Dil and she cuts his hair, however, she wonders if he is American. She then decides that he is Scottish. He accepts this and calls himself "Jimmy," not quite as generic as, say, "Jock," but still an outsider's "Scottishism."

Is Dil just, as the English would say, "a bit thick"? The film offers little information about her past, but a working-class black British transsexual hairdresser might have spent her life scrambling rather than becoming educated. Various hints in the film suggest she had experienced a lot of violence and her present boyfriend, Dave, isn't exactly upmarket. It would not be unlikely that Jody had in some sense "saved" her from a hopeless life, and his death has left her without much of a future. For her to be unable to tell the difference between an American, a Scot, or an Irishman is not impossible. Still, there might be something else involved.

When Fergus later tells Dil, "You're not a girl," she replies, "Details, baby, details." She seems to be quite comfortable with her identity as a woman unless someone outside interferes. Even when that happens, the interruption is brief. Her status as vacuum when wearing Jody's clothing might just follow the usual transsexual narrative, and mean that she is simply the woman she appears to be and thus lost in male clothing, but it might also be a denial of identity in favour of identification. She cannot imitate her other, which is Jody, but must rather imitate her own ideal of other as self, in her sexy dresses. It is not that Dil is from within a woman, has an ontology as woman, but that Dil identifies as a woman and there is nothing beyond that identification. Is "woman" in her nature or is it her nature to be unnaturally a "woman"?

For the boss, calling Fergus "Pat" is a conscious reduction, through which Fergus is limited to being an unimportant object in the boss's economic narrative. But, as one might say, at least he is right: Fergus is Irish. And yet he is right in the aid of a destructive imposition through which the boss's subjectivity is used against Fergus. Dil is wrong, her unconscious reduction does not limit Fergus's identity but instead moves him into her identification. Just as Dil's position as a subject is contained by her identification, so is her control of Fergus as potential love object. Fergus is not Scottish. So? Dil isn't a woman either.

## 9. How Do Homosexuals Read?

Poststructuralism has destabilized identity categories just at a time when contemporary society is beginning to accept that the hegemony must respond to minorities, such as homosexuals. Yet poststructuralism also offers modes of understanding that explain identities in ways that are less stable but more satisfying, as in Lee Edelman's *Homographesis*. In Edelman's opening chapter he pursues a careful argument that begins with the premise that homosexuals

> were not only conceptualized in terms of a radically
> potent, if negatively charged, relation to signifying
> practices, but also subjected to a cultural imperative that
> viewed them as inherently textual—as bodies that might
> well bear a 'hallmark' that could, and must, be read. (6)

In essence, although he would no doubt not like that phrase, Edelman is referring to gaydar, the ability to read others as homosexual. He is also commenting on the contrary desire to be seen as homosexual. This is changing, but in the past it meant to be seen as homosexual by other homosexuals but not to be seen as homosexual by heterosexuals. This is rather unlike most identity categories, where someone might prefer not to be identified by the hegemony but was usually inevitable. The African-American concern for "passing" was based on the assumption that only a very few could pass. Most homosexuals live under the assumption—or delusion—that they are "straight-acting."

Even more than other minorities, homosexuals are very concerned about being read and about reading as. This makes them unusually concerned perceivers. More than other texts, autobiographies of homosexuals and fiction about them represent them discovering themselves through literature. Each homosexual—and here I will refer to the male homosexual—must find a way to see the hidden homosexuals around him. Yet at the same time as he is reading such subtexts he is trying to hide the dangerous writing of homosexuality done by the self. Even before that he must have read his own text. He has found an identity category that is constituted only by the discovery that his self is different from the self that had been assumed by society and family. Homosexuality might be innate, but it is not a given. The homosexual must through introspection reach a point to decide that he is not heterosexual.

He must also read other nuances. In the past, homosexuality has coded various sexual activities. I once asked a boyfriend whether he believed our sexual compatibility was just luck. In that case, as in most of my personal experiences, we had not required any negotiation as to who did what to whom. He, devoted to phrasing resonant of his Guyanese background, said, "Dog know dog." Perhaps, but if this is general, as it often seems to be, it suggests a still more subtle form of "writing" and "reading." The homosexual not only can read a poem, he can tell a Shakespearean sonnet from a Petrarchan one.

What does it mean to me to read and to be read? I would argue that this creates a particular subject/object tension for the homosexual. Desiring both to be read by other homosexuals and not to be read by heterosexuals, he constantly reconfigures himself as an object to be observed. Similarly, while the subject is creating this ever-reconstructed object, he must also exert his subjectivity on the obscured objects of other homosexuals. This might seem like a confusing *mise en abîme* that is full of mirrors, from Dil's boudoir to the dress she wears when lip-synching at the Metro. The look, whether seeing or being seen, is the life of the gay man.

## 10. Is Anyone Here Gay?

In *The Crying Game*, Jody's blackness disrupts identity as does Dil's gender, but still more problematic is the category of sexuality. When Fergus vomits at the sight of Dil's penis, it could be from shock in the face of such a profound gender error. We all assume we can tell pink from blue, especially in someone at a kissable distance. It seems more likely to be homophobia. If Dil is a man, Fergus has been given a blow job by a man. If Dil is a man, Fergus has sexually desired a man. Fergus is beginning to look like a homosexual.

The recurring image of Jody after his death has been read by some as intimating Fergus's homoerotic desire for Jody. The image is emphasized at times when Dil's gender is an issue or when Fergus's sexual desire for Dil comes to the fore. Thus this might be the moment when homoerotic desire for Jody becomes homoerotic desire for Dil. It seems to me rather a heterosexual exchange. Jody's woman becomes Fergus's woman. Jody's image reappears because in a sense he has performed a typical male joke on a male friend, with a woman as exchange. The joke here, of course, is that the woman is a "woman."

The relationship between Dil and Fergus is set up through the bonding between Jody and Fergus, but as the film develops the earlier friendship comes to have more and more layers. At first it seems homosocial in the most obvious sense: two men who should be separated by being military enemies, by nationality, by race, use sport, a shared attraction to a woman, and an interest in story to overcome their differences. When Fergus falls for Dil, they both recognize it as a heterosexual triangle. Their bond restores Jody's relationship with both of them. Jody's ghostly presence could make both guilty; it does not deny but rather enhances their love that the memory of Jody is inscribed within it.

Then when Dil is revealed as a biological male, Fergus shares the audience's incredulity that the macho Jody might be homosexual and asks Dil if Jody knew her secret. Dil replies, "Absolutely." Although Fergus never openly reflects on it in the film, this seems to raise questions not just about Jody, but also about him and Fergus. Yet as Eve Kosofsky

Sedgwick suggests, the homosocial bond has an inevitable homoerotic element. The racial difference adds to this. In the chapter on the "dinge queen," I explore racial attraction in what Darryl Bem refers to as "Exotic Becomes Erotic." In the gay world, two men in an intimate conversation are not automatically assumed to be lovers, but if they are of different races, sex is presumed to be a given.

I would still claim that there is no homosexual in *The Crying Game*. Actually, my guess is that Col the bartender is gay, but that is at best my misplaced gaydar: there is nothing in the narrative to assert that this is the case. As to Jody and Fergus, I see no reason to label them as such. To see the eros in their bonding as defineably homosexual asserts a binary that the film is trying to escape. As to the relationships that either has with Dil, to see them as homosexual would be to deny Dil's worldview. To be homosexual requires a same-sex sexual desire so in this case there is no homosexual. If, as I claimed above, Dil as object defines the film, she must create the subjects as she requires them. I exist because I am perceived, but I must be perceived in the existence that I claim.

Fuss believes that Freud's view of identification makes the "normal homosexual" impossible. Only through heterosexuality can the subject incorporate the need for the absent other and fulfil the absurd inversion of becoming complete through establishing the lack. Homosexuality leads only to narcissism:

> What Freud gives us in the end is a Newtonian
> explanation of sexual orientation in which falling
> bodies are homosexual bodies, weighted down by the
> heaviness of multiple identifications, and rising bodies are
> heterosexual bodies, buoyed up by the weightlessness of
> desires unmoored from their (lost) objects. (77)

Dil performs an amazing reversal of this dichotomy. She erases homosexuality and reproduces heterosexuality as a deep veneer. She demonstrates that the lost object can become the container for the present subject.

## 11. Living the Phallus

Autobiography is usually introduced in literary criticism through a victim position. Autobiography seems to acclaim the authority of the self, yet in case after case, autobiography is used to show that the critic, by virtue of being female, or South Asian, or gay, is not part of the hegemonic critical order that has previously been hidden in apparent objectivity. Now this specific critic is revealed to inhabit a subject position that has been suppressed and oppressed by that hegemony. This can be compared to testimonio. In the latter the life writing is validated by the author's identity as member of a specific community, a representative sample of an oppressed culture. The victim position is usually central. Most attacks on individual testimonios have been based on claims that the author's life has not been as oppressed as she or he claims. The classic example, of both the genre and the attack, would be I, Rigoberta Menchu, but a recent autobiography of a rather elite figure was similarly treated, Edward Said's Out of Place: a Memoir. While Said's status as Columbia professor and past president of the Modern Language Association makes him an unlikely victim, the primary drive of his postcolonial criticism and of his memoir is his position as representation of the Palestinian. His Orientalism has obvious "objective" claims, but it also has "subjective" claims, as it names the Palestinian response to the hegemony of Orientalism.

So, to put it into vulgar psychologism, who has the phallus? In Sexing the Self: Gendered Positions in Cultural Studies, Elspeth Probyn sees the limitations of ontology, the category of being that leads to essential identities. Instead, she offers epistemology:

> Re-figuring the self as an image, we can begin to locate
> feminist speaking positions within a tactical use of
> images as points of view. In this way, the self works at
> a discursive level, operating epistemologically within
> various systems of thought. (92)

This is the category Said seems to be employing, especially in recent critiques, but in most cases of autobiographical criticism, the inferiority of this "speaking position" is the justification for taking it. I would go so far as to say many examples represent a state of abjection, the critic who must be listened to because she is from the position that cannot speak.

My sister's experience is, for many reasons, a representation of this position, unspeakable pain that has not spoken; so the other day I talked to her about being a victim. While words such as "abjection" are not part of her normal vocabulary, she agreed that being a victim is a troubling speaking position. Then she said that she is concerned more with listening than with speaking. I replied that I have never learned so much as when I have listened to her listening.

The listening position must seem in many ways to be denying the phallus. The listener is penetrated rather than penetrating. While I have constituted myself here as a gay man, with connections that have various values, I should also reveal myself to be what sexologists call "anal passive." In other words, while I have a penis and use it sexually, my sexual aim is not to insert that penis somewhere, but rather to have a penis inserted into me. Some might find this observation a vulgarly explicit revelation in what is ostensibly film criticism, but it defines me on Dil's side of sexual activity and it also defines me as a male who perceives himself as observer of the penis (phallus?) rather than a wielder of it.

In *Care of the Self*, Michel Foucault suggests that a major part of the classical task of "the cultivation of the self" is the pursuit of an active life and the rejection of the passive, whether construed as femininity or passive homosexuality. Or, in other words, the assertion of the subject. Thus when autobiography enters contemporary criticism, it asserts an abject position only in a process of reversal. The critic turns to autobiography because she does not have the phallus and is in a state of abjection or even absence, but through introducing autobiography, and through asserting the power of her victimization, she is able to speak.

## 12. Misplacing the Penis
When Fergus is guarding Jody, he takes him out to urinate. Jody stands there, but his hands are tied behind his back and he is, in this sense, impotent. After a bit of cajoling, Fergus is convinced to pull down his

fly, but that isn't enough. The screen focuses on Fergus's pained face while below camera range he pulls out Jody's penis. Jody says, "It's only a piece of meat." Afterwards they share some locker-room humour and Fergus concludes, "The pleasure was all mine."

The discomfort is of course homophobic, but it centres on one of the primary contradictions in heterosexual males. While the male tends to have an obsessive relation with his own penis, he wants to avoid all others, and certainly doesn't want to touch one. In this combination, however, Jody's penis has, as one might expect, a larger dimension. Frantz Fanon maintains that white male fear of black sexuality is the key to white racism, as in the lynchings in the American south. According to Fanon, in the imagination of the white man, the black man "is turned into a penis. He is a penis." (170) And Fergus has touched it.

When Dil reveals her penis, it doesn't look all that big, although no doubt it looms large to Fergus. No one calls it "only a piece of meat," but an attentive viewer will recall that phrase as Fergus is throwing up into the toilet. The other threatening penis, Jody's, is never seen. The one potential white penis, Fergus's, is never mentioned or seen, but is figured in when Dil gives him a blow job as the camera watches Fergus's face. Thus while the two black penises are the threat, in different ways, to the film's eyes, the white penis is an unstated source of interaction between Dil and Fergus. Dil bringing him to orgasm is one more example where she turns his subject into what her object requires, this time through the most subjective of responses, the sexual:

It is tempting to see this aspect of the representation of Dil as a joke on Mulvey's critique: "Ultimately, the meaning of woman is sexual difference, the absence of the penis as visually ascertainable, the material evidence on which is based the castration complex essential for the organisation of entrance to the symbolic order and the law of the father." (Mulvey 13) Jude is a phallic woman, with a big, big, gun, but she doesn't belong in Dil's script. When Dil reveals her body to Fergus, he and the audience are expecting the normal castration. Instead, the absent penis is still there. If Dil could do a better job of usurping the law of the father, I don't know how. The gaze is shattered all over the screen.

## 13. The Crying Game

I would like to take Dil's object lesson a bit further, as a possible figure for autobiographical criticism. Because the subject of the film is never Dil, she cannot control the agenda. Fergus makes the decisions. Her view of the world, however, seeps through the edges to produce her Fergus, to produce her audience. The name of the film shapes this transformation. It seems to give an ironic take on Dominic Behan's song "The Patriot Game" and therefore a rejection of the expectations of what an Irish narrative should be about. Still, "The Crying Game," the song that provides the title, is not new and ironic but rather a sappy bit of 1960s schlock that offers what could be called a chick-flick view of the world. It seems to enforce a victim position, with Dil as the hard-luck girl. But is she in the end a victim? Apologies to Neil Jordan, the film's director and screenwriter, but it seems that Dil brought her lipsynch tape to the audition and it somehow took over the movie when no one was watching. Or rather, when everyone was watching.

I am unable to define what autobiographical criticism should be. It should not set up the critic as more important than the discourse under consideration, even if the argument is that the critic as victim deserves this importance as some kind of affirmative action. I still want autobiography to act in a more overt way than has been normal in criticism to date, in acknowledgment of the subject position, but in a process of identification rather than identity. The elucidation of this identification should be provided in somewhat oblique ways which accept the multiple resonances of that process.

The scene of the opening credits is not Fergus's physical point of view. He is at the fair watching Jude and Jody. It might be his psychological point of view, looking through the dark at the fun fair that is Dil. Perhaps this is an artistic representation of Dil's view: in one scene, she

plays her own disc of "The Crying Game" while Fergus watches her sil-
houette. She inhabits the dark underbelly yet never lets it stop her life at
the fun fair, at least as long as she is able to keep the coloured lights. Or
perhaps the camera of the opening credits is the autobiographical critic.
The critic is trying to be, and by that I mean BE, in the shadows, under
the bridge, and yet provide some new look at that fun fair text, which is
presumably the reason the camera is lurking in the first place.

And join Dil in that final scene. Fergus, the author of the text, is imprisoned behind the glass, telling the story that Fergus heard from Jody,
that we have heard from Jody, that Dil has no doubt heard from Jody.
She is in a stereotypically feminine position as her man tells her a story
she knows as well as he does. She sits outside the glass, listening to her
text and responding to it as Lyle Lovett sings "Stand by Your Man." The
Crying Game might not be the most explicit metaphor for autobiographical criticism, but then that's not in Dil's nature. And perhaps it's not in
mine.

## 3. The Homosexual Child

Margaret Mead seems to have fallen on hard times. References to her work today are devoted to showing her to be manipulative, overly subjective, and just plain inaccurate. Anyone who reads her books, however, can see why she has been so popular. At first the behaviour she describes seems exotic, but then she shows it to be commonsensical and perhaps even suitable for trying at home. Her 1949 *Male and Female: A Study of the Sexes in a Changing World* includes the following:

> The American Plains Indians, valuing courage in battle
> above all other qualities, watched their little boys with
> desperate intensity, and drove a fair number of them to
> give up the struggle and assume women's dress.

> There seems in fact every reason to suppose that with
> the exception of the occasional anatomically confused
> hermaphrodites, homosexuality is a combination of adult
> expectations and fears and a possibility latent in many
> children that will never be fully expressed if it is not given
> social recognition or if the complementary position is not
> allowed for—as among the Iatmul. (107)

Mead's comments about "hermaphrodites" are certainly out of date, but the essence of that last sentence seems to encompass my memories of growing up. My developing sexuality was "a combination of adult expectations and fears and a possibility latent in [me] that [was] never fully expressed [as] it [was] not given social recognition [and] the complementary position [was] not allowed for." So today I look back and see how that came to be—and more important to the present book, how I came to be something that has been given "social recognition," although no doubt "never fully expressed."

The homosexual child is forever linked to Freud, if only because the sexual child is so linked. While there are many ways in which homosexuality, at least in the culture in which I live, has long overcome its assessment by Freud as inversion, as pathology, this same culture continues to be confused by the sexual child. Freud and his followers have offered a multitude of theories about how the child develops sexually. James Kincaid, in his fascinating study, *Child-Loving: The Erotic Child and Victorian Culture*, notes that scientists have found that observable sexual arousal begins before birth (172). In 1987, Theo Sandfort published *Boys on Their Contacts with Men: A Study of Sexually Expressed Friendships*, a book with an extraordinarily liberal view of childhood sexuality. In the introduction, the sexologist John Money writes, "For those born and educated after the year 2000, we will be their history, and they will be mystified by our self-imposed, moralistic ignorance of the principles of sexual and erotic development in childhood." (5)

So much for futurology. When doing research for this book, I spent a summer at the Library of Congress. I was able to request a variety of books on sexology without seeing a raised eyebrow, but when I moved on to books on pedophilia, the disdain of the staff handing me books was evident. Perhaps I should have worn a white lab coat with a "Dr. Goldie" nameplate. In 2008, society continues to see childhood as completely divorced from anything akin to sex. Even when a child imitates sexuality through kissing, marriage games, etc., adults view the action as imitating love rather than sex. Floyd M. Martinson, in his article "Eroticism in Infancy and Childhood," attempts to define sexuality in a way that accommodates child sex but also recognizes its limitations: "Sexual experience is of two kinds, reflexive and eroticized. Eroticized sexuality refers to sexual experience that one is conscious of and involved in." (25) "Any child, certainly by the age of five, is capable of being autoerotically awake and capable of autoerotic experience, including self-stimulation to the point of orgasm." (25) This, however, is reflexive, according to Martinson's distinction. He goes on, "It appears that a necessary component of rational premeditated sex is that the adolescent be well on the way to developing an identity of his own, separate from that of his parents." (33)

"Rational premeditated sex" might seem rather oxymoronic. Still, presumably our assumptions as to what constitutes "sex" require something akin to reason and premeditation. Sandfort and Peggy Cohen-Kettenis, in "Sexual Behavior in Dutch and Belgian Children as Observed by Their Mothers," state:

> By labeling the child's behaviors as sexual, the parents
> single out a particular set of behaviors and give it a specific
> symbolic meaning. By labeling these behaviors as sexual,
> parents might also attribute motivations to the child's
> behavior that are not necessarily present. This attribution
> of meaning to the child's behavior will affect the way
> parents respond to the child when he or she exhibits these
> behaviors. The child may not always understand why their
> behavior is responded to so exceptionally. (114)

In other words, the concept of "sex" requires a sense that the person engaging in "sex" must "mean sex," however that meaning is defined and manifest. This meaning of sex seems a presupposition within the concept of the "homosexual child." Thus Martinson's analysis appears to suggest that a child could not be homosexual before "developing an identity of his own," regardless of his actions. The process seems to be drifting towards Foucault, in which the social construct of the homosexual, here self-identified, defines homosexuality. Not that this is Martinson's purpose. In another article, "Childhood and the Institutionalization of Sexuality," he comes to the conclusion that

> ... a growing recognition of the affectional-erotic
> capacities and needs of human beings has contributed
> to an autonomous institutionalization of affectional-
> erotic sexuality free from its traditional association with
> procreation and free from its traditional association with
> marriage. Institutionalizing affectional-erotic sexuality
> in this way opens up a wide range of styles of sexual
> conduct: (1) with reduced distinction between male and

> female, (2) for both homosexual and heterosexual,
> (3) without regard to marital status, and (4) without
> regard to age. It is assumed that institutionalizing sex as
> autonomous will contribute to a broader acceptance of
> children as less dichotomized by gender and as capable
> of, and entitled to, affectional-erotic intimacy and sensate
> pleasuring. (276)

No doubt the psychologism of a phrase such as "affectional-erotic capacities" is off-putting to many, but the liberationist ideal of "institutionalizing sex as autonomous" is attractive, although also utopian. Our society might get beyond gender, sexual orientation, and marriage, but do we have any hope of erasing age? Kincaid aptly notes the importance of our

> ... division between adult and child, a dissociation which,
> I will claim, has been at least for the past two hundred
> years heavily eroticized: the child is that species which is
> free of sexual feeling or response; the adult is that species
> which has crossed over into sexuality. The definitional
> base is erotic: our discourse insists on it by loudly denying
> its importance. (6-7)

Kincaid asserts that sexuality in children is usually confined within that delightful word, "latency": "It simply disguises its activities, artfully making them appear as something else, just as a latent disease, masking itself as an absence, puts forward the symptoms of another disease that actually isn't there." (127-128)

Most people in our society see this childhood sexuality becoming active only when the latency is abused by some evil man, the monstrous pedophile that has become the bogeyman for all parents. Regardless of the constant reiteration by experts of all sorts that child abuse is primarily performed by members of the child's family, the lurking stranger pedophile remains the central icon. Sara Ahmed's *Strange Encounters: Embodied Others in Post-Coloniality* captures the sensibility behind this image:

> The discourse of stranger danger also involves the
> figuring, not only of the wiser subject who can move
> through dangerous places (a mobile subject who is
> racialized, classed and gendered), but also the vulnerable
> body, the one who is most at risk. Here, 'the child'
> becomes a figure of vulnerability, the purified body that
> is most endangered by the contaminating desires of
> strangers. (34)

The pedophile stranger is thus created at least partly by the assumption of
purity and innocence. Recognition that the pedophile not be an absolute
other might imply that the child is not absolute purity, that the sexuality
is not only within the predator.

Michael Ingram, in "Participating Victims: A Study of Sexual Offenses with Boys," comes to the following assessment of the pedophiles
he studied:

> The men viewed their own sexual development with
> disgust, and thought that childhood was a sort of
> perfection. They were impotent with men and women
> alike.
>
> They were men who loved children, and in most
> cases were doing a great deal of valuable work in the
> community. They all suffered much anxiety lest the
> disclosure of their indiscretions might wreck their careers,
> but complained that the children were so provocative or
> seductive that they had found abstinence impossible. (182)

This might be compared to Sylvia Warner's biography of the novelist
T.H. White, in which she quotes the following from his diary:

> I have fallen in love with Zed [ten years old]. On Braye
> Beach with Killie I waved and waved to the aircraft till
> it was out of sight—my wild geese all gone and me and
> lonely old Charlie [White's dog] on the sands who had
> waddled down to the water's edge but couldn't fly. It

would be unthinkable to make Zed unhappy with the
weight of this impractical, unsuitable love. It would be
against his human dignity. Besides, I love him for being
happy and innocent, so it would be destroying what I
loved. He could not stand the weight of the world against
such feelings—not that they are bad in themselves. It is
the public opinion which makes them so. In any case,
on every score of his happiness, not my safety, the whole
situation is an impossible one. All I can do is behave like a
gentleman. It has been my hideous fate to have been born
with an infinite capacity for love and joy with no hope of
using them. (277-278)

Yet, as Ingram suggests, the issue comes back to meaning:

Thus, I suggest that, though there may well be a
meaningful relationship between a loving man and an
unhappy child, and that a sexual act takes place within
the context of this relationship, nevertheless, the act is
sexually meaningful only for the adult, not for the child.
A large number of acts are mere horse-play, and the man
has to be content with that instead of the meaningful
relationship. (184-185)

Those who work with pedophiles describe their process of "grooming"
the focus of their attention. As an adult I have searched my memory for
someone who groomed me. In childhood I can remember no one, although
with hindsight I know one of my primary teachers was "grooming"
a young female classmate. I can think of one high school teacher. His
behaviour was scrupulous, however, even more than that of White, and
our time together was invariably spent discussing theatre or literature.
The collection of Shakespeare plays he gave me was the closest thing to a
provocative present. I of course have no idea what was in his mind, but
it would not surprise me if he was less "grooming" me as a target of his
sexuality than rather very obliquely mentoring me as a potentially out
example of the sexuality that he always kept carefully closeted.

One of the central questions is always how the target is chosen. Inferences about the sexuality of the objects of homosexual pedophiles are often attacked as blaming the victims, but it would seem likely that the pedophile of the sort exemplified by White and depicted by Ingram, someone who seeks love from a child, would choose a boy who seems likely to give that love. I can think of at least two heterosexual men of my acquaintance who were groomed as youths by pedophiles in ways that were recognized and confronted by their fathers but never resulted in what might be called "sex." This of course is just my inexpert opinion but my gaydar suggests that both could be gay. Their adolescent experience, however, made them quite homophobic. So much for homosexual recruitment.

This chapter, like all in this book, reflects my own experience. Thus it is very much about the beginnings of a homosexual identity rather than early homosexual practice, as I never had anything that could be called "sex" with anyone, male or female, before I was eighteen. This is very different from the Australian culture depicted by Gary Dowsett in *Practicing Desire: Homosexual Sex in the Era of AIDS*:

> Harry's not-so-furtive youthful fumblings (they took all their clothes off) and his initiation into anal sex are examples of one theme common in the lives of men in this study; the *perverse sexual experiences* of boys. Harriet, Barney, Harry, and Neil all told tales of boys and youths experimenting sexually, exploring bodies and seeking sensations, seemingly oblivious to the incursion of specific anti-homosexual discourse. (142)

> A striking feature of these life histories is the pre-adult sexual experience. Is Freud's notion of *sexual precocity* sufficient, even in its essentialism, to explain the downright permissive perversity of these youngsters? Is a *capacity* for sexual expression an adequate basis for understanding the subsequent sexual explorations among these boys? (246)

Perhaps the lack of such experience in my own life reflects a lack of that precocity or perhaps a lack of interest in the male-bonding that could have included such activity. I was much more interested in theatre and music than I was in the rough-housing that might have led to sexual experience.

But I was still developing sexually. When my mother realized I had begun masturbating, she suddenly brought up the name of a friend from band: "Did Theodore[4] teach you that?" The idea that masturbation was in some sense linked to homosexuality shows my mother to be a product of her place and time: she was born in the small town of Weyburn, Saskatchewan in 1907. Kincaid notes that masturbation was often seen as a dangerous disruption of the natural innocence of childhood, but also that this might not have been the larger reason it was proscribed:

> Was the anxiety over childhood innocence secondary
> to concerns about homosexuality? To what extent were
> children actually made innocent? To what extent were
> they protected from one kind of sexuality in order to be
> turned over to another? To what extent were they made
> available for adult desire, opened up to an eroticism much
> more complex and demanding than the masturbation they
> were being guarded from? (176)

Not that I recall any specific suggestions that my mother was concerned about pedophiles, although given her many fears for my life, that one likely was included somewhere.

It might seem surprising that my mother was not completely opposed to activities that the surrounding culture most likely would have considered to be completely female. Thus while it was my grandmother who taught me how to crochet and knit, my mother dedicated many hours to teaching me how to cook and sew. I suppose my mother's instruction could be dismissed as survival training, but mock duck and beef stroganoff were hardly your basic food groups, and she was not

---

4. I have avoided names of lovers, friends, and acquaintances throughout this book but this anecdote seems to require one, so I have made one up.

helping me learn mending but rather assisting in creations such as a pair of flowered bellbottoms. I presume my mother flinched at some of my choices, although she did not try to stop me. This was rather unlike my father, who was at times literally sickened by my appearance: any new look of mine could lead to a migraine. His succinct response to my pierced ear was, "Now that you look like an idiot anyway, can you get your hair cut?"

Still, the hair played into my mother's primary concern. She once said, "Why would you want hair like that given you are so large and manly?" With hindsight, I can recognize many moments in my youth when my mother diagnosed my homosexuality and tried to find some way to redirect it. Given that I spent little of that period considering my own sexual orientation, I see these moments now and marvel at her insights. While I lament her lack of openness to my sexuality, her age and the climate in Saskatchewan in the early sixties made it impossible to be otherwise. Within the limits of the culture and of my own naïveté I found my mother's reference to Theodore quite puzzling. Theodore was extremely non-physical in every sense. If anyone inadvertently touched him he became noticeably uncomfortable. The thought of him participating in anything as overtly physical as masturbation was mind-boggling. But I realize now that Theodore—his voice, his walk, every aspect of his presentation—was as gay as a three-dollar bill, although it had not crossed my mind at the time.

These thoughts about my lack of sexual activity make me wonder whether it was to my benefit or not. The type of energetic experimentation depicted by Dowsett was far from my character and thus would not have happened in any case. A more direct form of pedophile grooming would have been much more likely. Perhaps I would have had the reaction noted in so many abuse memoirs, such as that of the National Hockey League player, Sheldon Kennedy. He attributes his later alcohol and drug abuse to having sex with his coach as a teenager. The much less acknowledged alternative is that offered by Tom O'Carroll in *Paedophilia: The Radical Case*. He quotes assessments from various adults who had sexual experiences with older men when children. One hetero-sexual male states, "Paedophilia I find a more difficult question [than homosexuality]. I allow everyone love and happiness in all respects, but I cannot approve of this. I experienced no trouble myself, but not all become acquainted with it in such an understanding manner." (73) A woman says, "It certainly has done me no harm. It depends on what a paedophile does and how he does it, and if he really loves children (and that usually goes together) he will understand and be in sympathy with the child and thus know very well what he can and what he can-not do." (78) For myself, the situation is far too hypothetical to judge. I often have thoughts, however, that if I had been lovingly groomed as an adolescent, my life might have been much less bisexual and more ho-mosexual. Given that I am a devout believer that life is as it is, I neither lament nor applaud this process. My assessment is that I would be sad to have missed my heterosexual experiences, especially if the lack thereof had precluded having children, but I wish I could have explored my homosexual experiences with more clarity of identity.

But without that clarity, and without the sexual experience, why do I call myself the homo##xual child? Part of it is of course the belief that I was as a child who I am today.

Robert Kus sums up one side of the argument in his review of Rich-ard Green's The Sissy Boy Syndrome and the Development of Homosexuality:

> [Green] does not see homosexuality as a lifelong,
> irreversible state of being that is recognized by gay
> males in their teen years. On the contrary, the author
> imagines that gay male children do not exist, but rather
> are neutral boys who may 'become' gay. This is similar to
> the imagery of a cocoon that may, eventually, turn into a
> butterfly. (188)

Kus replies, "One's sexual orientation, like other nonchosen aspects of self, is a beautiful divine gift to be treasured and developed to its maximum." (188)

The "nonchosen" element is explained many ways. The claim that sexual orientation is genetic is constantly asserted and constantly refuted. One of the most recent versions of the biological explanation results from a study by Anthony Bogaert at Brock University. In "Men with Older Brothers More Likely to be Gay: Study Points to Biological Origins of Homosexuality," Michael J. Silverman summarizes Bogaert's analysis:

> "Most studies indicate there is probably a biological basis
> to men's sexual orientation," Bogaert said. "My study
> adds to that—it adds another fairly strong piece to the
> biological puzzle that underlies, at least in part, men's
> sexual orientation."
>
> The leading biological theory is the maternal
> immunization hypothesis, which suggests that something
> changes with each son a mother conceives.
>
> When a mother gives birth to her first son, she may create
> antibodies in response to the foreign male proteins of her
> baby. These antibodies can increase in the mother with
> each successive male baby, which may affect her son's
> brain, hormones, and sexual orientation.

Given that I have no older brothers, I can skip that one. Judging from the stories my family has told, after two daughters, my mother was yearning for a son, so I am sure any antibodies she created to defeat my male proteins were against her will.

Whatever the causes of homosexuality, looking back to the early moment when one recognized either an innate or developing homosexuality is the norm in any gay autobiography. This continues in spite of queer theory's many attempts to destabilize such comforting identity moments. In her book *Outside Belongings*, Elspeth Probyn questions "How are we to theorize the singularity of queer uses of childhood when the memories are cut of the same cloth as the typologies of quantitative social science?" (111) She offers an alternative:

> Against a trend to posit childhood as a point of departure

in the construction of queer being, a maneuver which
indicates a barely hidden yearning within some
formations of identity politics for something that
would ground difference ineluctably, I want to consider
childhood as the point from which we 'laugh at the
solemnities of origin'. (96)

I feel accused of not having a sense of humour in my consideration of
my past, but the idea that the child is the father to the man controls most
of our hermeneutics of self. On the other hand, I would be denying my
own subjectivity if I rejected her following comment:

I want a strategy for mining the richness of childhood,
a tone of writing that encourages a diverse exploitation
of childhood with an eye to present exigencies. I want
a tactic that enables certain formulations of belonging
but disables general statements about identity that would
ultimately stall the singular force of queer interventions.
(100)

Thus, the present discussion is an excursion not to the point of origin,
but rather an enabling of certain formulations of belonging. To continue
the figure through a common euphemism for homosexuality, what
follows is my description of how I came to be on the team.

Janis Bohan, in *Psychology and Sexual Orientation: Coming to Terms*, states,
"Perhaps the most common experience reported by LGBs, especially
by men, is the very early sense of being 'different.' This sense of difference usually does not have specifically sexual connotations prior to
adolescence." (143) "Difference" can certainly take various forms, but in
my case it often took apparently "gay" forms, such as a very early devotion to Broadway musicals (this has often been noted by friends as such
an obvious expression of my homosexuality that they cannot see how I
could ever have thought myself heterosexual). On the other hand, another major fixation of my youth was country music, which is instead
passed off as irrelevant, not a mark of *difference*.

Another element of my life that might seem opposite fits Bohan quite neatly, my early conformity to a rather conservative moral code, that difference through not differing: "Teens who feel thoroughly unacceptable because of homophilic feelings might strive to overcome both their own and also others' judgments by becoming 'the best little boy/girl in the world.'" (149) For a child who sees no potential for peer acceptance, parental approval becomes very attractive. The various academic awards I won gave me just that and my participation in musical theatre gave me something akin to a social life. A few years ago I attended a high school reunion and when the conversation turned to remembering the days spent skipping school and drinking beer in a local park, I couldn't partake: I not only had not joined them, I did not know where the park was.

Richard Friedman's 1990 book *Male Homosexuality: A Contemporary Psychoanalytic Perspective* is now almost twenty years old and so might be seen as somewhat out-of-date, but it remains a reasonable summary of a certain perspective. Friedman notes, "Many homosexual men who do not report cross-dressing, having feminine mannerisms, or preferring feminine activities in childhood nonetheless say they avoided rough-and-tumble play.... This may be the most common childhood trait of prehomosexual boys." (18) In his study, "All thirteen men reported that as youngsters they had had markedly negative feelings about their bodies. Ten of the subjects described themselves as soft and flabby." (19) "None engaged in even the modest juvenile sex-typed interactions described by the least aggressive preheterosexual youngster (e.g., actively pushing another boy in anger)." (20) All of this describes me.

Edward Stein, in *The Mismeasure of Desire: The Science, Theory, and Ethics of Sexual Orientation* (1990), states, "Together, the retrospective and prospective studies suggest that the experiences associated with being a gender nonconforming child are significantly correlated with homosexuality, that various features of parental family dynamics are somewhat correlated with adult sexual orientation, and that one's early childhood sexual experiences have no particular connection to adult sexual orientation." (238) This is of particular interest in distinguishing the different ways of becoming the homosexual child. The effeminate boy is more likely to become homosexual than either the object of a pedophile or the participant in the nascent homosexual activity described by Dowsett. In other words, this denotes the non-sexually precocious me, although, unlike the boys in Friedman's study, I never "felt chronically hungry for closeness with other boys." (19) Perhaps I was too busy with *Oklahoma*.

Yet I did have that closeness with certain boys, not that I recognized it as something unusual. I never had an identity moment like the narrator's description of the ideal lover in Edmund White's *A Boy's Own Story*:

> He would prize me for my sexuality, which was at once
> my essence and also an attribute I was totally unfamiliar
> with, like the orphan's true name, a magical identity he
> knows nothing of until the very moment of revelation.
> (198)

This would have required a self-awareness I was quite lacking. As I look back forty years later, however, I can see a basic pattern in my life from approximately the age of twelve through high school. I always had one "best friend" with whom I spent all my time during the day, and with whom I would have long phone calls in the evening. Over the years, four boys took that position, in a process of serial monogamy. None of us ever had a girlfriend, although we would discuss girls sometimes and periodically ask one out, usually to be rejected. I have lost touch with all of these boys but learned that they all proved heterosexual, with wives and kids too. I can remember little that was erotic in our relationships, although one did a penis dance once in the locker room when we were alone. He was not at all erect and we both treated the event as ridiculous. Still, while eros was missing, I now realize that romance definitely wasn't. I pined for those telephone calls, especially with two of the boys. When I returned from school I would count the hours until the call could be made. Holidays when we could not be in touch were very painful. I seem to have been experiencing "puppy love" without realizing I was at all canine. This was but one of many stages in my life in which 1) my own naïveté and 2) living in a culture with no sexual diversity, and 3) my lack of a constant erection at the thought of the perfect man made me fail to recognize the gay signals that my loving but homophobic mother was always picking up.

The non-masculine boy continues to have problems in our culture, as is documented throughout psychological studies and the popular media. Money notes, in *Venuses Penuses: Sexology, Sexosophy, and Exigency Theory*, that the "sissy boy" is a constant target: "It is either more exaggerated and frequent in boys than in girls, or else it generates more alarm in those adults who take action toward changing it. In our society today, sissy boys are severely stigmatized. Tomboyish girls are not." (249) Adolescent homophobia is more about appearance than identity: masculine boys who become gay men tend to have happier memories of their youth than effeminate boys who become heterosexual. The macho jock performs heterosexual masculinity no matter what his sexual orientation, but the limp-wristed straight boy is seen to be a ladies' man in only the wrong sense. In my own youth, one of my female dates was laughed at by a friend for going out with a "mama's boy." In a more contemporary example, a female friend of mine went through a rather fractious divorce but told me in a satisfied tone that her ex-husband's new young wife had produced what was turning out to be a "girly-boy." In spite of her financial and other troubles, her own son the boxer seemed to be giving her a competitive edge.

A short while ago I was in the dressing room of the local swimming pool when a gaggle of ten-year-old boys entered. Three who looked "different" separated themselves from the group and changed in a corner. While the others were either uncaring or flagrant in their nudity, these three undressed behind towels. What will be their sexual orientation? Just seeing these boys while thinking about this chapter made me wonder how much the effeminophobia, if I can coin a word, produces homophobia and even heterosexuality. We so often, following Monique Wittig and many others, believe that heterosexuality enforces strict gender codes, but what if strict gender codes enforce heterosexuality? I wonder whether a world that accepted my rather slight gender variance would have produced a more resolutely homosexual person. I was never terribly girly and I have never been terribly concerned about being masculine but I still recognize that I have often needed to be male. One rather consistent embarrassment in my youth was having a unisexual name. I most definitely did not want to be listed under the girls whenever I was a new participant in some organization. I wanted to be a boy. Perhaps much of the heterosexuality in my life is a product not of some innate desire or even of some socially constructed sexual orientation, but more a socially constructed gender.

Ellie Ragland-Sullivan, in *Jacques Lacan and the Philosophy of Psychoanalysis* explains the obvious confusion between that which seems somehow psychoanalytically ordained and that which is socially constructed and thus might seem to be chosen or even arbitrary:

> Lacan saw the effect of the Oedipal nexus as that which
> decides the assignment of sex, where sex is correlated
> with identity rather than gender (*Séminaire* I, p. 80). Every
> child is under an obligation to submit his or her sexuality
> to certain restrictions or laws of organization and
> exchange within a sexually differentiated group and thus
> find his or her place within that society. The Oedipal crisis
> does not occur because a child wants to possess its mother
> sexually, but when the child comprehends its society's
> sexual rules; the crisis is resolved when the rules are
> acceded to and accepted. (268)

Thus I can look back and see myself falling victim to compulsory heterosexuality, but to my memory the process was such that it is very difficult to see how this process could have been avoided. I comprehended and therefore I was.

Ken Corbett, in "Homosexual Boyhood: Notes on Girlyboys," captures much of my memory of childhood:

> Feminine identifications for homosexual boys are not
> so much an expression of a wish to be a girl (although

> often that is the manifest behavior and, at times, the latent
> wish) but rather an avenue to passive experience and wish
> fulfillment. Passive longings and feminine identifications
> reside alongside a masculine identification, often creating
> what one patient referred to as 'mixed gender feelings'
> during boyhood. (121)

I have no recollection of wanting to be female. Whenever questions were raised about some of my activities, I was pleased to note that Jacques Plante, the Montreal Canadiens goaltender, was known to knit, and that the great chefs were all male. I knew nothing about fashion, with the possible exception of the name of Chanel, and had not learned the stereotyped sexual proclivities of male fashion designers. It would be interesting to note, however, whether there are differences between these activities as performed by girls and by boys in terms of the relationships with their mothers. Many girls recall their first ventures into mother tasks as fraught with anxiety as their apprenticeship was prodded and poked. For me, I remember nothing except love and support. My happiest memories of childhood are with my mother in the kitchen: "The kitchen is a girlyboy domain.... Mothers have a way of recurring, and one repeatedly finds them either in the self or in the other. Analysts would have us believe that girlyboys find too much mother in themselves, and not enough in others." (Corbett 128) It should thus not be surprising that one of the finest works by Rodney McRae, a gay author and illustrator of children's literature, is My Mother's Kitchen.

The theatricality of the homosexual child often takes the form of cross-dressing. Corbett says, "Girlyboys have a feeling for artifice, beauty, and style. The body often becomes the avenue for this mode of aestheticism." (130) Shyam Selvadurai's novel Funny Boy describes a young Sri Lankan boy who begins his journey to discovering his homosexuality by playing the bride in marriage games with his female cousins. Richard Pleak, in "Ethical Issues in Diagnosing and Treating Gender-Dysphoric Children and Adolescents," says, "One finds that retrospective reports of the childhood behaviors of gay men and lesbians show a higher propensity toward cross-gender behavior than the general population." (39)

I had the opportunity to cross-dress in a somewhat public manner between the ages of ten and thirteen, when I visited my grandmother in Weyburn. A long-term widow, she lived with a friend who could be called "butch," but I knew nothing of their relationship. More to my point here, they lived in what had before been a shop, and thus had display windows in the front. I was allowed to dress up in their clothes and perform plays in the window. All I can say is I wish I had films of the experience. Still, I sense that this was less important to my development than the private cross-dressing I did in my mother's bedroom. This often consisted of wearing articles of her clothing, but one of my games is strikingly similar to the one recalled in Jody Norton's "The Boy Who Grew Up to Be a Woman," although mine was private while her performances were for an audience of friends:

> I never came out absolutely naked. My ultimate outfit was a single cloth strap looping over my shoulder, down my back, between my legs, over my erect penis, and back up to my shoulder. Since the strap was made of a firm material, my stiff penis held it away from my body, so that 'everything' could be clearly seen by the spellbound audience, with the intensely magnified eroticism that the illusion of reserve unerringly provides. One cannot satisfactorily be a peeping tom unless one has to peep into a place that is 'covered'—that is, symbolically designated as taboo. Scopophilia, indeed, is not simply the desire to see, but to see the object of a desire that is itself off limits, behind the veil, through the looking glass, and so on. My self-revelation became infinitely sexier, then, precisely because it took a feminine form of self-presentation: a striptease act through which I objectified myself as the 'female' object of the gaze, preserving my chastity—a nod to the feminine demeure—with the modest restraint of a thong." (265-266)

In spite of the penis, Norton's narrative is transsexual, a tendency that seems to have only a small part of me. For me, the act provided an erotic contrast, in which I could be either covered, the person without the penis, or revealed as the person with the penis. It made my own penis an erotic object in a way that it seldom has been for me, except as a tool for masturbation.

The penis was the focus for my nascent scopophilia. While I was interested in the developing shapes of my female peers, I did not find them arousing or fascinating. As an adolescent, I began to buy *Playboy* and similar magazines, and studied the photographs in an attempt to find an *attraction*, rather than just an attraction. When my mother found them, she seemed embarrassed but vaguely supportive, no doubt another moment in her how-not-to-bring-up-a-gay-son agenda. Because of my very limited involvement in team sports, I did not have a major opportunity for locker room play, but the normal physical education classes offered a few chances. I had one classmate who was very well-endowed and that offered me the fascination I did not find in *Playboy*. Of course, being "soft and flabby" and a late developer—my voice did not change until I was sixteen—I was in the difficult position of trying to hide my own body while watching others. As I learned later in the baths, looking without showing has its limits.

I suppose it is possible that my problem with my own body was the reason that, unlike Norton, my performance had no audience except the mirror. I think that in my private world, I could imaginatively transform my body into what I wished it to be. It might be worthy of note, however, that it was my mother's mirror. Whereas the kitchen was a place where I could publicly share my mother's presence, her bedroom—and given that my father had a different bedroom, it was very much *her* bedroom—was a place for private enjoyment when she was out. This was not just the eros of cross-dressing. Her toiletries held a strange charm for me and I still have as a keepsake a small plastic container in which she used to store her hairpins. Corbett says, "There has been no effort to entertain the ways in which a boy may identify with his mother as distinct from a regressive lack of separation." (129) Or to put it in terms of an old joke: "My mother made me a homosexual." "If I give her the wool will she make me one too?"

Friedman describes the way psychoanalysis reshapes the Oedipus complex to deal with the mother of the homosexual: "One theory holds that if a boy identifies with his controlling, seductive mother rather than with his indifferent father, he experiences the identification and the wish to be loved by his father as his mother would be in the form of homosexual erotic imagery." (25) While my father was somewhat distant, I do not recall such a desire to replace my mother in his affection. I did not find a "father gap" nearly as significant as my mother obsession. I do not recall any yearning for my father, sexual or otherwise. I suppose this is one of those elements for which my recall must be questioned. Presumably a sexual attraction to one's father is not a memory one would cherish fondly. Douglas Sadownick, in *Sex Between Men: An Intimate History of the Sex Lives of Gay Men Postwar to Present*, states:

> To be sure, the rejection of the boy by the father does not
> cause homosexuality. Rather, a boy is born with a special,
> erotic, twin 'brother,' who is felt to be the source of life,
> and it is this soul-complex that gets projected onto the
> father. So the wish for father-incest becomes the original
> nostalgic call to union with a primal homo source, and
> thereby the father (and father-complex) becomes the first
> filter through which love-hate shines. (162)

Instead, I recall primarily a fear of becoming my father, becoming that distant person, plagued by migraines, quick to anger in ways that made him not abusive but rather inarticulate and withdrawn, convinced of various religious and other conservative dogma, unable to connect with many people. When he discovered not that I was gay but that one of my friends was, he said, "Did you know?" When I said, "Yes," he replied: "Putrid. Putrid, putrid, putrid. Putrid." Rather than a distant figure of that erotic twin brother, someone to love and hate, he was someone who provided a model of how not to be. Whatever my life would be it would not be that.

This decision became even more emphatic when I realized, once I reached my twenties, that part of my father's problem might be his own sexuality. Although he had a very limited education, only various correspondence courses after leaving school in grade eight, he had achieved a white collar job and paid both significant money and significant attention to good suits. My earliest memory of him is being told not to touch him in case I disturbed his clothing. His one domestic activity was ironing his clothes, a choice made not to relieve my mother but because he was afraid she would not do it with sufficient precision. His most important memories, from all stages of his life, were of intimate friendships with a few individual men, perhaps five in all. He was devoted to gardening, for which he won awards, and he demonstrated an appreciation of flowers never equaled by his appreciation of his family, which tended to be more dutiful than romantic. His love of music was most evident in his intense emotional response to opera. I can still recall his face when listening to Callas in *Norma*, as he demonstrated all the characteristics of the classic opera queen.

If he seemed to have spent his life sublimating his love into a variety of other directions, my mother was exactly the opposite. Her whole life was family and for the latter part of it family meant me. Until she died, whenever she saw me she would wrap her arms around me and say, "My boy, my boy. Just let me look at you." My eldest sister sardonically observed that if I murdered someone, my mother would have asked, "Why did that nasty man put his back in front of my son's knife?" While I was often non-plussed by the power of this focus on my life, I also responded to it with my own devotion. Until a recent move, I continued to have a photograph of my mother in each room of my house, something I had not noticed until a female friend wryly pointed it out to me. Friedman's succinct assessment applies: "The homosexual men significantly more frequently than the heterosexual men had overintense mother-son relationships and unsatisfactory father-son relationships." (58)

Richard Green's *The "Sissy Boy Syndrome" and the Development of Homosexuality* states:

> The "recipe" approach to preparing a developmental
> model of homosexual orientation is a tempting tradition.
> A cup of father absence, a dash of maternal dominance, a
> sprig of peer rejection, and a pinch of early homosexual
> seduction combine to yield the homosexual man. (372)

While the psychoanalytic model is too facile to be an explanation, the number of gay men who have been prepared exactly according to this recipe is quite amazing. Although my mother has been dead almost twenty years, I had the sense that she believed in it. My adolescence was a combination of a continuing intense relationship with my mother and her attempts to somehow disrupt it. When I left home at seventeen to attend university she made it clear that she felt this would be better for me in the long run. As I look back I see this as her last attempt to produce me as a heterosexual.

Muriel Dimen, in "On 'Our Nature': Prolegomenon to a Relational Theory of Sexuality," states that: "The story of Heterophilia constitutes the Discourse of Nature." (133) This is the discourse we are all taught as the inevitable normal and so it seems a rather large gesture to oppose it. In the end I was not so simply "the homosexual child," because I did not find homosexuality to be inevitable for me, the choice that one cannot not choose. My life as a married heterosexual was not a lie but rather a partial truth, one that at times became difficult yet was often not difficult at all. I am tempted to say that one reason was that my sex drive, for men or women, has never been overwhelming. I have never performed that life-shattering pursuit of the object of desire so popular in fiction and film. Every time I see a film in which the protagonist simply must have sex with him/her and the resulting disintegration leads to homicide or suicide, I profoundly recognize that this could never have happened to me.

Thus for me it is not just a question of whether I am heterosexual or homosexual, but whether I am necessarily sexual at all. My choices to be sexual have often seemed more about other issues than about sexual aim and sexual object. Thus I feel comfortable deciding that I did live the life of the homosexual child, or at least the proto-homosexual child. If my sexual desires had been more ardent, this would have resulted in a more homosexual life. As Dimen suggests, heterophilia is an extraordinarily powerful force and one needs powerful urges to divert it. For me at least, those urges were—and for that matter are—a sometime thing.

## 4. Penis Envy

The title of this chapter is an obvious reference to Freud, who believed that women were guided by envy of the male penis. Common sense might suggest otherwise. There are many sexualities, the basic four being homosexual male, heterosexual male, homosexual female, and heterosexual female. I could not claim to have made a scientific study of their attitudes, but in my personal experience, if there is any penis envy, it is felt by the first two. Both homosexual and heterosexual males have penises, yet they often fear that it is not quite as large as someone else's.

Any women reading this might just say it is no big thing. One old joke is that women have trouble with math because men constantly tell them that eight centimeters equals six inches. Elements of sex are always comical, but penises seem to be a rather extreme example. It has become a standard game in university classrooms, in psychology, in gender studies, in almost all fields, to ask for lists of terms for the penis. This invariably leads to entertaining gender, age, and ethnic comparisons and usually comes up with at least a few idiosyncratic terms from childhood, such as "tea kettle." I trust you noted that "comes up with." The penis is such that in any discussion of it, it is impossible to avoid double entendre. Peter F. Murphy's *Studs, Tools and the Family Jewels: Metaphors Men Live By* is rather lacking in humour, in spite of the title, but it captures the extent to which sexual terms penetrate the language. Part of the lack of humour results from Murphy's earnest male feminism as in the following: "'Hard-on' relates also to the male view of the penis as a weapon to wield power against a foe. The foe in this equation becomes the woman in the relationship." (23) Yet, as Murphy claims, the penis as weapon seems to have a wide currency, as in references to a sexually successful heterosexual man as a "swordsman." Every man seems to be looking for a sheath, which, as many disgruntled feminist etymologists will tell you, is the root meaning—you see, it's impossible—of "vagina."

Bill Clinton's "I did not have sex with that woman" denial has been replayed again and again, but a number of analysts have pointed to the simple truth: he didn't "have sex" with her. Heterosexual relations are constantly described in terms of penis penetration of the vagina ("have sex") versus everything else ("did not have sex"). The idea of technical virginity is by no means a western invention, as many cultures in the South Pacific, in Africa, and elsewhere, accept sex play in adolescence as long as the hymen is not broken. This attitude seems at least part of the reason why anal penetration is so much the generic understanding of gay sex, regardless of the number of men who seldom or never practice it. Even in the gay world there is an assumption that a real man is looking for a place to put his instrument, as in names for sex clubs such as "The Toolbox."

There are perhaps exceptions. For much of my life I believed that the male devotion to his own penis was a myth. When I heard that some heterosexual couples have pet names such as "big fella," I was amazed. I knew that my desire to insert mine anywhere was limited and I assumed that the constant male claim of a biological imperative to get it into some receptive orifice was simply a justification for obsessive behaviour, whether in pursuit of women or in pursuit of men. Since then I have come to recognize that I am simply one of those males who is just as devoted to the penis as any other, it is just that the penis of choice is not my own.

Still, I should not deny my penis, in the manner of so many cultures that use the penis as a testimonial, often by holding it during an oath. My penis has served me well in a variety of contexts, including fathering children. In my youth I was as devoted to masturbation as the next boy, sometimes more than five times a day, to the point the skin on my penis became decidedly raw. I came to learn, however, that I was more interested in the orgasm than in the penis or the erection. My overdose on masturbation taught me that it was possible to have an orgasm without either erection or ejaculate, although this tended to happen when the penis had developed a rather flayed appearance. As I engaged in heterosexual sex, I learned that women expected penetration and I did as was expected. It took me many years to recognize that this was not what I wanted. By then I had discovered the type of orgasm I could have through anal penetration to the point that I rarely masturbated without it, as the resulting orgasm could never compare.

Some feminists attack Freud for over-rating the penis, but he certainly did not originate the veneration of the male member. A general survey suggests that the penis has been a dominant symbol of power throughout the world. One element that supports this premise is the wide-ranging devotion to and highly varied methods of male circumcision. While different cultures acclaim different meanings, the one continuity seems to be subservience. Whether the foreskin is removed as a gesture towards a god (or gods), a human master, tradition, or whatever, its removal is a recognition of a higher power. If considered in reverse, this suggests that the penis is itself extraordinarily powerful and thus it becomes the thing that is constrained as a symbol of submission.

While removal and embellishment might seem polar opposites, there appears to be support for my argument in Peter Ucko's article, "Penis Sheaths: A Comparative Study." Ucko concludes:

> From our review we see that penis sheaths in most
> societies have remarkably few phallic connotations and
> are, rather, symbols of modesty and decorum. This is
> perhaps not as surprising as it might at first sight seem to
> be, when we remember that most societies first adopt the
> penis sheath at or near puberty. The sheath is, in many of
> these cases, not simply a symbol of sexual maturity but
> one of social control of that sexuality. The penis sheath, in
> many instances, is not primarily a sexual symbol in itself
> but a visible sign of sexual restriction. (60)

While Ucko is careful not to overstate his case, a logical extension of his argument is that the penis sheath exists to contain that least controllable and most dangerously powerful of objects.

The role of the penis in heterosexual pornography is a marker of its power in western culture. The penis continues to be the maker or breaker in censorship. Today, full frontal nudity of a female is acceptable in many films with only mildly overt sexual messages, while the male penis is seen to be a problem in seeking anything less than a very restrictive rating. The erect penis remains limited to hard-core pornography, with very few exceptions. While almost never visible in mainstream cinema, ejaculation remains a marker in heterosexual pornography. The usual term is "the money shot," the act that defines why the film is worth the spectator's purchase. In heterosexual pornography, the man often withdraws from the vagina and ejaculates in a woman's face. As one porn director said, "That's the way it has to be. I don't know why, but that's the way it has to be." The obvious explanation is that it represents the woman's submission and worship, almost a sexual eucharist. In practical terms, however, it also shows, even more than penetration, that "real sex" happened. A defining product is presented, not hidden or even faked inside a vagina. Thus the "coming inside," which shows a woman accepting male power in "normal" heterosexual sex, becomes an absence of power.

Is the penis as powerful as our cultures have claimed it to be? While terms such as "phallogocentrism" make the phallus just as seminal to language as the penis literally is to biology, the connection between the phallus and the penis is both obvious and easily overstated. Lacan famously claims the phallus to be the transcendental signifier, but he also asserts that male dominance is a bit of a trap, as the male assumes his penis is the phallus, while it is a far more limited thing. Ellie Ragland-Sullivan, in *Jacques Lacan and the Philosophy of Psychoanalysis*, assesses why the Lacanian phallus leads to an over-rating of the penis:

> Difference, in other words, is not an intrinsic attribute of
> either sex. The penis, as a separate or third entity, signifies
> the difference. As we have seen, Lacan treats the penis as
> privileged because of a confusion of the virile member
> with a phallic signifying function. The Phallus introduces
> the alienating effect of difference into the pleasurable

and natural mother-infant dyad, and this Oedipalizing,
dividing effect gradually becomes substantivized around
the Name-of-the-Father. (290)

That is a rather large job for a small and often fragile object. No wonder
"erectile dysfunction" is such a growth industry. In *Impotence: A Cultural
History*, Angus McLaren uses the phrase "specter of impotence" a number
of times, to suggest that he thinks it is a very large spook indeed. He
concludes his book with the claim that progress has not made us less
fearful, "because sexual dysfunctions are spoken of more openly today
it is probable that the specter of impotence haunts more men than it ever
has before." (266) Boo.

Jeanne E. Hamming's article "Dildonics, Dykes and the Detachable
Masculine" considers the artificial penis, the dildo, and its relationship
to the phallus:

The dildo scandalizes identity categories of gender and
sexuality because it reveals that the penis is always
separate from the body, that the dildo is separate from the
penis, and that sexual pleasure can be disconnected from
sexual identity as well as from essentialist ideas of the self.
(330)

There is a sense in which the penis has always been separate from the
body, as suggested by numerous jokes on *Seinfeld*. As Elaine says in one
episode, "I don't know how you guys walk around with those things."
One problem is that men cannot walk around without them. This
was addressed by the music group King Missile in its novelty song,
"Detachable Penis": "I can leave it home, when I think it's gonna get me
in trouble." While the song is inveterately heterosexual, it is not without
double entendres: "Even though sometimes it's a pain in the ass, / I like
having a detachable penis."

The representation of the penis as emphatically a thing separate from
the body seems to be found in most cultures. Murphy looks at the various terms that suggest machinery, most particularly "tool": "The idea of
the penis as an instrument to accomplish something (usually penetra-

tion of a woman to have a quick and easy orgasm), or as an implement
to get a particular job done, pervades the way men think about their
sexuality." (31) Japanese woodcuts have a special appreciation for the lu-
dicrously large penis, including one in which an old man must carry his
own in a wheelbarrow. Craig A. Williams' *Roman Homosexuality: Ideologies*
*of Masculinity in Classical Antiquity* notes that statues of Priapus tended to be
rustic, as though not to mislead the focus on the oversized penis. The
god himself was of little importance, but his member was a thing to
beware. Williams states:

> An obvious but crucial point needs perhaps to be stressed
> once more: the Priapic paradigm, centered around the
> man as penetrator and noticeably unconcerned with
> the sex of his partner, necessarily implies that the
> fundamental antithesis informing Roman representations
> of men as sexual subjects was the opposition between the
> insertive role in penetrative acts, which was normative for
> men, and the receptive role in penetrative acts, which was
> not, rather than the opposition between heterosexual and
> homosexual behaviour. (160)

Yet it seems that the "Priapic paradigm" is not just about the man
refusing the receptive position, but also about the constant power of the
penis. This is one reason why I question Hamming's central claim: "In
other words, even if the dildo improves upon the penis, they are both
granted the same significance due to their relationship to the phallus."
(331) This assumes that the primary issue is Lacanian signification. Much
of the material I have read suggests rather that it is the power of the
penis itself that interests these various cultures, and particularly the men
of these cultures.

The power of the penis is not my primary concern here, although
I think it is worth asserting that our culture's concern for the phallus
seems mistaken. For feminists, it becomes an emblem to embody the
sexism of our society, but I question whether either the phallus or the
penis is the primary source of gender discrimination. Then there is the

new men's movement, which wishes to erect a phallus of male spiritu-
ality to protect the failure of modern manhood, as in James Wyly's *The
Phallic Quest: Priapus and Masculine Inflation*:

> Concretization—and perpetuation—of the phallic quest in
> the form of homosexual promiscuity has been a pervasive
> phenomenon of our time. It is distressing enough for men
> who identify themselves as homosexuals, for it endlessly
> complicates their lives and endangers their deeper
> relationships. It can be even more painful for men who
> continue to view themselves as committed to heterosexual
> relationships. A separation from *phallos* will certainly
> undermine a man's male-female relationships, for it will
> leave him powerless to deal with the devouring-mother
> aspect of any woman with whom he becomes involved. In
> that event, the temptation to flee to the apparent phallic
> security of a homosexual encounter can be extreme. (87)

I have found many things in "homosexual encounters," but "phallic
security" has not been one of them.

David Friedman's *A Mind of Its Own: A Cultural History of the Penis* is witty
and usually reasonable, although heterosexist, and quite wide-ranging
historically. He notes the importance of the arrival of Christianity in the
history of penis assessment, particularly as shaped by St. Augustine in
*The City of God*:

> For the Greeks and Romans, an erection was like a change
> in heartbeat: involuntary, and not susceptible to blame
> or praise. But for Augustine the cause *and* the effect of
> original sin is lust, the symptom *and* the disease is the
> erection. With this one stroke, this one man transformed
> the penis more than any man who had yet lived: the
> sacred staff became the demon rod. (39)

The question seems to be more than anything the apparent autonomy
of the penis. Our breathing, our heartbeats, and a variety of other

biological functions are more or less autonomous, but our external body parts tend to be pretty strictly controlled by our minds. The penis is rather an exception, often becoming erect when the owner would prefer that it not and failing to perform when the owner would dearly love to use it. In another episode of *Seinfeld*, Jerry tells George that he is repulsed by his girlfriend's personality but attracted to her physically:

> Jerry: It's like my brain is facing my penis in a chess game. And I'm letting him win.
> George: You're not letting him win. He wins till you're forty.
> Jerry: Then what?
> George: He still wins, but it's not a blowout.

Murphy's summation is that George is just too accurate: "As metaphors for male sexuality, these terms reinforce once again the insistent assumption that men have an uncontrollable need for sex and that their genitals are pre-eminent in their relation to women." (106)

One interpretation is that the penis simply does what it does, which shows the human to be a biological beast. The other, mooted by St. Augustine, is that it gets the human into trouble, it acts without reason simply because it represents trouble; it is controlled by forces opposed to reason, and opposed to God. One might think of the mime who pretends he is a puppet. He moves in various directions as though pulled by invisible strings. Each movement surprises him, as if he has no volition. This is the view of the powerful penis. There is a play about sex that was performed in Toronto in the 1970s, entitled *We Love You Baby Blue*. It was collectively written but with a set script. However, in one scene a woman magician performed a trick with a penis sticking through a curtain. She had a choice of two lines, one if an erection happened and one if it did not. In other words, far more than the proverbial theatrical sayings about the impossibility of dealing with children and animals on stage, the penis was an actor who would not take direction. How could this not be demonic?

Men seem to accept that it is that thing that defines us. Regardless

of pornography's obsession with breasts and genital references like the
rock band Hole, women might be represented as a series of body parts,
but they are not just one body part. The man is a penis, no more, no
less. Certainly not less. John Money, in one of his constant assertions
of scientific objectivity, states in *Venuses Penuses*, "The homespun wisdom
of medically unsophisticated people confronted with a newborn her-
maphrodite usually guides them to assign the baby to the sex that it
most resembles in external genital appearance." (133) Needless to say, he
claims that the medically sophisticated use a much more complex set of
diagnostic skills, from hormonal measurements to internal examination. But then, in another observation about parental explanations, he
concludes with a special case:

> A special problem of vocabulary arises when talking
> truthfully with parents, should a decision have been
> reached to allow a contradiction between gonadal
> structure and sex of rearing in their child—which should,
> for example, ordinarily be the decision when, despite
> testes, the phallus is clitoral sized. (142)

Medical sophistication seems to fly out the window in the face of a small
penis.

While being anally penetrated I often take some time to become
erect. In something that seems strangely akin to vaginal penetration for
women—and, as I note in the chapter on anal sex, I sometimes fantasize
that I am vaginally penetrated—I become lost in the experience and find
it difficult to focus on masturbating to create and maintain an erection.
When I become erect, I sense a general arousal throughout the genital
region, much more so than from just masturbation or from penetrating
a woman. When the orgasm arrives, it is not thrusting and spurting
but rather reaching the summit of a rather long climb. When I have described this to women, I have been told that this resembles a female orgasm. The ejaculation is like the overflow of experience at reaching that
summit. I find the effect becomes the whole body orgasm we are told
lies somewhere in the tantric beyond. While it is very much an orgasm

with ejaculation, the ejaculation is a culmination rather than a goal.

Yet again, my self-analysis is subject to my inability to see the hidden side of so many parts of my sexuality. As in my comments about cross-dressing and male feminism, it is possible that I am rejecting my penis as penetrator for some profound feminist or even, dare I say it, Freudian reason. I recall no dangerous sexual moment in my childhood, but neither have I ever been in psychoanalysis and who knows what I might have repressed. Is there an element of castration in my position? I recently received a note from a friend I have not seen in some years who said she had heard I had had a sex change. I laughed. It is not just that I do not see myself as a woman: I would not give up the penis that has given me a lot of pleasure over the years (in this case I mean my own penis). I suppose I could be avoiding the phallus but, as I just stated, I am more and more convinced that the phallus is the penis, with all its limitations.

But also, as I so often aver, its attractions. As a friend once said after a particularly energetic night: "I just had to wrap my lips around as many cocks as I could find." I have never been so obsessive about anything, much less fellatio, but I understand the basis of his drive. There is a moment when I face a new erection, knowing the prospective feel in my mouth, on my tongue, when the appeal of the penis is more than clear. At that point, all the evaluation, of size, shape, texture, begins to seem eminently important. It has always interested me that women seem to have rather limited interest in the penis. Thus the women's joke: "If you get a baby when you have sex, what do you get when you give a blow job? Jewelry." The usual claim is that fellatio is something that every man wants and that women offer under duress, out of kindness, or for future considerations, seldom sexual. I once asked a female sex worker who was known to be very good at cocksucking what made her so successful and she said, "I just think about what I would like if I were a penis." She seems a rarity, however, and her attitude might be explained as reflecting the type of person who would turn any job into a satisfying activity.

On the other hand, gay men often perform fellatio just for the joys my lip-wrapping friend experienced. When younger, he had a bad habit of hanging around heterosexual bars and picking up men who had failed to pick up a woman. His enjoyment of the various cocks was not deterred by the homophobic beatings he sometimes received after the men had been serviced. I have certainly given blow jobs to ostensibly heterosexual men, but never in such dangerous circumstances. The dismissive term "cocksucker," employed to represent demeaning subservience, has always struck me as mistaken. A good cocksucker is a skillful performer. One friend of mine gave a blow job in a toilet and then was beaten and robbed. Before he departed, the robber turned and said, "You know, you are really good at that." Small recompense perhaps, but my friend was somewhat proud to tell the story.

Yet, I feel the act is not just showing off a skill, nor is it only a gift to the person receiving the fellatio. It is not uncommon in the baths for the receiver to thank the giver. That terminology, "receiver" and "giver," suggests the assumptions follow the heterosexual paradigm, but all gay men know that this is not the case, that the seeker is more often the giver than the receiver. I'm sure the average heterosexual male would be amazed to know how often a gay man with an erection will pass up an offer to be sucked simply because there might be someone more ideal who will offer the same service a little later. Perhaps this is because, as so often claimed, the gay man is just a phallus worshipper and whoever has the top phallus is the top.

The connection between gay men and heterosexual women has long been recognized, particularly in the often pejorative term, "fag hag." In popular culture, such as the Bridget Jones novels and films, the gay man is a flirty person interested in fashion and boys and thus an obvious soulmate for the girl-about-town. Various books, such as *Straight Women, Gay Men: Absolutely Fabulous Friendships*, by Robert H. Hopcke and Laura Rafaty, and Catherine Whitney's *Uncommon Lives: Gay Men and Straight Women*, try to offer a bit more substance. Something similar might be lurking behind the common appearance of gay men as male feminists. Here, however, the image of gay men and feminists as sisterly comrades is more about gay men as similar victims of the patriarchy than as pursuers of the penis. I doubt that the gay male feminist is primarily envisioned as an inveterate cocksucker.

Freud codified the oral pleasures by comparing them to the genital. Thus in heterosexual oral sex, the female mouth is imitating the vagina. Deep kissing is a more restrained version of the same model (although I have no idea what Freud thought was happening when the woman thrust her tongue into the man's mouth. Perhaps this was one of those moments that tipped foreplay into perversion). One need not accept Freud's paradigms to acknowledge how profoundly sexual the mouth is. It is a commonplace to compare tasting food and wine to a sexual experience. Thus the process of fellatio engages the sexuality of the mouth as well as the penis. Perhaps the gay man is best able to appreciate that because he has a penis himself and because he already recognizes the apparent perversion of his sexuality and is likely to be more receptive to the appeal of a variety of parts. Just as an aside, few heterosexual males seem to recognize that their nipples are erogenous while few gay males don't.

This appreciation of what is received when giving certainly extends to the actual ejaculation. Some gay men spit out the cum in the apparently mistaken view that this is safer. However, if free from concern about STDs, gay men tend to luxuriate in the pleasure of cum in the mouth. Intimate friends will discuss the difference between one man's cum and another's, often with assumptions about race and ethnicity that reflect more prejudice than scientific accuracy. There is no suggestion of the common heterosexual female revulsion that "You let him do it in your mouth!?" Part of this is glorying in perversion, as in so many aspects of homosexuality, but more it is a recognition that taste and texture of the ejaculate is another sensual pleasure. When the process is energetic and the ejaculation forceful and voluminous, there is a gentle warm pleasure quite unlike the thrusting release of the receiver. He is finished while the giver is just luxuriating.

Regardless of how the various positions are explained, the homo-sexual male's attraction to the penis might seem easily explainable. It is difficult to understand, however, according to the paradigms our cul-ture is used to. The obvious reason is that Freud assumed heterosexual-ity to be not just the norm but the inevitable. A comparison of anatomy would lead to the assumption that the clitoris and penis are directly comparable: just rub until orgasm occurs. In order to naturalize het-erosexual intercourse, however, Freud believed the boy learned to rub his penis and then found sexual maturity by learning to rub it inside a vagina, a reasonably direct adaptation. On the other hand, the girl who had learned how to rub had to give up that pleasurable bit of expertise and hope that a penis inside the vagina might recreate the rubbing. The problem is that to succeed requires a success of indirection, where the thrusting of the penis leads either to pulling the skin around the clitoris or else to a rubbing of the male pelvis on the clitoris. It might happen, just as scratching your wrist might relieve an itch on your forearm. The difference is the first choice to relieve the forearm would not be to approach the wrist. Freud's naturalized view of male sexual maturity controls much of our thought on the penis. Thus Money states, "The very sexual performance of the boy is categorically different from that for the girl, in that his penis must be aroused to erection before he can begin; and it must ejaculate in orgasm if reproduction is to be effected. In the girl, by contrast, it is possible for conception to occur without either arousal or orgasm." (*Venuses* 210-211) "Sexual performance" requires an erection because without it, the male cannot "begin."

This still does not explain the apparent inevitability of penis attrac-tion for gay men. For Freud, the heterosexual male's search for the va-gina and the heterosexual female's desire for penetration were just nor-mal behaviours that supported the propagation of the species. On the other hand—again the inevitable double entendre—the gay man has no necessity to pursue the penis. Many gay men claim to love the "bubble butt" and some even express appreciation of the male nipple, but the penis is almost always the central concern. Perhaps it is just that we have been convinced that this is what makes the man and we want men. Any other explanation seems to be just functional, about the wonderful things that a penis can be made to do as it grows and thrusts, gets hard and shoots.

There have been many documented cases of ejaculation without erection and impregnation without penetration and without *apparent* ejaculation, but Money's premise that the male erection is male sexuality is very much the usual assumption. This has led to the plethysmograph, invented by Kurt Freund in 1965. Friedman notes, "'The availability of an objective method to determine the objects of arousal in the male is of considerable importance [as a diagnostic tool] for research,' Freund wrote in the *Journal of the Experimental Analysis of Behavior*." (231) Freund's primary purpose was apparently to identify pedophiles: "Frustrated with the subjectivity of standard research into deviant sexuality, which often relied on case histories, he was looking for a more objective way of measuring and, he hoped, preventing such behavior, especially the sexual abuse of children." (232) Friedman states that Freund was instead forced by the Czech government to use it to check for malingerers claiming homosexuality to avoid conscription and also to identify homosexuals who would be compelled to undergo aversion shock therapy.

Freund may not have wished to have his work so used, but there is clearly a series of continuities between his intentions and those of the state. He viewed pedophiles as a danger that needed to be identified. The government believed malingerers and homosexuals were dangers that needed to be identified. Both Freund and the state thought that the erection provided the identification. Throughout his book, Friedman seems to accept exactly this view, that the penis tells the truth. Thus regardless of how authorities, whether scholars or legislators, might feel about the technology of the plethysmograph or the uses made of it, they believe that the erection identifies the pedophiles, the malingerers, and the homosexuals. There apparently was no need—and no method—to identify female equivalents. On the one hand, this simply reflects experience: sexual violence is predominantly a male act, and it is often performed using an erect penis. That there is no reason to assume homosexuals are violent does not deny that the government believed homosexuals were likely to use the penis for something inherently evil. As well, however, the plethysmograph reflects the belief in the cultural importance of penis power, here being employed in its demonic mode.

But is the penis such an easy tool? Given the number of times the penis is marked as independent and undependable, it is difficult to see why it would operate so easily in an essentially oppositional environment. I have attempted to use my own erections as a marker of my sexual desire but have found them decidedly unsatisfactory. Any Freudian would simply say that my unconscious knows what my conscious does not, but I have spent many years attempting to assess my sexuality in as honest a manner as possible, and it seems to me that if anyone should be allowed self-analysis of the erection as denotative, I should. Besides the obvious contradictions provided by impotence caused by fatigue, alcohol, fear, etc., I have found only one way in which my erections are at least somewhat consistent. This is that they are xenophobic. I don't mean in racial or ethnic terms, as many of my lovers have been people of colour, etc. However, I am much less likely to get an erection, with a man or a woman, if I don't know him or her. Thus while my conscious self is interested in stranger sex and enjoys the baths, my penis is decidedly undependable in such an atmosphere, something that often deters me from going when I would like to go. Perhaps my inability to see my erections as accurate assessors of my sexual desire has led me to reject the penis as a guiding force and follow my body in more general terms. Perhaps if I had one of those all-powerful penises, I would have more respect for the argument by penis.

Still, this xenophobic penis could be part of my reason for being anal receptive. I think of myself as wanting insertion because of my response to the feeling, but perhaps it is also an aversion to my own failed erection. There is more to this, of course. As I maintain throughout this book, I assume that my personal physiological responses are not necessarily the dominant guide to my behaviour and my analyses, but they are certainly a significant factor. Thus my response to fellatio might be part of the key here. I have never had an orgasm when someone, male or female, performed fellatio on me. I have sometimes masturbated after fellatio, yet my assessment is that the fellatio made little or no contribution to the sexual stimulation that led to the orgasm. Thus all those jokes about blow jobs ("A bad blow job is a contradiction in terms") are about someone other than me. I enjoy fellatio by women, but I actually enjoy it more when not erect, a time when a mouth on the penis gives me more varied feelings than when erect. On the other hand, I don't like a male mouth on my penis at all. It is the time when some metaphysics of my femininity strikes me and I just find it wrong. I have never been able to maintain an erection when a male is giving me oral sex. For me erection is a means to an end, the thing that must happen—at least to some extent—before orgasm. This is not the erection as dominance so ubiquitous in many cultures.

It thus amazes me that so many scientists believe in the erection as not just symbolic but as a direct measurement of sexual desire. Benjamin Sachs's article, "Contextual Approaches to the Physiology and Classification of Erectile Function, Erectile Dysfunction and Sexual Arousal," considers the way behaviorists have tried to differentiate between erections that mean something and those that don't:

> Erection stimulated by touch outside the context of copulation is commonly referred to as 'reflexive' erection. When the perigenital touch results from *self-stimulation*, the term "masturbation" is usually applied. However, it should be noted that copulation is itself self-stimulatory, in that the male's own thrusting causes much of the genital stimulation that he receives from the vagina, and reafference from the thrusting movements may also be excitatory. When erection results from other than tactile stimulation, eg. from viewing, hearing, or smelling sex-related stimuli, or from recalled or imagined sexual stimuli, then erection has usually been termed 'psychogenic.' (542)

While Sachs questions these distinctions, he seems to wish to show them some respect. However, he himself notes the number of animal studies that show a similarly confusing complexity of erection possibilities, where they can happen hetero-erotically, homo-erotically, in response to non-sexual tactile stimulation, even as part of aggression in an attack. Perhaps I am being a speciesist, as an animal rights advocate might assert, but it seems to me that humans, having much more sophisticated powers of analysis, are likely to have a much more diffuse system of erections.

D. Richard Laws wrote an article with a title consisting of a rhetorical question: "Penile Plethysmography: Will We Ever Get It Right?" Given the way rhetorical questions function, it is not surprising that his answer is no: "I recruited several normal subjects and presented the pornographic films to them in several variations of an ABA reversal design. In the A condition I instructed them to allow themselves to become sexually aroused; in the B condition I instructed them to attempt to inhibit their arousal by mental means." (83) The result suggested that it is possible to prevent arousal through psychological control, which should produce at least some hesitation in those who see the plethysmograph as a legal agent to label people as one type or another. Laws then asked another question: "Is the phenomenon that PPG measures—penile erection—a valid measure of deviant sexual arousal (i.e. deviant sexual interest and preference)?" (90) His rather surprising answer is that regardless of the apparent incrimination, self-reporting is more consistent than the plethysmograph on questions of object choice and even on a history of sexual violence. In other words, if you want to find out someone's sexual predilections, rather than attaching electrodes to penises, it is more accurate just to ask.

Friedman notes a variety of complications for the Jewish penis in non-Jewish cultures. It was not just that the Jews were marked by circumcision, it was the nature of that mark. The Greeks believed that the revealing of the glans, an inevitable result of circumcision, was unseemly. If the penis is a power symbol, how much so the revealed glans, as in the title of a novel by the Canadian author Scott Symons, Helmet of Flesh. Jewish circumcision, like that in other cultures, is a statement of faith. God told Abraham to circumcise his male offspring as a covenant that they would be faithful and that God would make them fruitful. In other words, it might be that the circumcision is a weakening of the penis before God, in order that God will use his almighty power in the aid of those who have deferred their power as fealty to him, or it might be that the circumcision is a God-ordained strengthening, so it can now reveal his almighty power through the almighty power of the penis.

Friedman offers an ironic take on the results: "Some have argued that, by mimicking erection in this way, circumcision reveals the Hebrews to have been an early phallic cult. (This is not a widely held view)." (12) If a phallic cult sought circumcision, why is today's penis cult, the gay male community, so opposed to circumcision, as shown in the number of personal ads offering or asking for "uncut"? There are a variety of websites where men can learn how to reverse circumcision, represented as mutilation. The sexuality of those creating and using these sites is speculation, but those who reveal their orientation tend to be gay. One reason might be a desire to be "natural." Regardless of the association of gay men with interior decoration and the theatre, homosexuality seriously venerates the primitive, especially in sex. Another reason, however, might be transformation. I personally prefer a circumcised penis. This could be just because I myself am circumcised, but I honestly have no idea why I have this preference. I can see, however, that the erection of an uncircumcised penis offers a form of revelation that can be quite appealing. As that helmet of flesh surfaces from the folds of skin, it begs for attention.

I referred to Ken Corbett's article "Homosexual Boyhood: Notes on Girlyboys" in the chapter on sexuality in childhood. While I can identify somewhat with having been a "girlyboy" as a child, I do not feel transsexual. Yet I also can identify with the girlyboy's own appreciation of penises, and his anxious response to the general claim, that he himself has a phallus.

> Girlyboys have a penis, want a penis, and often identify
> with those who do not have a penis. This having,
> desiring, and lacking contribute to a unique gender
> experience. One feature of this experience is a particular
> form of anxiety: girlyboys frequently feel their bodies to
> be inadequately phallic. (125)

If one accepts the studies that say that girlyboys become gay men, but not necessarily effeminate gay men, it could suggest that in those early years the boy recognizes the attraction of the penis but fears the inadequacy of his own. This would suggest why the penis is such a scopophilic marker, but also why the adult gay man, no matter how phallic in demeanour and performance, might have a lingering fear that the penis is not quite sufficient to make up a phallus.

I suspect that the homosexual desire for the penis is directly related to our masculinist culture. It is not a narcissistic desire for that thing that the man already has, but rather an unusually direct desire for the thing that society has told him is so wonderful. Friedman describes a talisman carried by a young Roman man to show that he was a man who should not be penetrated sexually: "Known as a *fascinum*, this penis replica signified the boy's status and power as a future *vir*." (25) "Today, fifteen hundred years after the fall of Imperial Rome, anything as powerful or intriguing as an erection is said to be 'fascinating.'" (25) This could be one reason why a number of studies, such as "The Relation Between Sexual Orientation and Penile Size," by Anthony F. Bogaert and Scott Hershberger, claim that, after all those girlyboy fears, homosexual males have larger penises. Bogaert and Hershberger explore a variety of tangents, including the obvious one that homosexual men exaggerate more, but come to the decision that this observation, based on Kinsey's data, is true. In one reply, William Krisel makes the interesting note that Kinsey's analysis labels as "homosexual" anyone with significant homosexual experience, and it is possible that predominantly heterosexual men who have large penises are more likely to be approached by homosexuals. As Krisel himself comments, this seems "far-fetched," but it certainly conforms to any gay man's experience of stranger sex. In many bathhouses the "average" penis size is unusually large, no doubt reflecting the assumption of many men that if they are unable to display something fascinating, they might as well stay home.

The gay male obsession with large penises is difficult to dispute. Much of the desire for black men is attributed to their reputed size. Many pornographic websites are devoted to larger than average penises and there is even a label for men who commit themselves to the pursuit of the "big dick": "size queens." I personally see the attraction, but for me it is a bit like the heterosexual desire for large breasts: too much is fascinating but in the sense of a trainwreck, rather than sexual attraction. Presumably at least part of the attraction of size is related to anal sex and fellatio. What works best might be different for different people. I have certainly had sex with men who were too small for me to find the greatest pleasure, but if I was in an ongoing relationship it seemed a minor matter—is it possible to say that without a double entendre? On the other hand, I personally have yet to find a man who was so large that I couldn't adapt. I still have lingering memories, however, of a relationship with a man many years ago. Neither the largest nor the smallest—nor for that matter the most attractive in other ways—the shape and size seemed well nigh perfect in terms of function. This is quite a contrast with a friend's experience. He went to the bathhouse and was confronted by what he called a "beer can cock." He claimed it was exactly that, in length and circumference. He said he had no idea how to handle it, in any sense, and walked away. Presumably the owner meets this problem often.

Anyone who has seen many flaccid penises knows the variety involved, and erections just add to this. There is a website named *imagesize. com* that offers photographs of large erections but also small and, to say the least, unusual. While most on display in the bathhouse tend to be rather classic in formation and quite large, any nude gay beach or resort shows that the possibilities are endless. According to scientific studies, most notably Kinsey, the average size of an erection is about six inches and it is extremely rare to find one more than nine. Some websites advertise that their performers are as large as eighteen inches. It seems unlikely and camera angles can of course be quite creative but some seem to be at least eleven or twelve inches.

This claim of size is partly commercial, whether on websites or in "personal" ads, an assertion that the product for sale offers something other than what you can get for free, but it is also a general source of attraction, like large breasts. It is less common now for men to wear extraordinarily tight jeans, but a few years ago one could see "advertisements" walking by in gay districts. It is not that all men would pursue this, which is akin to those large-breasted waitresses in some bars: enough men want it that the value is there. I talked to one waitress who said that breast enlargement surgery increased her tips by $200 a week. In spite of all the claims, I doubt that penis enlargement would be as easy, but it might have the same effect in the right bar.

Friedman ends his study with some comments on the chemical penis, the use of drugs such as Viagra. While in the heterosexual community it seems primarily employed to rejuvenate aging penises, both in relationships and for casual sex, in the gay community it has become an aid to sexual play in the baths. A good example would be a twenty-seven-year-old acquaintance of mine who had no trouble getting erections, but found that Viagra enabled him not just to have sex but to perform for hours. It had the same effect as, say, amphetamines for long-distance truckers. I have tried it but found that it doesn't work for me, for whatever reason. I get the erection, but the orgasm seems somehow deferred, as though it is coming from some much less energetic place. Once again, if I was penetrator rather than penetrated it might still be of use to me, but since I am seeking not erection but orgasm, it seems pointless.

Thus, at the very least, I disagree with Friedman's conclusion:

> Now man can hold his manhood in his hand, confident in
> knowing who is in charge. When a man uses the products
> of the erection industry, his penis works for him.

> This is more than a temporary jolt in the balance
> of power. It is a paradigm shift and a revolutionary
> restructuring of the masculine mystique. That mystique—
> and the psychic vault of attitudes, aptitudes, and anxieties
> which give it so much confusing urgency—compels man
> to impose his will on the world. Yet man has not always
> been able to impose his will on his penis, the flesh-and-
> blood symbol of that mystique. The penis used to have
> a mind of its own. Not anymore. The erection industry
> has reconfigured the organ, replacing the finicky original
> with a more reliable model. But the price tag for this new
> power tool is hidden. Eventually, we'll learn if we can
> afford it. (306-307)

Once again, I feel both a part of the penis club and outside it. I recognize the importance of the penis and also the impact of Viagra, yet I do not feel that I possess such a "power tool." Since for me my penis is only an aid to an orgasm, it is still that "finicky original." To a certain extent, I value Viagra as something that gives more reliability to my partners. A female porn star was asked what she appreciated most in her male co-stars and she replied, "Good wood." Even then, however, I would rather have a convivial guy who has his ups and downs than an inarticulate jackhammer. There is a lot of fun to be had with a penis, but at the end of it there is always a man attached. One of the great penis hunters of recent years, the American photographer Robert Mapplethorpe, too often neglected the fact that in order to live with an erection, he had to live with its support system as well.

## 5. There is No Such Thing as a Bisexual

This title sums up a view that is commonly held by both heterosexuals and homosexuals. A recent Northwestern University/University of Toronto study examined the penile response of bisexual men to pornography. Their handy-dandy plethysmograph came to the conclusion that bisexual men are really homosexual. This idea is less novel than it might seem, however. There has long been a decidedly gendered view of bisexuality. Men who claim to be bisexual are actually homosexual but also homophobic. Women who claim to be bisexual are actually heterosexual but think it would be way cool and kinda feminist to get closer to their girlfriends. A lesbian friend of mine suggested that this model could be explained succinctly as, "The penis rules."

This might be just one more replay of an old song, but it seems much louder today because bisexuality has become quite respectable, at least as a personal history. A *Vanity Fair* cover story on Angelina Jolie—a contemporary emblem of rampaging heterosexuality—refers to her experience of "dating a woman." This could be just a film-star version of what undergraduates refer to as "bisexual until graduation," but it still gives a very public face to the experience. Such a walk on the Wilde side is still not normal for the celebrity male, but the examples of prominent lesbians such as k.d. lang and Ellen DeGeneres, who were followed by the coming out of various gay men in music and film, suggests that where women go, men might follow.

The jokes about bisexuality indicate that it creates a smorgasbord. Claire Hemmings, in *Bisexual Spaces: A Geography of Sexuality and Gender*, quotes the Sexual Freedom League from 1967: "If it moves, fondle it." (155) This has given rise to many variations: "If it moves, fuck it. If it doesn't move, fuck it until it moves." In other words, bisexuality means there is no human outside the realms of sexual possibility. Many bisexuals quote the Woody Allen line: "The good thing about being bisexual is that it doubles your chances of getting a date on a Saturday night." Yet, a female friend of mine who had sex with an out gay man pined that he would never have much time for sex with women because the chances of success are so much smaller. In other words, if you count the number of possible humans, bisexuality is the way of opportunity, but if you count the number of likely humans, men should stick to homosexuality.

The world still wants bisexuality to be a brief aberration in a comforting dualism. Thus the heterosexual experiments but then returns to his true nature. Similarly, the homosexual attempts to be heterosexual and thus "normal," but comes to accept his true nature. As Janis Bohan states in *Psychology and Sexual Orientation: Coming to Terms*, "Most work in the psychology of sexual orientation begins from the essentialist assumption that sexual orientation is a primary, nuclear quality of self with which each individual must come to terms." (9) While I disagree with the "essentialist assumption," I am most definitely concerned with that "primary, nuclear quality of self."

Thus I have found this to be the most difficult chapter to write. It is not that it is the most revealing of personal matters that many might find a bit too blatant: the chapters on anal sex and the penis are most definitely those. However, as I have remarked so often in these pages, my primary concern is an honest representation of a certain subject position. Thus constant analysis of what might be my sexual orientation has been somewhat of an obsession through my life. Some might find it surprising, but most of the questioning has been as an adult. For various reasons, I was less aware of "the problem" as a child and teenager than I might have been. While I note in "The Homo####ual Child" a variety of what I now see as proto-homosexual elements in my childhood—including a fascination with looking at penises—my earliest memory of a concern for sexual orientation is when I first had sex with a man, when I was twenty-two.

One difficult aspect of the honesty of this chapter is that I am a fifty-seven-year-old man trying to be accurate in my representation of myself more than thirty years ago—if anyone reads this who knew me then, he or she might see a very different person than he or she remembers. An obviously confusing part of this for me is the eagerness with which I pursued women, although my actual sexual activity was limited, beginning when I was eighteen. I am not concerned about the physical manifestation of sexual desire, the erection, because as I state in the chapter "Penis Envy," this seems to me to be rather arbitrary. However, there is no question that when I had a girlfriend, I tried to get to first base, second base, etc., and I demonstrated to her an ongoing interest in some kind of sexual contact.

My explanation, which I admit might just be self-deluding, is that I loved social relations with women and indeed often loved individual women, and I had been convinced that expressions of sexual interest were required to demonstrate that love. I don't think I realized it at the time, but I later recognized that in a relationship with either a man or a woman, I required frequent sexual activity as an affirmation that my partner cared for me. I know that this makes no sense rationally, and I know many relationships, primarily gay ones, in which there is undoubtedly a great deal of love yet there has been no sexual contact in years. Today, I either have come to my senses or just have aged, and now seek sexual pleasure for itself rather than as some security blanket. Still, I felt the way I felt for a long time. I believe my sexual "aggression" towards women in the first twenty years of my sexual life was not a result of libido but a result of emotional need.

Not that I have a firm clarity on my desires for men either. When I was in my early thirties, an older gay friend invited me to go dancing. I said I would love to, but "I am straight." My homosexual experiences were explainable as liberatory *jeux d'esprits* or some such. When I was in my early forties, I had a brief relationship with a woman, but I warned her before it began that "I am bisexual." I had come to the conclusion that sexual orientation is simply a statement of social practice. Since I had sex with both sexes, I was bisexual. Today I live with a woman but I say, "I am gay." I have come to believe that "sexual orientation" is a choice one makes and that individuals can choose how to define that choice. For all the reasons explored in this book, I choose to define myself as gay. I have been accused by many people who know me of prevarication. Rather, I have been trying to find labels for a situation that consistently confuses me. In my twenties and thirties, I accepted an essentialist view of sexual orientation. I knew that I did not feel compelled to have sex with women, but neither did I feel compelled to have sex with men. Since the latter seemed an absolute requirement for anyone who was gay or even bisexual, I was not either.

For many, the idea of the bisexual is closer to what a common joke refers to as the "try-sexual," the person who will try anything. There is another term that goes back to the early twentieth century: "ambisexual." The famed sex researchers Masters and Johnson used this concept to describe "men or women who had no preference whatsoever over the gender of their sex partners, had never become involved in a committed sexual relationship, and had frequent sexual interaction with both men and women." (371). Given that Freud and his associates used the term "bisexual" for something closer to "bi-gendered," the term "ambisexual" might seem less confusing, but it is also quite loaded in its emphasis on sexual liberation and lack of emotional commitment. This is far from what most bisexual organizations represent or promote.

On the other hand, perhaps bisexuals have too much concern for gender. This would apply to those who say not that they don't care whether they have sex with a woman or a man, but rather that they enjoy profoundly different experiences with each. Then, of course, there are those who assert that even the assumption that such dualism is possible is inherently flawed. As Kenneth Kipnis and Milton Diamond wrote in "Pediatric Ethics and the Surgical Assignment of Sex":

> The condition of intersexuality precludes the application
> of terms like hetero- and homosexuality that conceive
> sexual desire, and its idealized object, in relation to the
> subject's sex. Instead, we reaffirm the recommendation
> to substitute the terms androphilic, gynecophilic, and
> ambiphilic. (405)

Even in their terminology, however, each person is drawn to an idea of man, an idea of woman, or an idea of both. Many intersex activists would say this is still too restricted. In this realm, "bisexuality" is impossible except perhaps as an assertion of two valences in a multi-valence system.

Richard Friedman's psychoanalytic study of homosexuality offers a cogent response to the possibility of bisexuality: "Identity diffusion is a prominent part of the clinical picture and patients commonly feel be-wildered about the meaning of sexual fantasies in relation to their sense of identity (i.e., they wonder 'am I gay or straight?')" (131) Friedman has an obvious key here to those males who believe themselves to be bisex-ual regardless of when they get erections. On the other hand, Friedman comes closer to the usual view when he deals with a case study of what he calls "pseudohomosexuality" (140):

> I felt that Arthur's enthusiastic pursuit of a gay identity
> appeared to be an attempt to cope with diffusion in
> his sense of identity generally. This attempted solution
> allowed him to maintain sexual satisfaction while
> renouncing heterosexuality. Unresolved preoedipal
> and oedipal conflicts produced anxiety which, when
> added to the emotional pain resulting from his mother's
> illness, led him to avoid heterosexuality and to amplify
> the sense of pleasure from homosexual fantasy activity
> as a symptomatic attempt to cope. Interestingly, despite
> Arthur's (hypothetical) maternal identification, he did
> not become overtly effeminate following her illness and
> death. (137)

Friedman was writing in 1988. Since then views have changed about sexual orientation, but his reaction to bisexuality still seems representative of the majority of both gay and straight observers. He states, "Identity diffusion is the hallmark of the bisexual obsessional borderline syndromes." (141)

The bisexual activist Loraine Hutchins offers a game based on the

Kinsey seven point scale, which ranges from 1 (exclusively heterosexual) to 7 (exclusively homosexual). This includes my favourites, 2 and 6, which are "predominantly" one but only "incidentally" the other. I guess the word reflects a few "incidents," those embarrassing occasions when one isn't any too sure about anything. Most people, however, seem to believe themselves to be 1s and 7s. There are even gay T-shirts that proudly proclaim, "Kinsey 7." I think my sexual attractions are somewhere around 5¾ while my social life today seems to be somewhere around 1⅞. My sexual history is probably in the neighbourhood of 4. As the expression goes, you do the math. When Hutchins conducts workshops, she puts each of the seven numbers up and asks everyone to choose a number. After they do this, she then tells them that this is their number for the rest of their lives and any deviation will be severely punished. She thus proves that even those most committed to their number are not completely convinced of its permanence.

John Money and others have tried to modify Kinsey's scale, but arguably the most popular realignment is that provided by Fritz Klein, medical doctor and activist, and founder of the website *bisexual.org*. Klein goes beyond the Kinsey continuum to create the Klein grid that also includes:

A. Sexual Attraction

B. Sexual Behavior

C. Sexual Fantasies

D. Emotional Preference

E. Social Preference

F. Heterosexual ↔ Homosexual Lifestyle

G. Self-Identification. (16)

This makes obvious sense, but once so many subjectivities are involved, is there anything left? Can any of Klein's variables be reduced to gay, straight, and bi? Are all aspects of character part of the definition of sexual orientation? Klein notes, "Anna Freud has written that the sex of one's masturbatory fantasies is the ultimate criterion in homo- or heterosexual preference—an astute, even wise, observation on the face of it." (16) But what about those people who engage in masturbation without sexual object or even sexual thought, simply as a means of relaxation? Or is their claim to have no sexual thought simply a lie—or at least self-deceit? Part of the problem yet again is what constitutes a "sexual thought."

I must apologize to those who would prefer me to call myself bi-sexual. Bisexual activists have often said to me simply, "That is what you are." I certainly see the point. I would be required to deny my history to give an emphatic rejection to their argument. Still, I don't understand myself in their terms. For one, many bisexual activists are what I would call sex radicals. They believe that an ultimately liberated sexual expression is the goal. I am not offended by their goal but neither am I attracted to it. Others are closer to Mariana Valverde's description in her 1985 book *Sex, Power, and Pleasure*, in which she claims that "adult bisexuality … is not an innocent, pre-genital eroticization of all bodily experience, but rather involves the selection of properly gendered men and women as objects of desire within the context of fairly rigid rules about what constitutes real sex." (113) As in my comment on intersex and bisexuality, the bisexual subject requires specific gender ideals, and a belief in "fairly rigid rules." Otherwise, the subject might find sufficient variety in various sexual aims pursued with various sexual objects from one gender. Given that her book was published over twenty years ago, it is more than possible that Valverde would change this assessment today, but it still seems to me an accurate depiction of many who label them-selves bisexuals, as opposed to the vast array of people who have some kind of sexual relations with both sexes. Those who call themselves bisexuals have some faith that there is a difference, perhaps even an es-sential difference, in "sex" with a man or a woman. Even those who as-sume that label today, however, have not achieved a presence sufficient to deny what Valverde said back then: "Bisexuality does not exist as either a social institution or a psychological 'truth.'" (119) Thus labeling yourself "gay" or "straight" tends to be accepted by most listeners, but those who assert that they are "bisexual" seem to feel required to justify it. Still, they are sufficiently few in number that they are seldom heard. In spite of the obvious fact that many people, perhaps the majority, are in some psychological or even experiential sense bisexual, and that a significant minority call themselves "bisexual," "bisexual" bars, stores, or media remain rare.

Of course, the term "bisexual" could also be denied simply on its assumptions of binaries. What if, to borrow the title of Kate Bornstein's performance piece, *The Opposite Sex is Neither*? A central premise of the show is that it is ridiculous to live in a world of only two genders. In *Sexing the Body: Gender Politics and the Construction of Sexuality*, Anne Fausto-Sterling considers the reasons why medicine is so resolutely committed to this binary:

> In their suggestions for withholding information about
> patients' bodies and their own decisions in shaping them,
> medical practitioners unintentionally reveal their anxieties
> that a full disclosure of the facts about intersex bodies
> would threaten individuals'—and by extension society's—
> adherence to a strict male-female model. I do not suggest
> a conspiracy; rather, doctors' own deep conviction that
> all people are either male or female renders them blind to
> such logical binds. (65)

Presumably at some level, someone with an intersex body cannot be heterosexual or homosexual, which also precludes that person being bisexual. Or perhaps that person is an ideal, not the bisexual as both homo and hetero, but rather the bisexual as a convenient misnomer for omni.

This ideal often seems to be part of that choice to be "bisexual until graduation." The majority of people who call themselves "bisexual" are quite young. I have not seen a study on the subject, but my guess is that there are few persons over thirty who claim the identity "bisexual" and still fewer over the age of forty. I have no easy explanation for this observation, but I have a few thoughts, including the idea that the bisexual is as false a concept as many suggest and thus is an identity for those who are prematurely willing to assert an identity but are actually still on the road to their true identity. I would find another, somewhat similar, view more convincing. Given that "bisexual" is, as Valverde suggests, not an identity that society generally accepts, it is asserted primarily by people young enough that a coherent and acceptable identity is less important. Once they reach the age when a unity that fits the hegemony seems to be required, they will fall on one or the other side of the fence. An article by Alex Morris in *New York Magazine*, entitled "The Cuddle Puddle of Stuyvesant High School" (Feb. 6, 2006) considers a variety of bright young people who wander merrily between heterosexuality and same-sex flirtations. Morris states:

> This past September, when the National Center for
> Health Statistics released its first survey in which teens
> were questioned about their sexual behavior, 11 percent
> of American girls polled in the 15-to-19 demographic
> claimed to have had same-sex encounters—the *same*
> percentage of all women ages 15 to 44 who reported
> same-sex experiences, even though the teenagers
> have much shorter sexual histories. It doesn't take a
> Stuyvesant education to see what this means: More girls
> are experimenting with each other, and they're starting
> younger.

While the males with whom Morris talked are also kissing each other, they hesitate to go further as they seem to fear anything like actual sex with a man.

Another possibility for the age demographics of the "bisexual" is that no matter how often bisexuals claim otherwise, the very idea of "bisexual" seems to belie a monogamous heterosexual or homosexual relationship. Our society continues to have a penguin-like faith in the couple, regardless of how few couples seem able to keep the faith; thus the person who winds up in a male-female couple is a heterosexual and the one in a male-male or female-female couple is homosexual, regard-less of his or her sexual history. Not that the *bisexual* likes this view, as in the following comment by Michael Du Plessis:

> We have been told that bisexuality veers between
> homosexuality and heterosexuality as two distinct sexual
> orientations, without ever becoming an orientation in its
> own right; we have also been informed that it oscillates
> between two genders because it already androgynously
> contains masculine and feminine within itself. Experts
> and laypersons alike have wondered in a variety of ways
> whether it might be some rare fusion of sexuality, gender,
> and object choice. But we have also heard, over and over
> again, that bisexuality is merely a behavior which is fairly
> common but does not have an identity to back it up. (19)

One need not be a very subtle reader to sense that the syntax is carefully
chosen: he is fuming about what "we have been told" and what "we
have heard."

Not that it constitutes an answer to this frustration, but Maria
Pramaggiore's introduction to *RePresenting Bisexualities: Subjects and Cultures of
Fluid Desires* offers a more expansive view of that "fence" I mentioned:

> [Eve Kosofsky] Sedgwick's recognition that the closet helps
> to define our ways of knowing the world informs but
> does not circumscribe the work in this volume, writing
> which directs our attention to a related location—the
> fence—and its attendant epistemologies. 'Something there
> is that doesn't love a wall ... and makes gaps two can
> pass abreast,' writes Robert Frost. Those gaps rewrite the
> wall as fence, opening up spaces through which to view,
> through which to pass, and through which to encounter
> and enact fluid desires.
>
> Sedgwick's closet is a rich visual and spatial metaphor—a
> location and a way of viewing and dividing the world. But
> closets are not definitive: they continually dissolve and
> reproduce themselves. (3)

> Thus the fence, a permeable and permeating structure,
> is most akin to the mutually inclusive 'both/and' rather
> than the exclusive 'either/or,' just as Frost's mending
> wall is reconstructed and reinforced by persons on both
> sides: 'And on a day we meet to walk the line/And set the
> wall between us once again./We keep the wall between
> us as we go.' The attention required to maintain this
> exclusionary wall forces those on either side to recognize
> not only both sides of the wall but also the wall's position
> as a third term in between them which continually
> deconstructs itself. (4)

In the cynical twenty-first century, it is very difficult to accept Robert Frost as a model, but this idealized fence is the bisexual identity as seen by the bisexually identified.

In my own life, I seldom have felt attracted to the term as an identity. In my early thirties I was far from my family, doing research in Sydney, Australia. My nights were spent in gay bars and my days in the library. I found myself one day sitting at my desk and staring at all who entered. Lacking any meter to judge my erections, I tried to assess my own sexual desire for each person. I tried to include a sort of sliding scale for age and physical appearance to accommodate the obvious fact that a division only according to male and female would be insufficient. Within ten minutes I became hopelessly confused, almost to the point of tears.

Of course, claiming oneself to be bisexual offers little insight into bisexual practice or even bisexual attraction. David R. Matteson's "The Heterosexually Married Gay and Lesbian Parent" is primarily about parenting, but it also offers a subtle explanation for the person doing the parenting:

> These men frequently had thought of themselves as
> heterosexual because they were responsive sexually
> once they had an emotional relationship with a woman
> (kinesthetic). Only later, after their sexual inhibitions and
> homophobia decreased, did they recognize the fact that

their visual interest was homosexual. (140)

He follows this generalization with another one: "We can hypothesize that men tend to discover their sexual orientation through visual experience, and women through kinesthetic experience." (141) Matteson is here differentiating between gay male and lesbian but, for the bisexual man in the earlier quotation, the implication of this differentiation is that the homosexual orientation is "masculine" and the heterosexual orientation is "feminine."

This seems to raise the question whether the bisexual male is behaving sometimes as a male subject and sometimes as a female subject. This is presumably highly arguable. There can be no argument, however, that the bisexual male sometimes pursues a male object and sometimes a female. The obvious explanation is Valverde's, that the bisexual accepts a highly gendered world view. But is there something else? I have found the attraction of the penis to be sufficient that I have devoted a separate chapter to its attractions. But what of the vagina?

While I don't think I have the traditional heterosexual male desire to penetrate, penetrate, penetrate, it seems to me impossible not to recognize how much our society has constructed penetration as a goal. This has led to what I would call a general overdetermination of the meaning of sexual penetration. Historically, the father protected the daughter's vagina from other males and then awarded it to the husband. We usually refer to the daughter rather than her vagina, but I think one might as well focus on the prize bits. The unpenetrated hymen is the essence of this transaction. In many cultures, many things can happen to said daughter as long as the hymen remains intact. The new husband is concerned with just one thing, that the hymen has not been broken.

Thus while there are many things shown in pornography, and many acts are bought from sex workers, and many awful things happen to women within what we call "sexual assault," the key element is the penetration of the woman by the penis. This is less true than it used to be, but there has been a tradition in some lesbian cultures of eschewing penetration. The usual claim is that this is to avoid the imitation of heterosexuality, but perhaps the unconscious purpose is to avoid the meaning of penetration. It is my suspicion that this meaning is one of the forces compelling the male towards heterosexuality. It is not just that the male desires to penetrate, but that society has compelled him to believe this must be his desire—and that this desire is primal and visceral but also transcendent, to suit the theological interpretations of conception.

In the chapter titled "Up the Ass," I refer to Foucault's depiction of the classical belief in the necessity of the whole body, as in bodily health, that had absolute boundaries. As many feminists have since pointed out, if the 'normal' body could not be penetrated then the normal body could not be female, at least heterosexual female. Still, while this makes the female less normal, it also elevates the importance of penetration. Penetration of the female is 1) a definition of the female, 2) a very important aspect of the female that must be controlled by whatever male "owns" that female, and 3) something that must never be done by a non-owning male ("the worst thing that could happen to a woman"). I see this in at least the beginnings of my own attraction to women. The hegemony of compulsory heterosexuality created an attraction for that hallowed vagina that did not equal my visceral fascination with the penis but instead often replaced it.

To make a connection to yet another chapter, "Dragging Feminism?" links my experience of drag with feminism. Thus I would see my attraction to women as partly feminist, albeit with a rather paternalistic subtext. Many of my relationships with women have at least begun on the typical model of the straight woman and gay man as friends. Of course, if the same man is "really" bisexual, then the friendship can lead in other directions. On one occasion I became friends with a woman and after a night out at a club, we went back her apartment. As the expression goes, one thing led to another and we had all our clothes off when she said, "I better look after protection." She adjourned to the bathroom, I presume to put in her diaphragm, and then came back. We were back in bed, naked, when she said, "No." I replied, "Are you sure?" To which she replied something such as, "I just don't feel right about this," and so I left. While we still chatted when we saw each other, we never again went out together.

I have told this story often. Listeners, whether male or female, usually react with surprise that the process would go that far and then be stopped. I of course have told it with the pride of a male feminist, someone who realized that "No means no." As I consider the event today, however, I also realize that it is part of the story of the meaning of penetration. While we had engaged in many acts that could be called "sex," the stopping before penetration was the essential marker. Similarly, I wonder if I would have been proceeding towards that "marker" if I had not been convinced that this was the necessary goal for a male with a female. Finally, was my acceptance of my friend drawing the line simply a statement of my rational feminism or might it also be a reflection of the limitation of my desire? To put it in Freudian terms, for me penetration was a performance of ego or even superego, of purpose controlled by cultural assumptions, rather than id, the drive towards pleasure in the form that the body knew pleasure must be found. If I had been ruled by the drive to penetration, as our society presumes the heterosexual male is ruled, I perhaps would not have been so easily restrained.

If, as I suggest in "The Homo###ual Child," there is both reason (the belief in meaning) and an almost autonomic desire (that bodily urge for pleasure) in sex, definitions are always difficult to find. Bisexual activists often claim to get different—often expressed as complementary—pleasures from men or women. For me at least, I would put it somewhat otherwise. Much of my urge to have sex with men is expressed in the chapters "Up the Ass" and "Penis Envy." In terms of my own response, the former is about physical effect and the latter about my fascination with another man's sexual arousal. Yet, as I suggest there, that fascination with the penis is sufficient to see it as my arousal as well, in both a scopophilic and a tactile drive. My urge to have sex with women has been rather different. It has been more about my partner's pleasure. At times it has led to an almost complete limitation to cunnilingus as something that gives pleasure to the woman but does not require any of the confusion I associate with penetration. I cannot deny that this might be partly my id being warped by my male feminism, something I explore in the chapter "Dragging Feminism?" but it seems to be the primary goal in my participation in what could be called "heterosexuality."

In this moment of introspection I am attempting an honest assessment of what I have thought and felt, but even if I could do this—and I cannot—I could not achieve a similarly honest view of my sexual orientation. I could resort to the most simplified version of social science, quantification, which would achieve at least some version of objectivity. In *The Mismeasure of Desire: The Science, Theory, and Ethics of Sexual Orientation*, Edward Stein attempts a logical precision in his assessment of science: "The behavioral view of sexual orientation has the advantage of characterizing sexual orientations in a way that is objective and scientifically accessible. On this view, a person's sexual orientation is a matter of determining what sorts of sexual acts the person has performed." (42) As Stein notes, however, Kinsey's approach seems to offer a more accurate assessment given the nature of human sexuality: "The Kinsey view of sexual orientation is a dispositional picture of sexual orientation because it counts sexual behaviour, sexual desires, and sexual fantasies as part of a person's sexual orientation. Further, it allows that these aspects of a person's sexual behaviour may be discordant." (47) Ah yes, those "discordant" aspects, of which I seem to have found many.

Yet some of the most sophisticated and committed theorists seem able to sing loudly enough to drown out the discord. The title of Michael Warner's *The Trouble with Normal: Sex, Politics, and the Ethics of Queer Life* suggests his polemical style: he doesn't like "normal" much. This colours his view of identity:

> When Clinton set out to reform the military antigay policy
> after his election in 1992, he made a point of saying that
> the military should be allowed to punish people for their
> acts, but not for their identities; the focus should be on
> 'conduct, not status.' He was invoking the most central

>premise of lesbian and gay politics as a politics of identity:
>that sexual orientation is fundamental to one's personality
>and is not mere sexual behavior. (29)

This view of identity is interesting because of that word "mere." To Warner, the Clinton ruling is specious because the acts are the identity.

Stein raises a possible form of analysis that reflects my assessment of my own sexuality. He considers various theories based on experience: "According to such theories, at birth (or perhaps before puberty) we all have roughly the same potential with respect to our sexual orientations and sexual desires; our different experiences and environments account for our differences in terms of sexual orientation." (229) Among these theories are "operant-conditioning theory," which suggests that good sex with a man leads one to want good sex with men, and "early-experience theories," which include "seduction theory," that nasty man in the park, and "first-encounter theory" (232), meeting the hunky football player before the flirty cheerleader, and "parental-manipulation theory" (233), any combination of absent father, smother-mother, etc., etc.

But would such theories ever provide an adequate identification of identification? One of the most consistent scholars of homosexuality has been Jeffrey Weeks, who captures a salient contradiction:

>We are increasingly aware that sexuality is about flux and
>change, that what we call 'sexual' is as much a product
>of language and culture as of nature. But we earnestly
>strive to fix it, stabilise it, say who we are by telling of our
>sex—and the lead in this conscious articulation of sense
>of self has been taken by those radically disqualified for it
>by the sexual tradition. Since the late nineteenth century
>most western societies have witnessed a prolonged effort
>to realise a lesbian and homosexual identity, or identities.
>(186)

He responds to Erik H. Erikson's definition, in *Identity: Youth and Crisis*, of the "identity crisis":

> The quest for identity has characterised the history
> of homosexuality during this century. The finding of
> it has invariably been described in terms of homing
> in on an ultimate self buried beneath the detritus
> of misinformation and prejudice. It is like finding a
> map to explore a new country. Such a discovery has
> been the precondition for a sense of personal unity.
> Categorisations and self-categorisations, that is the process
> of identity formation, may control, restrict and inhibit
> but simultaneously they provide 'comfort, security and
> assuredness.' (188-189)

Thus the "bisexual identity" is a product of a cartographic process that is followed whenever a "new country" is discovered. Erikson's identity crisis begins with an assumption that identities exist. Such identities range from an individual, as in one's proper name, to a variety of collectives, gender, race, ethnicity, and age. Each provides "comfort, security, and assuredness," but each also "restricts." Presumably identities are most restrictive when they are inaccurate. They are most often perceived to be inaccurate when they in some sense forcibly deny that they contain those with a different or even opposite identity. This makes Weeks's "new country" a particularly apt metaphor. When the identity of the old country does not fit, then the new country seeks sovereignty. Perhaps the apparent success of "gay" made "bisexual" inevitable.

Most studies view bisexuality as a statement of sexual response. However, as Valverde suggests, it is also a statement about perceptions of gender. Weinberg, Williams, and Pryor, in their book *Dual Attraction: Understanding Bisexuality*, claim that "Ideas about gender and gender roles are crucial factors in how we think about our sexuality. As we develop sexual identities, our frame of reference generally is not sexuality *per se*. Instead of learning *directly* to eroticize one gender or the other, we learn to act as a woman or to act as a man." (49) This follows the premise that we begin as sexually undefined and through some process learn what should be our sex objects. They conclude, "bisexuality then emerges we suggest as a result of failing to unlearn, or rediscovering both same and opposite-sex gendered pleasures." (288)

Is this just freefloating? In the same way that someone might eat pasta six days a week and then rice on Saturday, a bisexual wanders through the menu. John Money has troubled many with his apparently scientific approach to sex and gender, his devotion to neologisms and in some cases his disastrous interventions in human lives. Still, his view of sexual orientation is worthy of note. It is both unusual and unusually commonsensical, enshrined in his strange word "lovemap," again a way of dealing with those new countries:

> A lovemap is defined as a personalized, developmental
> representation or template in the mind and in the brain
> that depicts the idealized lover and the idealized program
> of sexuoerotic activity with that lover as projected
> in imagery and ideation, or actually engaged in with
> that lover (Money, 1983, 1986a). A lovemap is rated as
> normophilic on the basis of what is ideologically defined
> by those with ideological authority as sexuoerotically
> normal and acceptable. (*Gay* 127)

The concept of "normophilic" is an interesting response to Freud's descriptions of the "perversions," which are here defined as "paraphilic." In other words, the "normophilic" is whatever sexual aim and sexual object are acceptable by the hegemonic society and the "paraphilic" is that which is not. Money presents an interesting alternative in that he sees both homosexuality and heterosexuality as potentially "normophilic" but veering towards the paraphilic according to sexual aims. His system of understanding raises the interesting possibility that those who perceive themselves to be paraphilic might be more attracted to bisexuality or even homosexuality: "Men with a paraphilic homosexual lovemap almost certainly have an advantage over those with a paraphilic heterosexual lovemap, insofar as paraphilias are more prevalent in males than in females." (147)

Another important element is that, at least since the nineteenth century, and in many ways before, society has associated the paraphilic with homosexuality. To return to Weeks's "country," it is something akin to the historical assumptions that exotic sexual practices are more common somewhere else. Thus everything from sado-masochism to masturbation has been seen as somehow homosexual. An episode of *The Sopranos* suggested that a male who practised cunnilingus was likely to be gay. This perhaps makes sense only to me. It becomes something like the old Australian joke: How can you tell a poofter? Someone who leaves his mates at the pub to go home to his wife. In other words, anything that deviates from that which the hegemony perceives as normal masculine behaviour becomes homosexual.

While I certainly see enough "tendencies" in me that are homosexual to identify myself as such, I cannot deny that the paraphilic implications of the category have been of interest to me. My sexual practices with both men and women have been normative, what gay culture tends to call "vanilla." Thus regardless of my reputation as "different," which has been with me since early childhood, my sexual difference is only evident through having romantic relationships with both genders. Thus while I am not paraphilic in my practice, I am able to flirt with paraphilia through my homosexual side. To take this even further, I am homosexually paraphilic in having a heterosexual side. It is common to see the male bisexual as someone who fears being homosexual, as someone who yearns for the conformity of heterosexual privilege, but my own willingness to be out seems to put the lie to that. Perhaps I am truly perverse, someone whose sexual choices exist only to disrupt assumptions of sexual choice.

Instead of suggesting that sexual orientation might respond to such paraphilic desires, Money resorts to "love." While this might seem an almost stridently anti-scientific premise, it provides a useful point of analysis given the couple obsession of our society. This is a long way from the plethysmograph, but it reflects the complications of what Money strangely calls "pairbondage." While my long-term relationships with men and women have taken a variety of different shapes, I would argue that most of the differences have been less about gender than about other issues. These range from the obvious, (such as geography in a long-distance relationship) to the less obvious (I dated a man for a time who constantly complained about me being vegetarian). A non-monogamous relationship can accept many sexual differences, but leaving the cap off the toothpaste tube can be the deal-breaker. Presumably many, if not most, long-lasting couples have limited interaction that would interest a plethysmograph, but much that reflects the cartography of the lovemap. My main claim to a variety of locators is that I know that, to the extent I can define something as amorphous as "love," I have been in love with both men and women.

The majority of people who identify as bisexual are women. The first possible explanation is suggested by the crowd at Stuyvesant High School. Women can see the attractions of a "cuddle puddle" in which actual performance seems undefined, but men fear that they might be required to accept an erect penis in an orifice that is not quite ready for one. A more philosophical answer is that women have less invested in the necessity of a unified identity. It might also, however, reflect the fact that heterosexual society rejects the bisexual male but flirts with the bisexual female. Television programs such as *Oprah* counsel women on how to identify a bisexual boyfriend or husband and to get rid of him. An article in *Cosmopolitan* magazine suggested that one danger signal is when a man looks at a strange man for more than ten seconds. (This conjures up the image of the Cosmogirl out there with one eye on her boyfriend and the other on her watch.) On the other hand, the very titles of the film, *Kissing Jessica Stein*, and the Jill Sobule song "I Kissed a Girl" suggest that bisexual females are good clean fun. At a raunchier level, "girl on girl" is a staple of heterosexual pornography, and swingers clubs eagerly seek females who touch other females during sex play while making it strictly off-limits for males to touch males.

That word "love" might present another explanation for the gender imbalance. It is not just that men are often viewed as emotionally limited and thus unable to "love," and women said to "love too much," it is more that our society has convinced men that "love" can be felt only for the optimum sex object. Women, on the other hand, seem to believe in more possibilities, including the possibility that love might create a sex object. Freud often provides answers that are too easy, but if these differing views of sex and love shape the mindsets of men and women, they might reflect his heterosexist view of penetration in which the penis pursues its destiny and the vagina accommodates it, in spite of the physiological fact that the clitoris might be better pleased by other activities. Thus for the female, "sex" does not make sense as the primary goal of heterosexuality. This might be one more partial explanation for studies that suggest that many more heterosexual women than hetero-sexual men are willing to accept that they could some day be part of a homosexual relationship. Most heterosexual men dismiss something that is sexually unattractive or even sexually revolting whereas at least some heterosexual women are open to a variety of possibilities of love. Yet even here, what are the definitions? I am at present in a relationship with a woman that looks permanent and I certainly hope will be permanent. My longest relationship before this was with a woman, in a marriage. Yet the closest thing to "love at first sight" has happened to me only three times, always with men. In each case, it led me to a relationship that was fraught in many ways and that caused me emotional pain, much more than I have ever felt with a woman. I might have had a slight touch of what Money, in *Gendermaps*, refers to as "limerence":

> Limerence has only two other counterparts in human
> experience, grief and religious ecstasy. All three may be
> abruptly sudden in onset, overwhelming in their intensity,
> fixatedly long-lasting, unresponsive to logical reasoning,
> and capable of leading to wildly irrational acts of self-
> sabotage. (113)

Yet even with these lovers I didn't reach this level, the love that exceeds and confounds reason, although they were closer to limerence than my relationships with women. Perhaps all my relationships with women, including the present one, can be attributed not to "love" but to an accurate assessment of my own emotional needs, a rational pursuit of what I need in a companion. In *Gendermaps*, Money quantifies the various types of "homo:hetero ratio" (118) available in bisexuality. He suggests that there can be an appropriate "pairbonding" between bisexuals with a similar ratio, but sees serious problems for "mismatching." "The relationship may be based more on nonerotic expediency and exploitation than on sexuoerotic bonding." (119) "Expediency" is one of those words that seem inherently pejorative. But what if "nonerotic expediency" means spending your life with the person you "love," regardless of the sexuoerotics of your homo:hetero ratio?

Generalizations about gender are both vexing and insupportable. Few comments tend to be as inaccurate as "men are..." or "women are...." And like most times those statements are made, I am using them as a preamble to make just such generalizations. I find women more suitable as friends than men. While I find men sexually attractive, I also find them confusing, particularly in what I perceive to be their emotional limitations. They are much less likely to discuss their feelings than to let their feelings overwhelm them in some explosion of anger. I have always identified with certain *bon mots* about the problem. Playwright Michel Tremblay was quoted as saying "I hate men. If I were not homosexual I would have nothing to do with them." In an episode of *Seinfeld* Elaine reacts to an acquaintance's misinterpretation of her sexual orientation: "I'm not a lesbian. I hate men, but I'm not a lesbian." Whenever someone jokingly refers to me as a male lesbian I refer to Elaine's resolve that no matter how irritating, men are the ones with whom you have sex.

So what borders have I drawn for this non-existent territory of the bisexual? Perhaps I should conclude with Hemmings. She begins with the 'fence' but then offers another possibility, although one that she suggests is denied by the bipolar hegemony: "Bisexuality becomes real only in heterosexual or homosexual contexts, but has no enduring context of its own: no one stays on a bridge for long." (3) One need not be a scholar of Robert Frost, however, to see that the bridge enables journeys while the fence offers only boundaries or, worse, the balancing act of being on the fence. As Hemmings suggests, the bisexual idealizes this bridge, but the rest of society says bridges are only a place of transition in the travels, not a destination. As Hemmings succinctly explains:

> One of the conditions for sexual subjectivity is that its aim be consistent over time … the formation of sexual identity requires not only that one make a particular gendered and sexed object choice but that one *continues* to make that choice. The present can only be validated by the anticipated future, which can only be validated by a past that is retrospectively given meaning according to the present. (25)

One is only bisexual if one continues to be bisexual. In terms of sexual experience, time will eventually run out, dissipating in monogamy or age-induced celibacy.

Perhaps "bisexual" is then just another word for "queer." I don't mean the "queer" in "queer nation," a term of activism, or the "queer" in "I think he's queer." It might be something similar to the "queer" in "queer theory," although "queer theory" is a notoriously slippery concept. In *Sex, Literature and Censorship*, Jonathan Dollimore, often represented as one of the primary figures of queer theory, gives the following rather disdainful summary:

> Queer theory is quintessentially metropolitan and, at its worst, little more than intellectual style-politics (for which, nevertheless, there should be a place in every fallen world). Its claim to a poised and perfect radicalism reflects the influence of a facile postmodernism, the kind which competes to be always on the forward edge of our own contemporary moment, and from there clamours to announce a profound new insight into the here and now, telling us that today radical change is in the air while

knowing that tomorrow it will all change again, and is
anxious to be in on the diagnosis when it does—hence the
prevalence in academic titles of 'post', 'after,' 'beyond' and
the like. (14)

In general I agree with him, but why would one not want to be "always
on the forward edge," especially if this means that "queer" is that perfect
form of sexual identity that enables everyone to be just as she/he/
whatever should be. Hemmings concludes by moving from geography
to what she terms a

... future utopic grammar..... This grammar constructs
a bisexual home of possibility that can only be sketched,
never built, an architect's fantastic blueprints that defy the
laws of structure and gravity. In this way the specificities
of what might constitute a bisexual home are endlessly
deferred by reference to an imagined future of bisexual
possibility. (171)

So it is not so much that there is no such thing as a bisexual but rather
that the bisexual is an ideal that we never can reach. This bridge that is
a fence somehow lives in a mythical land between those real worlds of
the heterosexual and the homosexual.

## 6. I Never Took It Up the Ass

There is a story the origin of which I have been unable to trace and so is possibly apocryphal. After his death, it became well known that John Cheever, the American writer, was bisexual. His inner circle was aware that Cheever had a variety of sexual encounters, but I have no idea if they knew the details. Thus comes the story: Cheever observed that his tombstone should read, "Never went down on a woman, never took it up the ass." The obvious inference to be made from this is that Cheever—or more accurately "Cheever"—was happy to acknowledge bisexuality but not cunnilingus or being anal-passive. As I note in the chapter on bisexuality, cunnilingus has been associated with homosexuality, presumably on the premise that overtly servicing a woman is emasculating. If one extrapolates from this view, then this "Cheever" was careful to say that, like Roy Cohn in the play *Angels in America*, he had sex with men but was not a "homosexual."

There are many possible reasons for an anal orientation in sexuality. The assumption is usually that the male is phallic. His desire is to put it in. For whatever reason, this has not been the goal of my sex drive. In my youth my behaviour suggested that this was very much my goal, but with hindsight, I realize it was more a response to a social construction than a sex drive. Hindsight—ah yes, the double entendres again—tells me that my preferred form of sex is anal, with me as the receiver of my partner's penis. Yet this could also be seen as overtly male in another sense. If the male desire to insert is simply to achieve orgasm, then that would reflect my choice: I have the most powerful orgasm when masturbating with a penis in my anus. I have been told by partners that my orgasm approximates a female orgasm, with a rising and extended climax that seems only partially connected to ejaculation.

When AIDS first became part of the popular imagination, I saw a delightfully homophobic T-shirt: "The asshole is an exit not an entrance." While I doubt the wearer had any idea of the classical heritage he was reflecting, this seems to represent the view famously noted by Foucault, that the aversion to anal sex is about an ideal of the male body as whole and complete and not to be entered. Craig A. Williams, in *Roman Homosexuality: Ideologies of Masculinity in Classical Antiquity*, notes the specific form of this ideal in Roman society. He comments on the importance of *pudicitia*, which signifies sexual integrity or chastity, but actually refers to penetration: "In other words, a claim that a man was *impudicus* usually functioned as a coded way of signifying that his masculine inviolability had been compromised, and ancient discussions of a man's *pudicitia* can almost always be reduced to this question: Has he been penetrated or not?" (173) In other words, the Romans viewed the male body in a way similar to that T-shirt: being anal passive represented a general moral failure.

Derogatory terms connected to anal sex have long been used to designate all homosexuals. Thus all gay men are "bumboys" and "shirtlifters." In the Caribbean, they are "battyboys" or "battymen." Gary Dowsett's *Practicing Desire: Homosexual Sex in the Era of AIDS* maintains that this association, if not the pejorative view of it, extends to gay men themselves: "Almost all gay men consider anal sex the symbolic center of gay identity. It is central to the social definition of male homosexuality and, therefore, claims its erotic core." (37) Sometimes the term designates the person as anal active, as in "arsebandit," but this is rare. One of the reasons is that it is common in many cultures for the anal-active person to be free from any pejorative label. This would justify the assumptions of the apocryphal "Cheever." Rather than a homosexual, he is someone whose phallic power is such that he can produce an erection suitable for any orifice. Rather than being a homosexual, he is a man whose sexuality can subdue and penetrate even a man. Edward Stein, in *The Mismeasure of Desire: The Science, Theory, and Ethics of Sexual Orientation*, notes the attitude in Mexico:

> *Jotos* are primarily anally *penetrated* by their sexual partners,
> while *machos* primarily anally *penetrate* their male sexual
> partners and also may have sex with women (involving

vaginal and/or anal penetration). If you asked a *macho*
whether he was gay (or homosexual), he would almost
surely answer in the negative (to him, that term would
probably be seen as applying exclusively to *jotos*). Similarly,
it seems unlikely that he would consider himself
bisexual; rather, he would say that he is a "normal" and
"masculine" man. (210)

The terms "top" and "bottom" have various interpretations in gay
sex. For those involved in S/M, the top is the dominator and the bottom the dominated. The words are also used, however, for what the
Mexicans call the macho and the joto, the inserter and the receiver.
I realize these are not the best terms, but they seem better than penetrator and penetrated or anal-active and anal-passive. The former pair
reinforces the assumption of dominance and takeover that is so much
a part of the semiotics of heterosexual intercourse, where the valiant
sperm penetrates the demure egg. The latter pair of "active" and "passive" assumes actions that often do not occur: it is not uncommon for
the "active" person to just lie there with an erection, or for the "passive"
person to expend all the energy. An extreme version of this is offered
by "Aaron" in Steven G. Underwood's *Gay Men and Anal Eroticism: Tops, Bottoms, and Versatiles*:

In one phrase, power bottom means, "Shut up and lie
down. I'll take care of the rest. Don't assume I'm going
to lie on my back and let you go away at it. You're going
to lie on your back and you're going to shut up and I'm
going to show you what really can be done." It's that
whole emotional, psychological thing. "I'm going to
engulf you; you're not going to penetrate me. I'm gonna
swallow you up whole. You're going to find out who's
really in control." (27)

This recalls feminist versions of reproduction, where the egg swarms
the sperm: the position of the speaker defines the narrative.

Dowsett presents an unusually perceptive analysis of male-male sex.

More than most sociologists he is an attentive and sensitive listener to his subjects, a variety of Australian men who had sex with each other in toilets, backrooms, etc. He commented on problems of language:

> This became more urgent on the issue of anal intercourse
> between men. The use of the words "penetration" and
> "penetrate" brought with it considerable baggage from
> discussions of heterosexual sex, baggage that obscured the
> radically different intentions, sensations, meanings, and
> context associated with that sexual activity for gay men.
> "Fucking" and "being fucked," as more appropriate terms,
> not only describe exactly how the men in this study think
> and talk about anal intercourse, they do not automatically
> collapse into the taken-for-granted analogue that
> penetrator/penetrated *equals* active/passive or powerful/
> powerless—a collapse I seriously wanted to avoid. (9)

One of the problems for such descriptions of gay sex is that every man has the equipment to be both inserter and receiver. I myself have never inserted my penis in another man, which makes me a pure bottom in the common parlance. Still, in my experience the more sexually active a man is, the more likely he is to be "versatile," someone who can act as both bottom and top. A friend of mine who claims to have had in the realm of a thousand sexual encounters told me that he learned to be a bottom for the simple reason that he realized there were tops who would reject his advances if he only went one way. To him, the specific sexual activity was less important than the pursuit of more men and more activity. Dowsett rejects even the applicability of tops and bottoms: "Gay men may not read the anus as passive or regard the erect penis as dominating in anal intercourse...." (115) He believes that those who simply apply feminist assumptions about man/woman to top/bottom are in error: "The interchangeability of position in homosexual intercourse renders the application of the readings as extremely suspect...." (115) He takes it still further: "If they are in the habit of using both penis and anus for sex, does the issue of power in penetration, as defined in heterosexuality, become simply irrelevant in homosex?" (154) The obvious answer, as noted by many bottoms and tops, is no. I cannot speak for the tops, but I know how often I have yearned to feel the power of the man I am receiving, even when he is less than powerful in many ways. Dowsett says, "It is for this reason—their actual experiences of sexual pleasure—that many gay men believe they know something about men and male sexuality that exclusively heterosexual men may never discover." (175) Yes, but I am not completely convinced that tops know as much as bottoms, as I have been told by a number of tops who have tried the other side. Dowsett himself says, "Any man who has taken another man's cock up his arse knows only too well that sex will never be the same again." (213) A rather well-known gay scholar told me that while he has always been a top, the one time he bottomed changed his whole understanding of gay studies. Perhaps it should be a requirement for all critical theorists no matter what their sexual orientation.

Of course, many gay men do not engage in anal sex. Studies suggest that it is significantly less common than mutual masturbation or oral sex. Dowsett notes that an Australian research project entitled "Social Aspects of the Prevention of AIDS" revealed that "although anal inter- course was regarded as the most 'physically satisfying' and among the most 'emotionally satisfying,' it was practiced by only about half the men in the sample." (80) There could be many reasons. One is fear of STDs, such as AIDS, which are more easily transmitted anally. Another could be that in various venues, such as parks or toilets, anal sex is de- cidedly inconvenient. One friend of mine said he had always avoided anal sex because he saw it simply as an imitation of heterosexuality. It could also, however, be viewed as a perverse inversion of heterosexual- ity. Such an act of opposition to the straight norm would appeal to many gay men. Douglas Sadownick, in *Sex Between Men: An Intimate History of the Sex Lives of Gay Men Postwar to Present*, suggests that the power of anal sex is anti- homophobic: "In a world that vilifies male-to-male intimacy, whether gay or straight, sometimes it does take the very intense emotional overload that comes with anal sex to flood a man's defenses about getting close to another." (220)

Then, there are many men and women for whom the pleasure of anal penetration is not worth the pain often caused when an erect penis enters the rectum. As the old joke goes, "A: The captain just screwed the cabin boy. B: Rectum? A: Damn near killed him." In his typically emphatic way, John Money states, "For those who are not readily role interchangeable, there is still no reasonable theory of orifices—no theory of why anal penetration is orgasmic ecstasy for some and anorgasmic torture for others, for example." (*Gay, Straight and In-Between*, 104) I am definitely the former. Receptive anal sex is usually a part of my sexual activity even with women. I have had women use strap-ons and I have used a double-ended dildo, with one end in the woman's vagina and the other in my anus. In other words, receptive anal sex for me is not limited to homosexuality. Yet I often wonder to what degree anal sex is a reason for my homosexuality. Freud and others see object choice as rather separate from activity, or what Freud called "sexual aim." Still, it seems to me inevitable that a desire for certain activities leads to a desire for those who seem best able to perform them. Dowsett asserts that "It is clear that the physical possibilities of human bodies play a definite part in what we call sexual pleasure; a prostate is a prostate and uniquely male." (37) As an adolescent, I experimented with various objects to insert while masturbating. At that point I had little knowledge of homosexuality and to my memory had no desire for men. However, even then I knew how my physiology worked. I did not know that I had a prostate that was massaged by anal insertions, but I knew how it felt to have something moving there while I was having an orgasm.

Yet this could never be just physiological. I have a much greater orgasm when entered by a penis than by a dildo. A woman friend of mine said, "The penis is the penetrator of choice." Apologies to lesbians, but I agree. There could be physical reasons for this, though I suspect it is more the metaphysics shaping the physics. Dowsett recounts that:

> Many men in this study talked of the intimacy and

pleasure of anal intercourse. It is this relational character
of sexuality and the vibrancy of participation in a
homosexual community that can be explored in life-
history work, as we seek to understand how gay and
homosexually active men got to where they are today,
how they understand that process and themselves, what
contributes to the history of their lives and to that of
the friendship circles, social networks, institutions, and
organizations that frame the living of lives and the loving
of men." (47)

Thus while Dowsett, like most gay analysts, wishes to deny the imitation
of heterosexuality in anal sex, he seems to describe it in terms that
approximate "making love," as the heterosexual romance would have it,
albeit making love within a large circle.

There are a number of articles on anal sex, such as one in the *Journal
of Sex & Marital Therapy* by B.R. Rosser, B.J. Short, *et al.* entitled: "Anodyspareunia, the unacknowledged sexual dysfunction: a validation study of
painful receptive anal intercourse and its psychosexual concomitants in
homosexual men." As that title suggests, however, most articles tend to
be dryly medical. The extreme is suggested by the following quotation
from J. Rogers' "Testing for and the role of anal and rectal sensation," in
*Baillieres Clinical Gastroenterology* 6(1).

... the rectum is insensitive to stimuli capable of
producing pain and other sensations when applied to
a somatic cutaneous surface. It is, however, sensitive to
distension by a balloon introduced through the anus,
though it is not known whether it is stretching or reflex
contraction of the gut wall or the distortion of the
mesentery and adjacent structures which is responsible for
the sensation. (184-185)

Rogers goes on to assert that "No specific sensory receptors are seen on
careful histological examination of the rectum in humans." (190) In other
words, while the rectum notices "distension," its various skin surfaces

do not respond. There is a rather large distance between the experience of anal sex and that description. I seem to feel quite a few "specific sensory receptors."

Underwood's collection of observations by Aaron and his friends is certainly interesting, but it is a bit like a collection of narratives from guests on *Jerry Springer*: a variety of gay men disclose why they like anal sex. It reaches its highlight in the account of Cole Tucker, a porn star best known for his cigar-chomping representations of macho stereotypes such as marines. He asserts:

> When I bottom, or I lick boots, or I suck dick, or I take
> a dick or an arm or anything up my ass, or even when
> I'm dominated, I don't feel any of that compromises my
> masculinity. At times, I feel more masculine as a bottom.
> Some of the things I do, only top guys can do. It ain't for
> the faint of heart. I'm a pretty strong, vibrant, powerful
> man and I take that to my bottom side. (154)

More useful for my purposes is anal sex's medical guru. Jack Morin's *Anal Pleasure & Health*, which begins with a reference to "My 25-year stint as Dr. Anal" (3), offers a number of observations that suggest why anal sex provides sexual pleasure: "In both men and women the PC [*pubococcygeus*] muscle contracts randomly during arousal and rhythmically during orgasm." (51) Among his observations: "It has been almost universally reported to me that the range of anal muscular activity—contraction *and* relaxation—increases as arousal builds, especially for those whose anuses have become more relaxed generally." (89)

If a transsexual has genital reassignment surgery it is common to create the vagina through inverting the penis. The logic of this seems to be self-evident and suggests the obvious correlation of sexual desire between male and female genitals. A perhaps surprising analogy to this procedure is the various medical articles on creating a vagina from a colon. This has been done for women who had no functional vagina and wished to have heterosexual intercourse. According to the article "Laparoscopic-assisted formation of a colon neovagina" by M. Possover,

J. Drahonowski, *et al*, published in *Surgical Endoscopy* 15(6): 623, a woman who had a radical hysterectomy was given a "neovagina" that "allowed normal sexual activity." Whether this suggests anything about anal sex, I have no idea.

There is another form of sex that I have difficulty categorizing: this is what is called fisting, the insertion of the partner's hand in the anus. I have employed this in masturbating, often with a female partner, but for whatever metaphysical reason it does not have the same power as the penis. And yet sometimes, particularly with a male partner, the fisting goes to another level. In this case, it usually takes a long time and becomes quite emphatic; going beyond a few fingers to something close to the whole hand. I do not masturbate during it, in fact, do not touch myself at all, but instead enter a kind of revery. It might fit the category depicted by Stein:

> I want to claim that a desire is sexual insofar as it involves
> (in the appropriate way) the *arousal* of the person who
> has the desire and that a behavior is sexual insofar as it
> involves (in the appropriate way) the arousal of at least
> one of the participants in a behavior. By arousal, I do not
> mean the various physiological manifestations of arousal
> (for example, having blood flow to one's penis or clitoris),
> but to the *psychological* state of being aroused. (69)

According to Sadownick, I might not be alone in this variant form of arousal. He quotes from a book I have been unable to find, Purusha Larkin's *The Divine Androgyne*:

> Purusha saw "hand-balling" not as S&M but as an act of
> pure love—"the most reliable ecstatic ritual of our time."
> The man receiving a fist revisits the primal womb-birth-
> nursing states of consciousness whereby he can "return to
> our present everyday consciousness bathed in the glow of
> that earlier ecstasy and unified consciousness." (135)

Foucault claimed fisting was invented by gay men, but I surmise that it has been around since the cave people, practised by all the possible gender combinations. Still, I doubt it is "primal," although my personal reaction certainly takes me far beyond the rational or even the simply sexual. I often don't have an erection but instead find myself moving into an erotic space far removed from the simple physical experience.

 With a lot of moaning. I have no idea whether this is "normal." I have touched a few male anuses, but never engaged in fisting as an inserter. I have not heard men moan in the baths, nor have I seen it depicted in pornographic films. I tend to moan in any kind of fisting and women seem to appreciate it. At least one male partner seemed completely put off by my sounds and left the bedroom and refused to come back. Another loved it, but he was a dominant bisexual and this was just part of his enjoyment of what could be called my feminized sexuality. I am not saying my behaviour is female, but observation suggests that the sound effects resemble some female sexual response. For him, to find a male who was not transsexual but had long hair, enjoyed lingerie, etc., was the best of both worlds. As I attempt to account honestly for my sexuality, however, I must admit a flirtation with the transsexual when being fucked by a man. I find that when I am being penetrated by a penis, I sometimes fantasize about being penetrated vaginally. This has a certain frisson, but it is not an aid to orgasm. In order to fully enjoy the penetration and to bring myself to orgasm I need to return my mind to the fact of anal penetration.

Intriguingly, I found one of the best explanations of the meaning of anal sex in an account of female physiology, Anna Burton's "The meaning of perineal activity to women: an inner sphinx," published in 1996 in the *Journal of the American Psychoanalytic Association*. The abstract states:

> Female anatomy and physiology are so arranged that
> the action of perineal and sphincter musculature also
> stimulates the genital. This fosters overlapping mental
> representations of vagina and rectum which in turn
> affect body image and unconscious fantasy in women.
> The experience of perineal contraction acquires complex

> psychic meanings with both libidinal and aggressive
> charge. The libidinal aspect is the largely covert erotic
> sensation that informs the mental representation of
> the genital and is destined to be integrated into female
> sexuality. The aggressive component may present as an
> unconscious fantasy of possessing an inner, powerful,
> and dangerous organ—a focus for conflict between anal-
> sadistic wishes and early elements of the superego. (241)

The last phrase is for me a bit too overwhelmingly psychoanalytic, but I understand the "dangerous organ" within. While the woman likely has had a vaginal experience with which to compare the anal (something that the male could experience only as fantasy), all humans have the perineal connection that stimulates the genital. I would say "the mental representation of the genital is destined to be integrated into gay male sexuality," at least this gay male.

Even if the gay male body is not "feminized" by penetration, it arguably is feminized by the role as object of the male gaze, as noted by the gay male obsession with the gym and the tendency for young gay men to wear much tighter clothing than that worn by the average heterosexual male the same age, although no doubt not in comparison with the average young straight female out on the town. I flirt with this process in my comments on *The Crying Game* elsewhere in this book. I think, however, that the gay male body is also different in being represented as a body performing sex, most obviously in anal intercourse. Jennifer Harding, in *Sex Acts: Practices of Femininity and Masculinity*, claims that:

> The female body is rendered a universal fact by virtue
> of being seen to be outside of, and prior to, history and
> culture. A universalised and naturalised version of the
> sexed body has been produced and perpetuated through
> medical discourse. This version of the body has also been
> maintained by feminists who demonstrate that gender is
> culturally constructed but do not also interrogate the ways
> in which the body is invested in culture and, in particular,

> do not examine the construction of anatomical differences
> upon which gender relations are built. (72)

It is interesting how often both sexists and feminists treat the female body as unchanging and universal. The same is true of both homophobes and gay men. The former see "sodomy" as a form of sin that has existed throughout time but that must be suppressed. The latter see homosexual desire as something that has existed throughout time and must now be liberated. Receptive anal sex has been treated exactly this way. The terms noted above are an obvious aspect, but so is identification of gay men through anatomical remnants of passive anal sex. The American army used anal inspection as the primary assessment of homosexuality. If you were a macho Cole Tucker look-alike just aching to go out and kill, but you had a funnel-shaped anus, you were a 4F homo. If you were a limp-wristed skirt wearer but didn't have a funnel-shaped anus, you were a malingering heterosexual.

The "naturalized" version of the sexed female is reflected in the moaning of women in heterosexual pornography. As far as I can tell, this recurring oral performance is rarely if ever heard in "real life," but in pornography it denotes the insatiable female vagina that yearns for a penetration that will touch some animal core. It is easy for me to dismiss this representation in film, but I find it difficult to see my own very similar response to fisting as somehow false: it comes from some inner depth and seems to be my unconscious reaction. I can control it somewhat, or else I would have caused some commotion in various semi-public venues. Still, if I do not stifle myself, it can be somewhat otherworldly.

In any case, the moaning does not seem attractive to most gay men. On one occasion when I was in the baths, there was a man who appealed to me. He was shortish, stocky, with short grey hair and significant body hair. We had entered the venue at the same time and so I was pleased to see him reclining in the whirlpool. I entered the pool near him and there were the usual "inadvertent" touches of the feet, etc. As my hand began to stray up his leg I found an interesting erection, not very large but very hard. In my experience, this is an excellent target for such an encounter as it enters the anus easily. Often a stranger is not good at—or just not interested in—foreplay and a large or soft penis can be problematic. My friend's would have worked well. But when he began to finger my anus and I began to moan, that was the end of that. This was a very public space with many men around. It is possible that he found my behaviour effeminate or even just surprising. I think I would have remained silent had I been prepared for him to touch me there, but I was caught off guard and reacted thusly.

I like the thought that fisting reaches some realm beyond the conscious to which I otherwise have no access. Frank Browning's attempt to describe something similar becomes quite florid in *A Queer Geography: Journeys Toward a Sexual Self*:

> Like Shelley gazing upon the face of Mont Blanc, I had
> been propelled by the act into a sublime and timeless
> moment 'where silence and solitude were vacancy.'

> For most males raised in the Judeo-Christian tradition,
> the initial experience of being penetrated is profoundly
> disordering. It is a challenge to one of the most
> fundamental principles by which we have been taught
> to know ourselves as masculine. But then to dress
> penetration in the terrifying imagery of the body's own
> rot and decay, precipitated by the particular penetration of
> an unseeable virus, opens us to the possibility of touching
> all the unknowable terrors and beauties of nature. (139)

Browning emphasizes AIDS as penetration, but presumably this "unknowable" is the penetrated male with or without the virus.

The most often quoted analysis of the anally unknowable is Leo Bersani's essay "Is the Rectum a Grave?" AIDS is central to Bersani's argument, yet his view of the glories of abjection is based simply on the experience of being penetrated anally:

> But if the rectum is the grave in which the masculine ideal

(an ideal shared—differently—by men *and* women) of
proud subjectivity is buried, then it should be celebrated
for its very potential for death. Tragically, AIDS has
literalized that potential as the certainty of biological
death, and has therefore reinforced the heterosexual
association of anal sex with a self-annihilation originally
and primarily identified with the fantasmatic mystery of
an insatiable, unstoppable female sexuality. It may, finally,
be in the gay man's rectum that he demolishes his own
perhaps otherwise uncontrollable identification with a
murderous judgment against him. (222)

Thus the process of anal sex overcomes patriarchal dominance. This
might be compared to Kaja Silverman's tellingly titled *Male Subjectivity at the
Margins*. The book's cover employs Mantegna's painting of Saint Sebastian,
long a central image of gay culture. The figure is clearly homoerotic,
but also much more. This is a man persecuted for his devotion to a
desire greater than self-preservation. He is also a man who embraces
penetration no matter what pain it might cause. This Sebastian seeks his
arrows.

Again, I am somewhat lost in an attempt to see myself. Given that
I am clearly subject and object throughout this book, this is always a
danger, but much more so when the topic is the loss of subjectivity. Suf-
fice to say I have never been involved in S/M beyond very mild bondage
and I see no masochism in my character. Similarly, I have no particular
interest in the scatological. I don't want to fall into the trap of viewing
gay "fucking" as an imitation of straight "fucking," but there remains
the obvious fact that for a female the vagina is the expected entrance to
the body, while for a male there is only the anus. Thus, in heterosexual
pornography a woman requesting anal sex is likely to say something
such as, "Do it in my dirtbox." Anal sex in the heterosexual world has
at least the aura of excremental intention. For most gay men, it is, first,
just "fucking."

The argument in Calvin Thomas's *Male Matters: Masculinity, Anxiety, and the Male Body on the Line* has limited attractions for me. His premise might seem quite similar to Bersani: "Insofar as it follows the logic of the *corps propre,* phallogocentrism must exclude the excremental as such and identify that devalued element with the feminine." (83) Note, however, that he emphasizes not anal sex but the excremental, in a particularly Freudian mode, as he shows in a statement on the difference between him and Bersani:

> The fact that my concern is with anality as a site of
> production, or unproductive expenditure, rather than as a
> site of penetration should not occlude the fact that for gay
> men anality involves a mode of sexual practice outlawed
> and despised by dominant culture, and hence a site of
> conscious political struggle. (186)

As Dowsett asserts, "Every man knows when he engages in anal intercourse with another man that he is engaging in something perverse." (37)

While I agree with Dowsett, I am less convinced by the associations claimed by Thomas. When I read his words, I looked in the mirror and asked whether this "site of production" is somehow associated with my sexual enjoyment. I think not. Rather, such "production" strikes me as a somewhat messy side effect of anal sex. I have done what I could to avoid it and would be highly alienated by any partner who drew attention to it, especially as a part of sex play. This confusion was reflected in 2003 in "Savage Love," a syndicated sex advice column written by Dan Savage. In his anger at the homophobic statements of American senator Rick Santorum, Savage proposed to use "santorum" as the name for "that frothy mix of lube and fecal matter that is *sometimes* the by-product of anal sex." While Savage is not known for delicacy in his treatment of sexual matters, he attempted quite a balancing act in trying to be at once in favour of anal sex and against Santorum. Arguably Savage is not actually *against* santorum, but knows that Santorum would be, and thus would be livid about the new terminology.

As Thomas suggests, however, all gay men know that, regardless of the aim of the desire, anal sex must deal with the fact of defecation. Once at Gay Pride in Toronto, there was a bootblack sponsored by a local bathhouse. He had various rates for his services, from the traditional spit polish to bootlicking. His only clothing was army boots and a jockstrap. Unlike the usual bootblack who crouches or sits on a stool, this one bent over and moved around in a way that left nothing to the imagination. There is no question he was displaying both an entrance and an exit.

While gay men will often attempt to describe the process of anal sex as other than a pursuit of filth, it retains that patina no matter what. This makes it less than surprising that most gay men do not talk about it at all, or, even if they do, seldom with the complex descriptions often offered for fellatio. Many a man will supply great detail about every vein of a cock and every lick that traced it but will never reveal that he takes it up the ass. One of the reasons is that it cannot escape its associations. In The Politics and Poetics of Transgression, Peter Stallybrass and Allon White note:

> The grotesque body, as Bakhtin makes clear, has its
> discursive norms too: impurity (both in the sense of
> dirt and mixed categories), heterogeneity, masking,
> protuberant distension, disproportion, exorbitancy,
> clamour, decentred or eccentric arrangements, a focus
> upon gaps, orifices and symbolic filth (what Mary Douglas
> calls "matter out of place"), physical needs and pleasures
> of the "lower bodily stratum," materiality and parody. (23)

All of these elements are part of gay views of anal sex, as shown in various examples of ironic terminology. The title of Edward Albee's play Tiny Alice might seem an obvious reference to Alice in Wonderland, but it also refers to a tight anus (the Toronto restaurant named Slack Alice's offers the opposite). Mary Douglas's classic text, Purity and Danger: An Analysis of Concept of Pollution and Taboo, captures the way this reflects a balancing act between the rules of the past and the rules of the present:

> … it is impossible to make any headway with a study of

> ritual pollution if we cannot face the question of why
> primitive culture is pollution-prone and ours is not. With
> us pollution is a matter of aesthetics, hygiene or etiquette,
> which only becomes grave in so far as it may create
> social embarrassment. The sanctions are social sanctions,
> contempt, ostracism, gossip, perhaps even police action.
> But in another large group of human societies the effects
> of pollution are much more wide ranging. A grave
> pollution is a religious offence. (73)

It intrigues me that this was published in 1966. I wonder what Douglas meant by "ours" forty years ago when "our" culture today is still so overwhelmed by the "religious offence" of the "grave pollution" of anal sex. Attacks on gay marriage by various Christian religions are laden with references to reproduction and the importance of two genders within marriage, but many of the statements contain cryptic references to "natural order" and other phrases that seem to imply that entering the male anus is not part of a natural order. Thus regardless of the other arguments, central to the opposition to gay marriage is the fear that men might be *impudicus*.

This is far from simply social embarrassment. In an article on "Bergson's Conception of Difference," Gilles Deleuze questions what he sees as Jonathan Dollimore's faith in the purposefulness of transgression:

> It would be wrong to associate the exhilarating sense of
> freedom which transgression affords with any necessary
> or automatic political progressiveness (Dollimore 1985).
> Often it is a powerful ritual or symbolic practice whereby
> the dominant squanders its symbolic capital so as to get
> in touch with the fields of desire which it denied itself
> as the price paid for its political power. Not a repressive
> desublimation (for just as transgression is not intrinsically
> progressive, nor is it intrinsically conservative), it is
> a counter-sublimation, a delirious expenditure of the
> symbolic capital accrued (through the regulation of the

> body and the decathexis of habitus) in the successful
> struggle of bourgeois hegemony. (201)

This argument might seem itself a rather "delirious expenditure" of a Deleuzian sort, but the assessment seems to work particularly well in the orgasmic context of anal sex. This would appear to be a particularly delirious expenditure, as Tim Dean suggests in *Beyond Sexuality*, in his comment on Scott O'Hara's *Autopornography: A Memoir of Life in the Lust Lane*. O'Hara, a porn star and writer, refers to being fucked as "surrender." (73) Dean responds:

> O'Hara's formulation makes clear that sex is often
> less about bodies or physicality than about fantasy,
> about accessing the disincarnate form of the Other's
> *jouissance* through someone else's body. This can feel like
> "possession" in both subjective and objective genitive
> senses: possessing the Other's *jouissance* by becoming the
> Other's possession—that is, by surrendering to the Other's
> alien *jouissance*. (166)

This again might seem feminized, but the *jouissance* of the receiver thus literally incorporates the *jouissance* of the inserter. Who possesses whom?

I realize this view is highly subjective, yet I think the transgression is more profound for the receiver. The entering of the male body, that being that is naturally whole, reverberates against some of our foundational beliefs, but much more so for the body being entered. Jonathan Sawday's *The Body Emblazoned: Dissection and the Human Body in Renaissance Culture* claims that the Renaissance saw anatomy as in some sense obscene: "The taboo which has been violated is, perhaps, one of the oldest known to human beings—that the inferior recesses of the body are not merely private to others, but peculiarly private—that is expressly forbidden—to the owner or inhabiter of the body." (14-15) Think of how seldom in the cycles of history it has been acceptable for the female to appreciate erotically the touching of the inside of her body. This is the case in spite of the fact that our culture has consistently claimed her body is made to be entered. That touching the inside of the male body should be a problem should not be surprising. Or rather, it should be no surprise that the male body is surprised to be entered.

Sawday believes that even in the Renaissance, the male object of the male gaze had to be reconfigured to be acceptable in a heterosexual context. In other words, the homoerotic is not simply a means of attracting the hidden homosexual desire in the heterosexual male. It is also a transposition of the male into a form that the male can contemplate as object. This goes a long way in explaining why even the most overtly masculine male nude usually seems to have elements that could be called feminine:

> ... for the male body to become the explicit focus of male
> desire (where "desire" could encompass both knowledge
> and sexuality) it first had to be re-created as female.
> It is this fourth element, for example, that helps us to
> understand the "feminization" of the male body (akin to
> that "feminization" of Christ in the passion which we have
> already encountered) when it lay on the dissecting slab;
> or the transformation of the body of Marsyas in Golding's
> translation of Ovid into "one whole wound." (Sawday 213)

The image of Christ's "one whole wound" takes the idea of penetration to another level. It is not just that anal penetration might be feminizing in mimicking vaginal penetration. Anal penetration imitates the ultimate vulnerability of the opening of Christ in the stigmata. Thus as Saint Sebastian's multiple arrows mimic Christ's penetration, so do they add to the image of the gay man as being opened.

Sawday considers Freud's view of the female body as unheimlich. Sawday responds,

> But is it only the female body which (to men) is held to
> be both "heimlich" and, following the logic of Freud's
> "Sandman" analysis, "unheimlich"? For men and women,
> the sexually undifferentiated body-interior is a region of
> eerie unfamiliarity made doubly eerie (and thus uncanny)

> by the knowledge that this unfamiliar geography is also
> part of ourselves. (Sawday 160)

If the anally penetrated body is all the things that Sawday suggests, then the ultimate attraction for the homosexual penetrator becomes more and more explainable. There are so many instances in male-male love in which the name of "homo" is met by emphatic difference between sexual partners. Thus as the anal passive body becomes *unheimlich*, it achieves the "eerie unfamiliarity" that convinces the penetrator that he is entering unexplored regions.

At the end of the day, it is the act itself that causes what might be called sodomyphobia. There are various acts, most of which anyone might do. Certain of them are rarely done, some of them are done by everyone. Some people feel compelled to do certain acts, others feel compelled to refuse to do certain acts. How much choice one feels generally or specifically and how much social pressure there is to do or not do such acts is always relevant. A prime example is body modification. The one extreme would be cutting one's toenails. The other extreme would be elective amputation. Cosmetic surgery, gender reassignment surgery, hair dying, tattoos, haircuts, and body piercing are on a continuum between. All must be considered in the contexts of issues such as degree of social pressure (unmarried male academic in large North American urban university versus married woman in small Aboriginal community pre-invasion), degree of permanence (elective amputation versus haircut), importance of act in terms of general social values (visible tattoo in Toronto 1960 vs visible tattoo in Toronto 2008).

So, this is an act that I choose to do. Perhaps I am compelled by sexual desire, but it is more than possible that my desire is less "compelling" than that of others who feel sufficient social pressure that they never do it. And here I have no doubt that my willingness to be so explicit about my acts, to a degree that still seems rare, is partly a belief that while it is pollution in some circles, in others it is at least potential sacrament on the altar of progressive politics, such as feminism. This is not necessarily because it is feminizing. It also could be because, once more with a glance towards Cole Tucker, the gay man manifests the hypermasculine and then perverts it through the anus, as so neatly described by Maurizia Boscagli in *Eye on the Flesh: Fashions of Masculinity in the Early Twentieth Century*:

> In other words, the Nietzschean figuration of masculinity
> stands as an instance of gender trouble. By citing the
> abject sexuality of the homoerotic male body, the image of
> the athlete-soldier-strongman puts normative masculinity
> under erasure while impersonating and performing its
> very laws. Signs of this complex, antiphallic masculinity
> can be detected in the erotic display of the male body
> that early twentieth century European culture both
> allowed and tried to manage. Repeated spectacles of
> masculinity from Thomas Mann's Aschenbach to Edgar
> Rice Burrough's Tarzan show a male body resexualized
> under the sign of abjection: The desire of these subjects
> that their bodies be seen enacts traces of a masochistic
> pleasure of showing off, of making an erotic sight of their
> suffering, degradation, and self-sacrificing discipline. As
> a mechanism for eroticizing lack, masochism therefore
> appears in this period as a chief means of phallic
> divestiture for the male subject. (6)

Obviously, this entire book is a performance, a spectacle, a showing-off (and no doubt will be criticized by many for exactly this reason). Yet, the inevitable rejoinder in this chapter is that I am showing off what most would deem to be abjection, pollution—or even erasure. Sawday refers to the texts that metaphorically ask the lover to perform a dissection:

> The lover who seeks anatomization is demanding
> from the beloved anatomist access to a form of sexual
> self-surrender, which, whilst it hints at transgressive
> fulfilment, also endlessly defers the moment of
> dissolution. The corpse and the anatomist, or the lover

and the beloved, rely on one another to produce a timeless
signification, a release from punishment, an entry into
a remoulded world of spectacle. But, this economy of
domination and surrender, flowing between corpse and
dissector, is also a public activity, a voyeuristic fantasy of
peering and prying which takes place before an audience.
(Sawday 84)

Sawday's account resonates of both Deleuze, and Dean and O'Hara: sex
as dissection.

Earlier, in this essay, I suggested that for me anal sex and fisting are
quite different things. However, perhaps my participation in anal sex
is rather a precursor to the Bersani-like dissolution that I find in fisting.
This returns the discussion to AIDS. The fact that I am writing this book
in the early part of the twenty-first century is important in many ways,
but particularly in the context of the gay plague. In the early 1980s, I
shared the usual gay paranoia that I had done something sexual that
would lead to my slow disintegration that would end in a quick death.
In the 1990s, I shared the survivor-guilt of middle-aged gay men who
were HIV-negative. In 2008, however, I write this in the context of Andrew Sullivan's "Not Dead Yet: An Apology," published in what arguably
remains the most prominent gay publication in North America, The Advocate. Sullivan notes how many both within and without the gay community resent the health of HIV-positive people such as Sullivan. Rather
than disintegration, those well-suited to available medication (Sullivan
included) are finding the virus to be less troubling than diabetes.

Yet we are still in the shadow of the association of anal sex and AIDS.
Underwood notes that "It appears that as far as the medical establish-
ment is concerned, male fucking didn't even exist before the onset of
AIDS." (5) Dowsett presents this as a dividing line between the straight
and gay worlds:

... for gay men the sexual activity now called "unsafe"
was not an unfortunate or dangerous behavior; it was
ordinary sexual behavior, validated historically by

homosexual communities, their cultures, and political
struggles for the decriminalization of that specific sex act.
It just so happened that a virus got in the way. (81)

In other words, on one side were heterosexuals, for whom gay anal sex
is the source of AIDS, and on the other side were gay men, for whom
AIDS is an evil effect of a good behaviour, like cholera from drinking
water. To Dowsett, having sex without a condom—what is known as
"barebacking"—is not suicidal lunacy but a refusal to let AIDS prevent
normal acts:

> Having another man's semen inside one's rectum is
> an insistent motif in much gay poetry and fiction, and
> its forfeiture is a serious issue to deal with for safe sex
> education. It would appear that women are not the only
> ones with worries about wet patches, and that there is a
> greater dispersal of pleasure in male anal intercourse than
> is captured in the idea of "genital primacy." (177)

I can only resort to my usual subjectivity to say that I do not have this
attraction to barebacking. Before AIDS, I believed it to be more of a
convenience: condoms were for heterosexuals. I don't feel I am missing
something by using condoms. However, I certainly agree with Dowsett
that anal sex is much more complex than a search for dissolution:
"What these men teach us, in contrast to Bersani's disintegrative
revolution, is the enactment of sex as centrally constitutive of men's
sexual subjectivity." (212)

I continue to be convinced by Dowsett. What I just referred to as "my
usual subjectivity" is largely constituted by "the enactment of sex." In
many ways, this is the most intimate chapter in this book. This is partly
because of the act itself, regarded by many people of all sexual orientations as too intimate for discussion, but also because of both its symbolic order, offering an entrance to the forbidden interior of the body, and
because of its resonance. My own response, both the orgasmic and the
beyond/beneath/outside of orgasmic, leads me to incomprehensibility.
I am intellectualizing, attempting to reason, about something in myself

that seems completely beyond the powers of reason. There is a dimension here beyond that which I could ever hope to grasp:

> The actual sensations of sex between men are what
> contribute to the counterhegemonic capacity in
> homosexuality. This calls into question the notion that
> it is gay identity that is actually subversive—a notion
> privileged in much sexuality writing. Only sensation—the
> bodily sensations of sex—have the power to contradict
> prohibition. (Dowsett 151)

To go one step beyond Dowsett, perhaps these "bodily sensations" have not been just a contradiction but an affirmation. In anal sex I have no great interest in the "counterhegemonic" or in Bersani's disintegration. Instead, during the act I disappear into my self: I become who I am in a way unlike any other at any other time. "Up the ass" provides the moments of ultimate autobiography when I write my life, but far more, when I "right" my life.

## 7. Dinge Queens and Racists

Some time ago I read an article in the gay press on racial relations in the gay community. It suggested that a typical white attitude is "I'm not racist: I love to fuck black men."

The gay community is founded on sexual desire. At one level it is a community of shared values. As in most minority communities, the individuals see themselves as different from the hegemony and the hegemony has a similar view. Thus gay men find spaces, organizations, events, in which they can enjoy an association with others who are "the same." Various claims are made about what constitutes this sameness, but in the end there is only one constant link: these are all men who sexually desire other men. Yet, contrary to what heterosexuals often seem to think, this does not mean that all homosexuals desire all men. The gay community generally accepts that each gay man responds to "a type." Whereas the heterosexual world tends to believe that even a male who says "I prefer blondes" is engaging in narrow objectification, the gay male world believes saying "I only get turned on by big guys with a lot of body hair" is more than reasonable.

But some choices are more reasonable than others. Attraction by race continues to be a major turn-on for some and a major turn-off for others. One of my students, a very attractive, extraordinarily slim young man of Asian descent, with a lovely feminine face, held forth in one class against the stereotype of the Asian gay as Madame Butterfly. Given that he was speaking in a soft, delicate voice, it seemed somewhat incongruous. I might be wrong, but I can't see a big burly lumberjack with a voice like George C. Scott rejecting the image of the "bear," the gay fetish of the man who looks rough, usually is overweight, and invariably displays as much body hair as he can produce. Of course, this could just be the gay aversion to effeminate stereotypes and attraction to masculine ones. Still, gay black men similarly reject the hypermasculine images of the black stud.

Gay white men seem to think that homophobia gives them some unusual sensitivity to other minorities. Hearing misogynist jokes in a gay bar should give the lie to that one. As Essex Hemphill says in the introduction to *Brother to Brother: New Writings by Black Gay Men*, "It has not fully dawned on white gay men that racist conditioning has rendered many of them no different from their heterosexual brothers in the eyes of black gays and lesbians. Coming out of the closet to confront sexual oppression has not necessarily given white males the motivation or insight to transcend their racist conditioning." (xviii-xix)

In the past, some American gay bars had entrance regulations that look like Jim Crow with a slightly limp wrist: whatever style was the latest mode in the black community somehow offended the bar's dress code. Of more interest in the contemporary scene is the view depicted in another observation by Hemphill about bars less concerned with the social than with the sexual:

> At the baths, certain bars, in bookstores and cruising
> zones, black men were welcome because these
> constructions of pleasure allowed the races to mutually
> explore sexual fantasies and, after all, the black man
> engaging in such a construction only needed to whip out
> a penis of almost any size to obtain the rapt attention
> withheld from him in other social and political structures
> of the gay community. These sites of pleasure were more
> tolerant of black men because they enhanced the sexual
> ambiance, but that same tolerance did not always continue
> once the sun began to rise.
>
> Open fraternizing at a level suggesting companionship
> or love between the races was not tolerated in the light
> of day. Terms such as 'dinge queen,' for white men who
> prefer black men, and 'snow queen,' for black men who
> prefer white men, were created by a gay community that
> obviously could not be trusted to believe its own rhetoric

> concerning brotherhood, fellowship, and dignity. Only an
> *entire* community's silence is capable of reinforcing these
> conditions. (xix)

According to Hemphill, racial designations are not acceptable in a community.

The present chapter is guilty of a significant elision of geography in the treatment of such racial designations. In most of the following, the term "black" is used as though all representatives of the African diaspora are the same, which is of course not true. Hemphill, like most of those quoted here, is discussing the African-American situation. Some, particularly Isaac Julien and Kobena Mercer, are part of the black British community. Frantz Fanon concentrated on the francophonie, particularly France, Martinique, and Algeria. My own experience is primarily in Canada, in Toronto. Given the Canadian demographics, this means that almost all of my sexual and social experience is with Canadian immigrants from the Caribbean, with a few Black Britons and African Americans, when either they were tourists in Canada or I in their country. Steve Pile's *The Body and the City: Psychoanalysis Space and Subjectivity* considers the spatialization of sexual relations, as in Fanon's situating of the black man in a white community in much of the discussion in *Black Skin, White Mask*. This is particularly important in the discussion here, because in Canada, black and white are still considered spatially: the black person is thought to be originally from somewhere else. This is not just a white assumption. One of my black students was asked by another black student whether she was going to a Caribbean dance. She said, "No." He asked her, "Where are you from?" She said, "Mississauga" (a suburb of Toronto). He then said, "Where are your parents from?" She answered, "Grenada." "Then you should come," he said. She replied, "Ask my parents."

If the subtleties of racism cause confusion, so do the nuances of homophobia, especially assumptions of who are the most phobic. Wesley Crichlow, in "Buller Men and Batty Bwoys: Hidden Men in Toronto and Halifax Black Communities," explicitly rejects any vilification of Caribbean heterosexism as somehow worse than others, yet he notes "the Caribbean origins of buller man and batty bwoy [Caribbean terms for male homosexuals] contain venomous connotations." (76) Carolyn Cooper's *Noises in the Blood: Orality, Gender, and the "Vulgar" Body of Jamaican Popular Culture* observes that in dance hall music "the homophobic thrust of Jamaican style machismo is evident in derogatory references to homosexuality and cross-dressing. In Jamaica, cross-dressing is a clear sign of other crosses: taking sleep to mark death." (149) In one of his songs, raggae star Buju Banton went beyond such a sign to suggest shooting gay men (Julien, *Darker*). In my experience, the dismissal depicted in these examples lurks in the consciousnesses of most black homosexual men in Toronto. As Crichlow notes, theirs is not just a North American experience: they are never just "gay."

On the other hand, in the United States, even the most roots-oriented black person or the most racist white person—either one of whom might be prone to "Back to Africa" rhetoric—tends to accept the African-American as *prima facie* American, but also most assuredly black. Some kind of racial designation is always assumed and usually given. In all three of these societies—the United States, Canada, and the United Kingdom—and perhaps in all societies, racial designations seem inevitable. South Africans used the term "racialist" to reject an attitude that might not be racist but still too easily accepts race as a system. As even post-apartheid South Africa has learned, however, while "race" might be a false consciousness, in its specious claim that skin colour and other physical features have some inherent meaning, it remains central in our culture. To be black, to be white, tells the world something.

Many of those involved in gay relationships with men of another race have attempted to deny the political imperatives. The naïveté of some statements in *Black Men/White Men: A Gay Anthology*, published in 1983, is striking, but I continue to hear comments from my friends similar to the following by Darryl Towles:

> I'm a Black male with a sexual preference for White
> men. It's really no different than preferring vodka to

scotch, except that I'm often judged because of it. But the
development of my sexual tastes is very logical: When I
was growing up, most of the male images I was exposed
to were virile, masculine, all-American White types. (92)

One of my black boyfriends similarly attributed his attraction to white
men to having attended a British boarding school while his brother, also
gay, was interested in black men because he had stayed in the Caribbean
for his education. Michael Smith, the white founder of National
Association of Black and White Men Together, said to Thom Beame:

> But, if I may turn this defensive stance into something
> more prideful, let me state that we interracialists are an
> entity as real and sincere as any other. We hurt when
> White—and Black—non-interracialists poke at us. And
> we resent their assigning us their racial hangups—we
> have enough to deal with. We also have our special
> joys. Any person who's come to grips with his own
> minority—be it racial or sexual—is, in one sense,
> grateful for the 'affliction.' For it gives him or her the
> opportunity to become a better human being. Gay and
> lesbian interracialists are dealt an even greater 'affliction,'
> and those of us who weather it take a special pride in the
> accomplishment. When you ask me if I'm glad I'm an
> interracialist, I'll ask you if you're glad you're gay. And if
> you say 'yes,' I'll tell you to double that feeling. (194-195)

Smith's "interracialism" has not triumphed. Many gay black men would
agree with Hemphill's view of the dinge queen—sucking black dick in
the baths and avoiding black faces on the street.

Few treatments of gay "interracialism" look to the heterosexual example, as depicted in Rey Chow's comments on sexism in Fanon:

> Miscegenation leading to the mixing of races and cultures,
> the threat of impurity, the danger of bastardization—this
> much is common knowledge. Is this the reason why

> women's sexual agency is tabooed and excommunicated—
> since, as Fanon portrays it, women are consciously or
> unconsciously prone to miscegenation? What dangers does
> a *female* tendency toward miscegenation hold for a theory
> of community formation in the aftermath of colonialism?
> (46)

The male homosexual similarly interrupts community formation as when Ron Simmons questions Marlon Riggs, creator of the film *Tongues Untied*, a liberation manifesto for gay black men, about Riggs' white lover:

> As one reviewer put it: If you state in the video's
> conclusion that 'Black men loving black men is the
> revolutionary act,' then why aren't you 'acting?'"

> It's a tricky question because as another reviewer
> commented, the issue of interracial love is 'unresolved' in
> the tape.... My only defense is that what I was searching
> for at that stage in my life was not so much a lover because
> I already had a lover at that point who is white. (193)

Riggs continues:

> Many people do interpret 'black men loving black men'
> solely in terms of a sexual, romantic affinity, and love.
> But what I meant was love in the sense of friendship,
> community, family, and fraternity, which was far more
> important, in nurturing me as a black gay man, than the
> love of a particular lover who is white. (194)

This seems reasonable, a social community of black gay men, for whom the race of sexual partners is not the essence of that community. Still, the film does not seem to reflect that philosophy. Riggs' film recognizes the necessity of a politically appropriate desire, but Riggs was unable to reject his own politically inappropriate desire.

One might turn to many sources for paeans to brotherhood in the gay community. Chow, like most feminist scholars, assumes a power imbalance between men and women. No matter what the ethnicity or race, heterosexuality means that in some sense a woman is "sleeping with the enemy." On the other hand, there has long been a claim that homosexuality means first of all comradeship among the lovers and potential lovers. The first ardent modern philosopher of this view was Edward Carpenter, but he was only articulating what Walt Whitman had long praised in poetry. Regardless of obvious differences in class and economic status, and even just the obvious differences between any two lovers of any gender, the concept of "same-sex love" led to belief in the ultimate ideal of a love between equals, something far beyond the sad imbalances recorded in a myriad of star-crossed heterosexual lovers throughout history.

Yet race is another matter. A black man's white lover does more than disrupt brotherhood. Chow says of female sexual agency, "Once we put our focus on this 'tabooed' area of female sexuality, we see that female sexuality is what interrupts the unidirectional force of existential violence that is otherwise justified in Fanon's theory of postcolonial nation-building." (48) Black nationalists view heterosexual interracial couples as failing to build the nation by creating at least the potential of the "half-breed." Sexual relations are not always a happy blending through "love," as commercial sex and sexual assault attest, but offspring of an interracial sexual encounter are an integral statement of integration, regardless of the nature of the meeting that led to their conception. There is no biological progeny from a homosexual union, but there are various inferences of children and descendants. It is as though a sexual association inevitably suggests reproduction, especially where that implied reproduction is of a sort often proscribed. It might seem too great a leap, but this would suggest that the interracial homosexual couple must confront the spirit of the mulatto in addition to homophobia.

Understandably, most of the black observers have been primarily concerned with the snow queen. Darieck Scott outs himself as a black man with a white lover in an article tellingly named for Spike Lee's film,

"Jungle Fever?: Black Gay Identity Politics, White Dick, and the Utopian Bedroom." He describes what he sees as the general black view of him:

> The black partner in the couple, it is assumed, does not
> value, indeed detests, blackness, and therefore detests his
> brothers and hates himself; he is beguiled, enchanted,
> by a white standard of beauty, by 'whiteness' itself, and
> consequently has an exclusive desire for a lover with
> Nordic features. Moreover, his political, social, and
> cultural allegiances are to 'white' gay politics, to white gay
> men, and to 'white' cultural forms. (299-300)

This snow queen is an Oreo cookie: black on the outside, white on the inside. One famous snow queen, the filmmaker Isaac Julien, sees it differently. His film *The Attendant*, in which an apparently closeted black museum attendant seeks to be whipped by an aristocratic white man, is one of the most troubling examples of gay interracial interaction I have seen. Julien treats "interracial desire as a transgressive act of affection. Trust is the bonding necessary in interracial desire, as in S/M." ("Confessions" 9)

Julien's link of interracial desire to S/M through "trust" is insightful. Many theorists claim that S/M enables the individual to rework oppressive systems of power. Sexual abuse of the child is one of society's most feared forms of such oppression. Yet in the S/M scene, the person who has experienced that abuse, or perhaps even just has a phobia about its possibility, can repeat it in a theatrical form as a slave. The master who dominates him also loves him. The "abuse" rehearses the past but now in a form controlled by the slave, as the "bottom" always establishes the limits of any S/M scene. This "abuse" almost invariably ends with the master demonstrating that it is only part of a sexual love that the master offers to the slave. He reconfigures oppression as love. Still, it might be more pleasing to liberal viewers of *The Attendant* if the master were black, if he were someone who reversed slavery and dominated the elite white slave, albeit in love rather than hate. Instead, the black man rehearses slavery, to turn one of the primary evils of history into something that he can embrace and even love. To follow my usage in the last sentence, Slavery becomes slavery becomes love. As Julien suggests, this can happen only in a setting where there is a phenomenal trust between the partners. They must believe that they can at least begin to expiate such a horrendous sin of history through their scene rather than reinstating it, as the outside world might expect.

There is not a lot of trust out there. The common black perception of the white lover of black men begins with that found in Fanon's *Black Skin, White Masks*, where the dinge queen might be described as "White Fear, Sexy Black": "the Negrophobic woman is in fact nothing but a putative sexual partner—just as the Negrophobic man is a repressed homosexual." (156) Fanon goes on to refer to "men who go to 'houses' in order to be beaten by Negroes; passive homosexuals who insist on black partners." (177) Fanon assumes that the dinge queen is seeking something akin to what I have found in anal sex, an orgasmic dissolution of the self through sexual experience. The most sophisticated commentator on homosexuality in Fanon, Kobena Mercer, has written at least six different pieces on a specific American dinge queen who might seem like the poster boy for Fanon's argument, Robert Mapplethorpe.

It seems impossible to justify Mapplethorpe's point of view, and difficult enough to explain it. Patricia Morrisroe, in *Mapplethorpe: A Biography*, records the memory of his friend Lia Fernandez: "Robert's relationships with blacks were all terribly sexual, but he didn't actually like them. He constantly called them 'niggers,' and said they were stupid. He may have been in love with Milton [Moore], but it was very different from the love other people feel." (254) Fernandez's memory might be questioned, but her view is only a more extreme version of that of many others quoted by Morrisroe. Earlier in the book, Morrisroe stated, "In a rare moment of self-reflection, Mapplethorpe confided that his goal in sex, and in art, was to stop himself from feeling: 'When I have sex with someone I forget who I am. For a minute I even forget I'm human. It's the same thing when I'm behind a camera. I forget I exist.'" (193) It would seem that Mapplethorpe sought that dissolution of self, which suggests why he might have had such a demeaning view of his sexual partners.

Of course, as most reviewers have noted, Morrisroe is surprisingly insensitive to the culture in which Mapplethorpe lived. She does not seem to understand interracial relationships, S/M, or even homosexuality. When she mentions any man who died of AIDS, she labels him as such, regardless of how tangential his role in Mapplethorpe's life. Perhaps there is a non-homophobic reason for this detail, but I am unable to see what it might be. A much more perceptive source for the present discussion is Mercer, who over the course of ten years moves from antagonism towards Mapplethorpe's iconic photographs of black sexuality to ambivalent acceptance. He describes his first response to the nudes in Mapplethorpe's *The Black Book* in the context of a general black gay readership:

> We wanted to look, but we didn't always find what we
> wanted to see. This was because we were immediately
> disturbed by the racial dimension of the imagery and,
> above all, angered by the aesthetic objectification that
> reduced these individual black men to purely abstract
> visual 'things,' silenced in their own right as subjects
> and serving mainly as aesthetic trophies to enhance
> Mapplethorpe's privileged position as a white gay male
> artist in the New York avant-garde. (Mercer 1996, 282)

Given Riggs's comments, this "we" is revealing. It is as if Mercer believes in a black gay community with a coherent taste. "We didn't always find what we wanted to see" is the type of psychological construction that tests the potential of the implied unity of the first person plural no matter what the topic and no matter what the community represented by that "we." In the end, however, Mercer—and perhaps "we"—comes to accept what might be called the gay argument, although now it slides into that ultimately slippery British pronoun, "one":

> One can see in Mapplethorpe's use of homoeroticism
> a subversive strategy of perversion in which the liberal

humanist values inscribed in the idealized fine-art nude
are led away from the higher aims of 'civilization' and
brought face to face with that part of itself repressed and
devalued as 'other' in the form of the banal, commonplace
stereotype in everyday culture. (Mercer 1996, 289)

Mapplethorpe's gayness interrupts the performance of authority in, say, a
male photographer's image of a female object. Mercer had been convinced
that Mapplethorpe had the phallus, that transcendental signifier of
power in society, but now suspects he might not. Mapplethorpe moves
from white observer to gay participant. Compare this with bell hooks
on sexism in black politics:

The discourse of black resistance has almost always
equated freedom with manhood, the economic and
material domination of black men with castration,
emasculation. Accepting these sexual metaphors forged
a bond between oppressed black men and their white
male oppressors. They shared the patriarchal belief that
revolutionary struggle was really about the erect phallus,
the ability of men to establish political dominance that
could correspond to sexual dominance. (58)

The black man seeks the phallus but is at the same time doomed to
embody its physical counterpart. Fanon claims, "He is turned into a
penis. He is a penis." (170) Forty years later, Essex Hemphill comments
on Mapplethorpe's photographs: "The penis becomes the identity of the
black male which is the classic racist stereotype re-created and presented
as 'art' in the context of a gay vision." (*Brother to Brother* xviii) Mercer offers a
more detailed analysis:

One might say that, despite anatomical evidence, the belief
symbolized in the fantasy of the big black willy—that
black male sexuality is not only 'different' but somehow
'more'—is one many men and women, black and white,
straight or gay, cling onto, because it retains currency

and force as an element in the psychic reality of the social
fantasies in which our racial and gendered identities have
been historically constructed. (Mercer 1996, 285)

How do you argue that the black man is prevented from having the
phallus by asserting that he *is* the penis? David Friedman, in *A Mind of Its
Own: A Cultural History of the Penis*, suggests how important the black penis
is in the history of white racism:

> Despite their different starting points, most racial thinkers
> based many of their most important conclusions on the
> same criterion—the African's penis. It was stared at, feared
> (and in some cases desired), weighed, interpreted via
> Scripture, meditated on by zoologists and anthropologists,
> preserved in specimen jars, and, most of all, calibrated.
> And, in nearly every instance, its size was deemed proof
> that the Negro was less a man than a beast. (106-107)

Regardless of facts, the very thing so often presented as a triumphant
feature of masculinity, the large penis, is used to denote the black man
as incapable of ruling because he is too masculine to be civilized.

Hemphill's poem "Black Machismo" provides a sensitive and subtle
answer to this penis that denies the phallus, as viewed by the black man
himself:

> Metaphorically speaking
> his black dick is so big
> when it stands up erect
> it silences
> the sound of his voice.
> It obscures his view
> of the territory, his history,
> the cosmology of his identity
> is rendered invisible.
>
> (*Ceremonies* 130)

In an earlier response, Mercer, with Isaac Julien, proffered one theory of the white containment of the emasculated penis in Mapplethorpe's famous photograph, "Man in the Polyester Suit":

> The black subject is objectified into Otherness as the size
> of his penis symbolizes a threat to the secure identity of
> the white male ego. Yet, the phobic object is contained
> by the two-dimensional frame of the photo, thus the
> white male viewer is made safe in his identification, and
> at the same time he is able to indulge that commonplace
> white curiosity about the nature of black sexuality,
> and black male sexuality in particular. As Frantz Fanon
> argued in *Black Skin, White Masks*, European myths about
> the aggressive, violent, and animalistic 'nature' of
> black sexuality were fabricated and fictioned by the
> phallocentric anxieties and fantasies of the all-powerful
> white 'master.' In Mapplethorpe's imagery, the stench of
> racist stereotypes rotting in the soil of violent history is
> sanitized and deodorized by the clinical precision of his
> authoritative, aestheticizing master vision. In reiterating
> the terms of colonial fantasy, his pictures service the
> expectations of white desire, but what do they say to our
> wants and desires as black gay men? ("True Confessions" 169-
> 170)

I neither should nor can delineate the "wants and desires" of black gay men, but I can provide at least a hint of what might be called their sexual position. One aspect has been suggested by the various recent discussions of "the down low." This refers to black men who have sex with other black men but live closeted, "heterosexual" lives. It became such a *cause célèbre* that it received extensive commentary on an episode of *Oprah*. The "scientific" view is suggested by Millett et al in "Focusing 'Down Low': Bisexual Black Men, HIV Risk and Heterosexual Transmission," in the *Journal of the National Medical Association*: "Black men who have sex with men (MSM) and women but who do not identify as gay or disclose their bisexual activities to main female partners, also known as men 'on the down-low,' have been cited as the main reason for the increase in HIV infections in black women." (525) The article raises questions as to whether the down low (DL) has contributed to the rise in HIV, but its scientific rigour cannot deny the image of the rampant black penis once more wreaking havoc. More relevant to the present chapter is the opinion expressed by Juba Kalamka in "How Can I Be Down? A bisexual black man's take on 'the down low'":

> While gay and straight white academic communities
> and the popular media continued to engage in rote,
> inflammatory, sensational, and racist demonizing of black
> sexuality, the black community, gay and straight, has
> not been able to get a handle on the discussion either.
> This failure was largely due to the dynamic overlap of
> homophobia and class privilege that has stunted most
> discussions of the way unchallenged patriarchy and
> sexism are integral to the experience of those on the DL
> and those they may infect.
>
> As I've gotten older and more experienced, it has become
> clearer to me that many of the men I had encountered
> in the black community, who were either suspected of
> being homosexual or had confided in me that they did
> indeed have sex with men, would have been exclusively
> involved with men had they had a supportive community.
> More often than not, though, they were engaged in
> sexual relationships with black women because doing
> so was what made them black men, what made them good
> men, according to the community they did have. That a
> community all too invested in creating "Million Man
> Marching Great Black Fathers" and in making "Straight
> Black Dick" the measuring stick—the barometer of
> verity, the only thing of real intrinsic worth—is also a

community willing to have women die at the end of one
should come as no surprise. (39)

Racism has led black men to have a particular need to seek a verification
of "real intrinsic worth" and homophobia denies that "only thing."

If the white man is attracted to a black man because he is a black
man, he is a racialized object, as suggested by Lee Edelman, in Homographesis: Essays in Gay Literary and Cultural Theory:

> We can recognize, in the fetishization of the visual as
> adequate to discern the hypostatized difference that the
> 'racialized' body must inevitably reveal, a borrowing
> from—and a repositioning of—the scopic logic on which
> the prior assertion of sexual difference depends. 'Racial'
> discrimination, in both senses of the word, like the
> project I have defined as 'homographesis,' is propped up
> on, or, as Freud might put it, occupies an anaclitic relation
> to, the privileging of the scopic drive in the psychic
> structuring of sexual difference. (46)

Like many other theorists who use Lacanian psychoanalysis as a base,
Edelman's language can be extremely difficult. The important element
to note here is the visual. Edelman's concept of homographesis assumes
that the homosexual is always writing himself and also always being
read, as noted in the chapter on the closet. If the homosexual is thus
someone who overvalues the visual, he becomes like the person who
overvalues race, because in most instances race is identified by external
markers. While every substantial thinker tells us race is false—physi-
ologically, sociologically, philosophically, etc.—many of us continue to
make it a paramount identity. Edelman links this to the general paradigm of "sexual difference," the system through which heterosexuality
recognizes large breasts or a fine beard. Yet in the homosexual world,
other visual elements must be established as reasons to find the partner
sufficiently "different" to be attractive as a sexual other, even if that
"different" is constructed as what the outside world sees as the same,
as in the appearance of some gay couples who look like identical twins.

Even there, no doubt even more there, Edelman sees the scopic drive as the primary source of sexual difference. Thus, the white man's attraction functions through the visual, and, like Freud's comments on scopophilia, is arguably an over-determination of the visual. The inference is that the subject's emphasis on his perception of the Other, his reading of him or her, is a further limitation on the Other's ability to assert his or her subjectivity through interaction with the subject. Any person who functions primarily as something that is seen has limited opportunity to perform all the dimensions of personhood. The careful discrimination through the gaze leads to discrimination.

In an article in *Psychological Review*, Daryl Bem offers a theory that he calls "Exotic Becomes Erotic," or EBE:

> The central proposition of EBE theory is that individuals
> can become erotically attracted to classes of individuals
> from whom they felt different during childhood.
> This feeling of being different is the theory's implicit
> definition of exotic, and it is important to note that it is a
> phenomenological state that is neither equivalent to nor
> reducible to some objective or externally defined measure
> of dissimilarity or unfamiliarity. The subjective state of
> feeling different from a class of individuals can have any
> of several antecedents, some common, some idiosyncratic.
> (395)

This seems to have no effect on some and a profound effect on others. It produces difference in the face of the claim that gay sex is about pursuit of "same." The snow queen and dinge queen, men who society says are "homo," use race to reproduce the relationship as "hetero."

I recognized this attraction in myself at the age of nineteen when I first saw a naked black man. But why? And for that matter, why is it so threatening to so many observers of a variety of races? Edelman suggests that Fanon captures a cultural assumption that there is a direct link between racism and homosexuality:

> In this way the terrorizing force of white racism—a
> racism historically expressed, as Fanon makes clear,
> through the specific violence of castration—acquires
> visibility through the demonization of male-male sexual
> relations: relations popularly construed as themselves
> effecting, though for the most part 'only' by metaphor,
> a similar sort of castration or violent alienation from
> the cultural authority for which the phallus serves as
> signifier. Made to articulate the 'racial' dynamic of a
> masculinist culture, homophobia allows a certain figural
> logic to the pseudo-algebraic 'proof' that asserts: where it
> is 'given' that white racism equals castration and 'given'
> that homosexuality equals castration, then it is proper to
> conclude that white racism equals (or expresses through
> displacement) homosexuality and, by the same token, in a
> reversal of devastating import for lesbians and gay men of
> color, homosexuality equals white racism. (55)

There are many inflections to this argument. As hooks noted, the black male fear of castration inscribes racism within a particularly masculinist domain. Here, the primary problem of racism is that the black man will be castrated, as often was done literally to the corpses when white American racists lynched black men, an action that was commonly a response to a black man's perceived threat to white womanhood. The secondary problem of racism is that the black woman will be raped, which can be read as less an invasion of the black woman than a usurpation of the black man's property, a usurpation in which the black penis is replaced. Thus once again he is castrated, albeit symbolically. Homosexuality, in its failure to use the phallus in reproduction, is also castrating. If it is seen as a "force," as something that produces the homosexual, and if homosexuality is deemed to be white, as it so often is in black communities, then the black homosexual is a castrated man produced by white homosexuality. If the castrated black man is consistently the key figure of white racism, then homosexuality is clearly a force of white racism. Whether confronting white guilt or confronting black anger, the black/white relationship reproduces in that one couple the racist implications of homosexuality. Like most phobias, it creates a negativity that combines the worst of an opposition: it implies the production of miscegenation and the end of production through castration.

Marlon B. Ross, in "White Fantasies of Desire: Baldwin and the Racial Identities of Sexuality," makes the following claim about interracial gay relationships:

> The white partner in the interracial couple helps diminish
> the fear of what two strong black men together might do.
> In addition to stirring up anxieties in a white audience, the
> representation of erotically tinged devotion between two
> black men can be troubling to some African Americans
> concerned with respectability or reproductivity of the race
> as principles of black cultural integrity or nationalism.
> Thus, in some black nationalist and Afrocentrist
> literature, such images have been conveniently policed by
> overstressing the natural whiteness of homosexuality, its
> intrinsic alienation from original African and historical
> African American culture. (38)

On one level, he is right. In my personal experience, two black men create more obvious anxiety in the straight black community than an interracial couple. However, I have found that the overt homophobia is greater in the white community's response to an interracial couple than to a white couple or for that matter to a black couple. The white community does not assume that two black men show that homosexuality is a black thing, but they do assume that two black men are not a white issue. A white couple might be just friends. In a world with no assumptions of interracial brotherhood, however, an interracial couple immediately foregrounds homosexuality. At one point, my then boyfriend and I were walking through a predominantly straight, almost completely white, neighbourhood. My boyfriend said, "Everyone knows we are gay." I said, "Why?" He replied, "Why else would we be together?" In the black context, it is more than possible that the interracial couple elicits that noted by Ross: a perhaps complacent but also deep-seated homophobia in the black community, but a homophobia that then can be associated with white emasculation. The interracial couple allows the black community to assume that homosexuality is a white thing—and a bad thing.

I haven't addressed the reason for the dinge queen's desire, nor that of the snow queen. I have asked black lovers and friends and have received no answers better than the EBE theory or Towles' belief in vodka over scotch. When I asked one white friend why all his boyfriends were black, he said, "Is that true?" Uh-huh. However, I will offer one possible diagnosis for the dinge queen, again from Edelman:

> The figure of impeded closure here speaks to the
> persistence of an opening, a hole, in the protective
> 'armour' of white male identity—a hole through which
> the integrity of the white man's body, which was secured
> by its difference from the black man construed as 'the
> unidentifiable, the unassimilable,' is now represented as
> subject to a violation, a destructuration, precipitating fears
> of psychic dismemberment. For that hole, that impeded
> closure, bespeaks the negation of the penis, the fetishized
> part in which the wholeness and coherence of the subject's
> identity is invested. (64)

This "psychic dismemberment" can be a fear, but it also can be an attraction. Coherence is not always the ultimate goal of the subject, as suggested by Mapplethorpe. And this is not just limited to those who are anal receptive. The orgasm, whether male or female, is often described in terms of disintegration through "the unassimilable"—the orgasm as "*petit mort.*"

Even if one could assume that something that could be called "disintegration" is the goal of the dinge queen, is there any possibility of finding why someone—why I—would pursue disintegration? As I note in the chapter on anal sex, arguably I am pursuing disintegration in my sexual aim, so I might well be in my sexual object. I could be internalizing that reversal of slavery, which would make me an even better white liberal than I am when not having sex. Perhaps I am simply pursuing the unassimilable, a non-answer if there ever was one. Maurizia Boscagli, in *Eye on the Flesh: Fashions of Masculinity in the Early Twentieth Century*, turns to primitivism, in particular the primitivism seen in European art at the beginning of the last century. The timing is certainly right as it is contemporary with the rise of a small culture in Europe of black-white homosexuality, to which many such as James Baldwin reacted in the period immediately after World War II. Boscagli claims, "For the western male subject under threat and seeking to recover phallic plenitude, the encounter with the primitive promised to be both rewarding and dangerous: His immersion in tribal culture and his identification with the native could produce a further dissolution of his rational subjectivity, and with it, of his masculinity." (167)

Perhaps. But all these explanations are far too reductive. Even sophisticated thinkers such as Hemphill and Mercer seem to offer answers too simple to be satisfying. There is a drive here—or better still, there are drives here—which are key to certain sexualities, but no analysis can explain them. Each time I come to a conclusion I have none. I would say that my desire for black men preceded my sensitivity to the political imperatives of the history of slavery, although nothing ever comes before ideology. Perhaps my sexuality is reversing a history of white hegemony on a very small canvas—or rather, bedsheet. It is possible that I need the heteroracial to introduce difference into the homosexual. Perhaps I am just another racist looking for the big black dick.

When I presented a version of this article as a paper, a black friend said, "Have you no sense of self-preservation?" One white lesbian in the audience said, "This is disgusting." My explanation for exploring the subject is largely that suggested by Robert Reid-Pharr in *Black Gay Man: Essays*. He notes the number of black intellectuals, such as Julien, who have revealed themselves as snow queens. "What is striking, given the tradition that I have just outlined, is the fact that so few white artists, critics, intellectuals of all stripes, male or female, lesbian or gay, have found it necessary to cover themselves in the mantle of dinge queen, rice queen, or what have you." (87) He continues:

> Why, I have asked, do we see so little work by white
> gays and lesbians that directly addresses the question of
> cross-racial desire? I have suggested that we might at least
> begin an answer by paying attention to the way in which
> speaking to these issues, admitting to the reality of beauty
> that is other than white, throws into disarray the idea of
> whiteness as universal. (97)

So am I back to viewing myself as the racist gazing at the Mappletho-rpe photograph? Perhaps. Christopher Looby suggests that Mappletho-rpe's images have an inevitable suture:

> Mapplethorpe's photographs coercively install the viewer
> in the position of the xenophilic white male homosexual
> desiring subject, whose attraction to the black male body
> cannot help but be a guilty one—a desire contaminated
> in some degree by the white supremacist imaginary's
> construction of that object. (The way Mapplethorpe's
> photographs turn the viewer gay is probably an important
> source of their shattering power and scandalous odor.)
> It may seem bleak to hold such contamination of desire
> to be inevitable, but this strikes me as a necessary
> implication of the understanding that erotic desire is
> socially and historically constructed. But if the white male
> subject's desire for black male flesh cannot ever escape
> entirely from the ideological inscriptions of the history of
> white racism, that doesn't render such desire useless for
> more utopian purposes. (99-100)

The utopian move made by the world of lesbian pornography attempts to claim the potential subjectivity of the sexual object. As Isaac Julien suggests, the black/white gay relationship offers a nexus for the interrogation of still multiply unacceptable desires. Perhaps this is why more than twenty years after the founding of Black and White Men Together, there is still no community for us. The BWMT organization recently held its twenty-second national conference in the United States, but it remains very small. And there remain many examples even within the organization that avoid the telling of untellable desires. Thus the Chicago chapter has changed its name to "Men of All Colors Together." Shades of vodka and scotch. Continuing the scenario described by Hemphill, we continue to fuck more than we talk. And we certainly fuck much more than we talk about fucking. At Pride Day in Toronto a few years ago, an interracial couple was walking hand-in-hand. The white man had a T-shirt with a simple slogan: "I am not a black man." Nor need he be.

## 8 Dragging Feminism?

The term "drag queen" apparently is a development from the combination of "draggle-tail" and "queen." If a fox has a wet tail, it drags it and presents a "draggle-tail" look, depressed and somehow deficient. Similarly the woman who does not look after the train of her dress or who has a dirty or hand-me-down gown looks draggle-tailed and becomes a drag queen. The journey from this to the man dressed as a woman is not a long one. the drag queen is thus a draggle-tail woman. Still, "drag queen" remains one of those terms that everyone understands but no one uses with precision. The performer imitating Joan Rivers in a gay bar is a drag queen, but is it the right term for that strange Margaret Thatcher look-alike in the drugstore?

Richard Ekin's *Male Femaling: A Grounded Theory Approach to Cross-Dressing and Sex-Changing* uses terms such as transvestite and transsexual, but not as definitions. (54-58) Instead he refers to "body femaling," in which the emphasis is on body modification, such as genital surgery and breast enlargement, "erotic femaling," manifesting elements of a female appearance for sexual satisfaction, and "gender femaling," in which the emphasis is on replicating the "real girl," in style or appearance. It is impossible to find comfortable and accurate demarcations. All are invested too much in the subjectivity of the person using them. Ekin is seeking a sociological approach that encompasses all relevant behaviours without implying anything inferior or superior about any of them. On the other hand, Janice Raymond's *Transsexual Empire* treats all male femaling as attempts to infiltrate and usurp womanhood. To her, distinctions between such patriarchal ventures are meaningless. As Judith Butler states in *Bodies that Matter*, Raymond "places drag on a continuum with cross-dressing and transsexualism, ignoring the important differences between them...." (126) Butler, however, erases her own distinction when she, without justification, uses drag as a category for Venus Xtravaganza. In the documentary film *Paris is Burning*, Venus is a particularly pathetic figure, a Latin street hustler whose aspirations to the glories of becoming a white suburban housewife are cut short by what seems like her inevitable murder by a bad trick. She has elements of the drag queen, but is more a stereotypical transsexual. Jay Prosser's excellent book, *Second Skins: The Body Narratives of Transsexuality*, details Butler's misdiagnosis of Venus. But there is another possible error, in using the term "drag" to designate Venus as not a "body femaler" but a "gender femaler." "Drag queen" should at some level be the latter, because the emphasis is not on the transsexual to explain the person within, but rather to create an image. And the root of drag queen, the draggletail queen, is a designation based on appearance. Thus it is highly appropriate that the primary use of the term "drag queen" is for performers, such as female impersonators in nightclubs. It represents not the internal female, the goal of Venus Xtravaganza, but rather the female as display.

This distinction between the transsexual and the drag queen can be extended. Butler states that Venus seeks "a certain transubstantiation of gender." (130) Prosser's lengthy critique explores the "Eucharistic sense" (50) of transubstantiation, but he ignores the "reality" of transubstantiation in the Catholic liturgy. The bread and wine *really* become the body and blood of Christ. Regardless of how one perceives transsexuality, such a transubstantiation, a *real* change, seems to be the goal. In a surprisingly doctrinaire comment in the otherwise nuanced arguments of *Volatile Bodies: Toward a Corporeal Feminism*, Elizabeth Grosz denies this possibility: "Men, contrary to the fantasy of the transsexual, can never, even with surgical intervention, feel or experience what it is like to be, to live, as women." (207) This statement is similar to scientific dismissals of the claim of transubstantiation. One of the traditional distinctions between the Catholic and Protestant cosmologies is that the latter sees the Eucharist as not transubstantiation but metaphor. The mass is not a physical process that incorporates transcendence, but rather a physical process that provides a figure for transcendence. Whereas the Catholic elevates the spirit through recognizing the physical as transformed into spirit, the Protestant elevates the spirit through sensing the spiritual in something that is treated as the physical becoming spirit but is actually only part of the mundane. So here, to follow this very loose analogy, the drag queen might seem more like the Protestant. The goal is not transubstantiation, but fantasy and metaphor.

Prosser analyzes the many examples in transsexual autobiographies in which a mirror provides a key moment of identity. While most transsexuals claim that they have essential genders that come from within, they are concerned—at times obsessed—with seeing glimpses of it in the apparently wrong-gendered image in the mirror. When they first cross-dress, the inner self can see a physical reflection of that psychological truth. Prosser notes that many transsexuals exert great effort to take photographic self-portraits that provide a permanent view of this body of the identity. This seems to follow Althusser's concept of interpellation, although perhaps in reverse. The process is not the way in which the hegemony labels you, names you, but rather the way you can manipulate that labelling to be interpellated as you would wish to be.

I have included two photographs of myself in drag. In my own life, I have found such shots have an importance that cannot be met by mirrors. The fluidity of the mirror, in which my subjectivity and myself as object are both very much in motion, creates a situation that is too dynamic for me to judge. Every time I see the image I pursue—the femaled me I imagine—some aspect of my male self escapes through a movement, through some particle of inadequate presentation. Although the essence of the process is that I am within the object, I need to be able to judge the object, which requires separation. As in the transsexual autobiographies, my reading of myself in these images is obviously subjective. My notes give the credits for the photographs, but I would like to emphasize here that the photographers are both "real girls." and heterosexual women. The clothing is my choice, but the style and presentation were primarily under the control of the photographer (both photographs were taken in spaces chosen by the photographers). There is a dimension in which these images are defined by someone other than myself, far more than if I were just looking in the mirror. In yet one more twist of subjectivity, however, I have selected these photos that suit my argument.

In the present context, the drag queen is homosexual. Prosser provides a series of distinctions that help to explain this specificity:

> In contradistinction to the transsexual, the transgenderist
> crossed the lines of gender but not those of sex; in
> contradistinction to the drag queen, the transgenderist's
> feminine gender expression was not intrinsically bound
> up with a homosexual identity nor could its livedness be
> made sense of through drag's performativity. (176)

For me, the "livedness" is defined by exactly these parts, the "intrinsic" homosexuality and the performative, although they are not without pejorative dimensions that have often been attacked as demeaning and stereotypical, products of heterosexist misunderstandings of homosexuality. One is the homosexual male as essentially effeminate. There are many contradictory examples in which homosexuality is shown as an excess of masculinity rather than a lack. This is a cliché of

gay pornography, but it is also a philosophical claim by figures such as
André Gide. Others have claimed that the drag queen is a representation
of the female that allows the homosexual to avoid having anything to
do with biological women. As Butler notes, compulsory heterosexuality
views drag as a necessary pathology for homosexuality:

> ... the only place love is to be found is for the ostensibly
> repudiated object, where love is understood to be
> strictly produced through a logic of repudiation; hence,
> drag is nothing but the effect of a love embittered by
> disappointment or rejection, the incorporation of the
> Other whom one originally desired, but now hates. (127)

It is not difficult to reject this, yet another illness theory for our
behaviour. It might be placed in the same category as the usual ridicule
of the pathetic drag queen, from the cross-dressed hula dancer in Walt
Disney's *The Lion King* to schoolyard epithets such as "your father wears
a dress."

However, drag could be a sexual object without constituting embit-
terment or repudiation. In *To Wong Foo Thanks for Everything, Julie Newmar,* a
film almost universally derided by the drag community, there is one
moment worth considering as a positive insight. In this, the Wesley
Snipes character claims that drag is a manifestation of homosexual excess, of too much sexual energy to be contained in male clothing. The
last photograph here particularly fits this premise. The attire and the
posture present the drag queen body as, in Butler's terms, "a place" of
"love"—a feminized sexual object.

When I first presented a version of this essay at a conference, I
thought of dressing in drag, but I decided against it. This is not simply
because I feared ridicule. Drag is always to some degree ridiculous, as
I know from experience. What could be more ridiculous, for example,
than walking in drag on the main thoroughfare of downtown Toronto,
on a Saturday afternoon when there were no similarly flamboyant characters to deflect attention away from me. Still, although I could not control the reactions, I had considered the possibilities and felt ready to deal

with them, even felt eager to experience a bit of antagonism. Whether walking down a busy street or lecturing at a conference, drag cannot be removed from a situation. If it is first and foremost appearance, it must be seen in a context, *can* be seen only in a context. Thus for the conference I presented not "me," but these photographs of me, distancing the person and creating a more isolated context. I was able to frame the photographs in a way I could not have framed my own performance as the lecturer. A display is never only what the person producing the display claims it to be, especially when it is a display in action, especially when that action is not primarily about producing that display. Being in drag would have been very different if, for example, I had been on a stage as Maria from *West Side Story* singing "I Feel Pretty." This is one element of the performativity of drag. Butler maintains elsewhere:

> ... performance as bounded 'act' is distinguished from
> performativity insofar as the latter consists in a reiteration
> of norms which precede, constrain, and exceed the
> performer and in that sense cannot be taken as the
> fabrication of the performer's 'will' or 'choice'.... ("Critically
> Queer" 24)

As Butler notes, "within speech act theory, a performative is that discursive practice that enacts or produces that which it names." (*Bodies* 13) The classic example is the marriage ceremony and the "I do's."

This returns to context. The drag queen in performance could be, as so many female impersonators over the years have claimed, a "normal" man in women's clothing putting on a show. The representation is contained, or if not contained, tricks the performer himself. Drag as performative, in a non-performance space, is intended excess. "Intended excess" seems a good description of me walking downtown that day, especially given that in heels I am about six-foot-seven. This does not mean that I controlled the meaning. Can any such drag queen understand him (her?) self? This presumably is one reason why I like the photographs, which give me a controlled context, if only as an historical moment. While I cannot claim to control the meaning you take from them, I can take my own meaning for the present analysis.

It is almost a cliché of commentary on cross-dressing that the best drag queens were Mae West and Marilyn Monroe. The essence of the drag queen on stage is a performance of femaleness, and who could do this better than a woman who had devoted her life to such a performance? In *Gender Trouble*, Butler states, "In imitating gender, drag implicitly reveals the imitative structure of gender itself—as well as its contingency." (137) West and Monroe seemed to highlight this contingency but they were not so much performing gender in general as they were performing a particular aspect of gender, female sexuality, and specifically the sexuality of the seductress: West the manipulative and Monroe the innocent. This is something quite different from someone such as actress Sharon Stone, who might radiate sexuality but does not make a similar coherent performance of it.

And yet perhaps in the drag queen I am presenting, in the emphasis on performativity, Sharon Stone is a better example, someone whose sexuality seems to exceed a contained performance. Once again it is sexuality that provides the mark. The professional drag performers who concentrate on stars who do not perform a similar sexuality, such as Carol Channing or Barbra Streisand, still emphasize the more sexualized elements of the originals. This is the focus for many attacks on drag queens by feminists. They claim, accurately, that they are just one more example of the male objectifying women, although in this case the male inhabits the object.

I do not quibble with the argument that drag queens operate through a fetishized sexuality. I also do not question that the aspects of female sexuality that are highlighted are often those that many progressive women reject. The last of my photographs here represents availability, accessibility, and probably a desire for a dominant sexual partner. It highlights elements of the body that are usually deemed most sexual. And it highlights them in ways that emphasize contrast with maleness, whether shaving legs and chest or adding jewellery seldom seen on men. The specifics of these things as sexuality can be seen in heterosexual pornography where the males are often nude but the women are partially clothed. The items the women wear are often specifically fetishistic, such as stiletto heels, but they include such apparently absurd elements as very feminine hats. The sexuality is from the feminine as well as from the female.

My own sexual experience while in drag is limited. I have never attracted a partner while in drag. I once advertised in a personals column and while, in the always particular taxonomy of the personals, I did not categorize myself as a drag queen or anything trans, I mentioned that I did drag sometimes. I received a few responses that focused on that aspect of my description, but they all had a tone that I found off-putting. Perhaps this just shows how prim I am; the respondents seemed to be fetishizing the drag—and my height—in ways that I was not prepared to pursue. Thus I never replied. On the other hand, I have had a couple of relationships with men that included me in lingerie and nylons. These were with men who called themselves gay but had significant sexual experience with women. In both cases, the lingerie was used as a "surprise" that I would introduce from time to time. With one partner it was mentioned euphemistically—"We haven't seen your playthings lately"—the way one might refer to a sex toy. In other words, it was quite clearly fetishistic rather than a part of our usual sex life. If it had been the latter, it might have been more a part of my definition of my role in the relationship.

Something that for both women and drag queens crosses between the body and the dress is makeup, again something foregrounded in heterosexual pornography. Makeup is a way of writing on the body, particularly in the case of the drag queen who stays within the limitations of what has been called "glamour makeup." This is the makeup that is always recognized as makeup by even the most myopic straight male and is described as "highlighting" or "enhancing," establishing some ground rule that says the original is not changed in any profound sense. This might be compared to one of Grosz's comments on the way the body is offered to the world:

> The notion of corporeal inscription of the body-as-surface
> rejects the phenomenological framework of intentionality
> and the psychoanalytic postulate of psychical depth; the
> body is not a mode of expression of a psychical interior
> or a mode of communication or mediation of what is
> essentially private and incommunicable. Rather, it can be
> understood as a series of surfaces, energies, and forces,
> a mode of linkage, a discontinuous series of processes,
> organs, flows, and matter. (120)

In my chapter on the film *The Crying Game*, I note that while Jude is the "real woman," Dil, a transsexual, is the one whose femininity is validated. One aspect of this opposition that many feminist critics have found difficult is that Jude seems unable to read Dil as biologically male, a statement either of Dil's success at representing female or at Jude's inability to see beyond surfaces. Thus it should not be surprising that the difference in their makeup seems to suggest a difference in their 'make-up.' At one point, Jude says of Dil, "A bit heavy on the powder isn't she?" Dil replies, with a similarly third person reference, "A girl has to have a bit of glamour." In other words, Dil justifies her makeup through a rather clichéd phrase about simply highlighting her self as a "normal girl." We as audience accept her justification because we realize that Dil's special needs might require a bit more assistance. This contrasts with Jude's similarly overt makeup in this section of the film where she is clearly performing the part of the femme fatale. In other words, Dil is only using a necessary prosthetic while Jude is employing a nefarious agent. In both cases, makeup is the performative but also a performing reality. Jude is a girl playing a girl while Dil is playing the girl she knows herself to be.

Today much of society accepts that the man presenting as male might use foundation or an eyebrow pencil. The justification for the man wearing makeup as a man is that it is not feminizing but rather enhancing. This is not the case for either Dil or the drag queen. The drag queen uses makeup partly for Dil's reason, to overcome the blandly masculine normal and replace it with feminine beauty. He also, however, uses an overt makeup, such as false eyelashes and unusually emphatic eyeshadow, to perform feminine sexuality in a more obvious way than would most "real" women. While the first move seems like Dil's, to cover the masculine in something that pretends to be just glamour, there is an ironic tension in the admission, never stated but always implied, that the man always remains within.

This is particularly important in the "drag queen" as I am depicting him here. There are very few cross-dressers who are truly not readable. Even in those cases part of the illusion is the form of highly feminized cover-up, heavy makeup, tight short dresses, high heels, etc. Thus they become readable in the many situations where almost no woman would appear that way. It is interesting that people such as Janice Raymond are so opposed to such objectified sexuality because often it is the very element that makes maleness so clear. While it objectifies femaleness, it also separates the drag queens from the representation of "real women." Potential readability is always at least part of the drag queen component. Butler's *Bodies that Matter* provides an extensive analysis of the goal of "realness" in *Paris is Burning*. The very term "realness" requires some category of unrealness. If the simulacrum is absolutely identical to the original then it is not "realness," it is simply real. So even if a drag queen is not at all readable, her readability is an essential—I use that loaded word intentionally—part of her drag queen-ness. This is especially true of the gay male who does not perceive himself as transsexual. To achieve the status of being unreadable would be to embody the female in a counter-productive way.

But what is the sexual component of such appearance? Ekin provides a specific category of the "erotic femaler," but arguably all "male femalers" have to some degree an erotic intention. Fetishism, in a quite strict psychoanalytic sense, has been the emphasis of many theorists of transvestitism in its various forms. If the most important aspect of the drag queen is the "real" male within this object, then presumably the drag queen embodies the phallic woman. If the phallic displacement in the fetish is the explanation for all focus on non-human objects of sexual desire, then it clearly applies here. According to Marjorie Garber's extensive exploration in *Vested Interests*, "The history of the fetish in representation ... indicates that the fetish is the phallus, the phallus is the fetish." (121) If the goal of the cross-dresser, particularly the heterosexual one, is an erectile response to the sexualized synecdoches of female garb, this would be an appropriate interpretation. However, in a broader view of sexualization, there are other possibilities.

The sexualized space is not found only through the fetish, or at least the fetish as usually constituted. Many women have rejected the idea of a simple equation of phallus as sexual drive. In *Space, Time and Perversion* Grosz provides a very complex argument on lesbian fetishism. She comments:

> ... the masculine woman takes an external love-object—
> another woman—and through this love-object is able
> to function as if she *has*, rather than *is*, the phallus. As
> with the fetishist, this implies a splitting of the ego: it
> is this which inclines her to feminism itself, insofar as
> feminism, like any oppositional political movement,
> involves a disavowal of social reality so that change
> becomes conceivable and possible.... The categories that
> Freud proposed as universally relevant—the function of
> the phallus, the Oedipus complex, the ubiquity of the
> castration threat, and women's status as passive—surely
> need to be contested in order that social relations
> themselves can be transformed. (153-154)

Drag is not in itself a political statement, an attempt at a broader transformation of social relations. However, it can suggest this through its act of disavowal. Psychoanalysis presents "disavowal" as a profound erasure of reality. It is not just a rejection. Instead, it includes an implied recognition of the absolute truth of something, a recognition that is denied because of an absolute need to reject that truth. It must be something that undeniably is but that the subject denies in order to be.

To follow Grosz, drag is a disavowal that goes beyond simple questions of the phallus and the role of castration. Perhaps in the present context it would be better to describe sexual desire as a multiplicitous space. Butler provides an alternative, with, instead of one phallus, many:

> If what comes to signify under the sign of the phallus
> are a number of body parts, discursive performatives,
> alternative fetishes, to name a few, then the symbolic
> position of 'having' has been dislodged from the penis as
> its privileged anatomical (or non-anatomical) occasion. (89)

Here Butler seems to go beyond the many-lipped sexualities of various French feminists, but the symbolism remains rather genital. I accept Grosz's argument in *Volatile Bodies* that while the "Body Without Organs" of Deleuze and Guattari seems very attractive, in the end its very amorphous attraction leads to vapour. (167-174) Still, something like this might be a worthy direction to pursue. Butler observes that Monique Wittig offers a "model of a more diffuse and antigenital sexuality." (*Gender Trouble* 27). Butler suggests that this can be taken to a level that could be called "postgenital." If such a term can be applied to the drag queen, it provides an interesting contradiction to the view both of drag as fetish (the pursuit of the false genital) and of drag as a simulacrum of the transsexual, for whom the genital is not a fetish but an object that can transform the subject's gender into something closer to the category of sex.

For this drag queen, the whole "thing" is sexualized, not just a series of associations. It has become a commonplace in sexual therapy to explore beyond the genital. Judging sexuality by some technical device that gauges the engorgement of the penis is far too simplistic. Perhaps psychoanalysis might make the same move. If the body represents all the body, everything at once connected to and divorced from the mind, then it is more than the phallus. A balance of self and philosophical not-self can be represented through a more expansive sexual geography, such as this "place of love," the drag queen. The fetish tends to be seen very much as an object. It can be an object in action, such as the whip, but it is first an object. However, gender performativity offers many more possibilities to the motion of the object. In her various spaces, the active embodiment of female sexuality becomes the goal, regardless of the sex of the body embodying.

One important contradiction is the place of drag in the gay community. While it is generally esteemed as performance, its performativity is often derided. Drag hookers do well, but most define their customers as heterosexual, although obviously heterosexual with a bit of a kink. One gay friend of mine who has never done drag said rather cynically that he always believed gay men did drag to avoid sex. I have never felt that myself, but I can see the argument, especially in that as a come-on to the homosexual male it seems to have little success. But while I hesitate to see myself as so internalized, narcissism seems a reasonable explanation of this process. Drag is a way of inhabiting desirability, regardless of whether the object desired responds. It offers the "feeling sexy" so often asserted in advertisements for commodities that convey female sexuality.

I have often questioned gay men about their response to the female sex object. It has always surprised me that so many claim to have no interest whatsoever. Those who admit a glance or two explain it in a few different ways. One is to place the gay male at some point on the transsexual continuum, and therefore in some sense a feminized gaze narcissistically interested in depictions of female sexuality. Another is to see the sexualized female as an aesthetic object and therefore fitting the gay fascination with art. A third is to see it as performance and thus fitting another stereotype, the gay male as theatrical. I would expect the gay male to be interested for another reason, however: the objectification of sexuality as a specifically female thing. This might seem a strange proposition, especially in a gay context. Magazines such as *Details* and *GQ* exist on the assumption that men want to present themselves sexually. It is difficult to see why all those tight-zippered tops existed in the eighties if men are not sex objects. But contemporary western society has evolved to the point where this is very much a minority culture.

We seem to have gone quite a distance from the human peacocks of the Renaissance courts.

The first explanation is the obvious one given above, that the body is the female body and therefore the sexualized body is female sexuality. Wittig goes so far as to say in "The Point of View: Universal or Particular": "There is only one: the feminine, the 'masculine' not being a gender. For the masculine is not the masculine, but the general." (64) To return to the comment about the effeminate homosexual, drag could be the search for a gender that the not-masculine homosexual lacks. But the specifics of drag's sexuality present something else, once again in opposition to the phallus. In *Bodies that Matter*, Butler considers the philosophical tradition that emphasizes the materiality of the female. If material is female does female garb make the male body more materially sexual? It becomes less the confusing general power of the phallus-that-is-not-the-penis and instead the specifically sexual power of the tight dress and displayed cleavage.

There are many other possible explanations. One would seem to be the route that has been followed by the hegemony of male heterosexual power. With the various waves of feminism, the female subject position has become more and more a part of everyday discourse, but our society has strongly asserted that the norm, the default option, is the male heterosexual. Thus it is only logical that the primary object should be the female heterosexual. Perhaps as a corollary, it has been assumed that if the heterosexual female is the subject, she does not respond to the male object in the same way. The logical example is *Playgirl*, a magazine that many claim is of more interest to the homosexual male than to the heterosexual female. (I should note here the many observers who have claimed that women appreciate the visual representation of sexuality much more than this suggests. Regardless of the accuracy of the assumption of the lack in the female gaze, it has been a guiding philosophy in the commercial representation of sexuality, where the male gaze, whether heterosexual or homosexual, is by far the dominant market.)

My own, admittedly limited, interest in pornography is for the heterosexual version. This is once again a space in which my introspection will no doubt be questioned. Can I decide why I am attracted? My answer, to the extent that I can ascertain the focus of my gaze, is that I find male performance, the erection in action, to be the primary focus of my gaze. But therefore why not homosexual pornography, where I could see a man who represents me interacting with that erection? My best explanation is that this is one space where I find that my inner drag queen becomes transsexual. I identify with the female role as she eagerly pursues the penis, whether as object of oral sex or as penetrator. My interpretation of my own response is that I have been sufficiently interpellated by the hegemonic view of the female sex object that I find the heterosexual narrative is my preference.

Of course, this might be still too simple a view of the pornographic scene, as Slavoj Žižek suggests in "The Seven Veils of Fantasy":

> Suffice it to recall the standard pornographic scene
> whereby a man is doing 'it' to a woman. The spectator
> of the film does not identify with the man who is fucking
> the woman. The woman is as a rule asserted as the
> exhibitionist subject who fully enjoys doing it, and who
> is being viewed by the spectator while doing it, in clear
> contrast to the man who is reduced to the pure, faceless
> instrument of the woman's enjoyment. The spectator, far
> from identifying with the male actor, rather identifies
> with the 'third,' implicit position, which is that of a pure
> gaze observing the woman who fully enjoys herself. The
> spectator's satisfaction is of a purely reflective nature; it
> derives from the awareness that a woman can find full
> satisfaction in phallic enjoyment.

> As a rule, the fantasizing subject does not identify with
> his or her own appearance in the fantasmatic space (with
> his or her 'oppositional determination,' as Hegel would
> have put it). More radically, fantasy creates a multitude

of 'subject-positions,' among which the (observing,
fantasizing) subject can freely float." (193)

Žižek's Lacanian analysis is complex, but sufficiently amorphous that
I find it quite convincing. All I can offer here, however, is the same
process I offer throughout this book, my own introspection. I have
interrogated myself and my identification seems not with the third but
with the second, the woman, a category that Žižek interestingly does not
consider, perhaps because he does not believe the male gaze could be the
female as "exhibitionist subject."

The primary male sex objects of the cinema are seldom hypermascu-
linized, male versions of Mae West. To consider a couple of exceptions,
Arnold Schwarzenegger and Sylvester Stallone, it is interesting to see
how recent they are and how often ironized. Others, such as Mont-
gomery Clift, James Dean, Clark Gable, and Brad Pitt, all have different
sexualities to offer, but the male Marilyn Monroe is not one of them.
This suggests that in our contemporary society, while male sexual performance is a constant subject of discussion, the performativity of male
sexuality is nebulous, at times obscure, and often rather skewed. When
the Wall Street lawyer in a Hugo Boss suit is discussed as a sex object
it erases the dividing line between power and sexuality, a dividing line
that might be narrow but that still exists. If there is a performativity of
male sexuality in the mainstream culture that is separate from economic
power, it is very difficult to define. Attempts to represent the male stud
muffin seem plagued with difficult definitions. A recent radio program
asserted the United Parcel Service delivery man as sex object. This is not
Stanley Kowalski, but what it is I am not at all sure. According to the
program it is something to do with those nondescript brown uniforms.

But what of the body within? I have suggested that the male body is
an important element of the drag queen, regardless of the many possible
interpretations of that body. And regardless of my comments about Mae
West and Marilyn Monroe, there is a *frisson* to the male within that creates much of the energy without. To offer just one experience, I went
in drag to an academic banquet. The response was ongoing, includ-

ing appreciative laughter from many heterosexual women and scornful stares from many heterosexual men. My subjectivity enjoyed both sides of this reaction. And in at least this one small, over-educated crowd, it led to an evening of discussion of gender, well beyond the usual topic of whether drag demeans women. For example, when I applied lipstick while sitting at the table, the straight man next to me stated that it was tacky to apply lipstick in public. I presume he would not have said this if I were a real woman. The result was a lengthy discussion of what private/public means in terms of gender, particularly in light of various beauty regimens and regimes.

But I again seem to have slipped away from the body per se. I think I have good company in this in that two of the most prominent body theorists, Butler and Grosz, often do the same. At at least one level it is difficult to see how this is to be avoided. Grosz provides the best analysis of the mind/body split I have encountered, particularly in her assessment of the concept of the body image:

> The body image does not map a biological body onto
> a psychosocial domain, providing a kind of translation
> of material into conceptual terms; rather, it attests to
> the necessary interconsistency of each for the other,
> the radical inseparability of biological from psychical
> elements, the mutual dependence of the psychical and
> the biological, and thus the intimate connection between
> the question of sexual specificity (biological sexual
> differences) and psychical identity. (*Volatile* 85)

As the jacket blurb by Butler states, *Volatile Bodies* sets "a high critical standard for feminist dialogues on the status of the body." And yet does Grosz's focus actually move the body from raw substance to focus? Is she not caught within the mind of the body? And is the mind of the body ever the body? The usual response to this binary is the claim that one cannot separate the mind from the body. In this case, the even more troublesome game is the attempt to split the body from the mind.

Regardless of the emphasis on surface and clothing that I am making, the packaging of the drag queen reconfigures the male body to look like the female body. Butler notes that the female body is traditionally the material, in opposition to the mind of man. Grosz polemically asserts:

> Corporeality must no longer be associated with one sex
> (or race), which then takes on the burden of the other's
> corporeality for it. Women can no longer take on the
> function of being the body for men while men are left free
> to soar to the heights of theoretical refection and cultural
> production. (*Volatile* 22)

By dressing in female clothes that create the figure of the female body, the drag queen at once impersonates this corporeality, this position as the body, and yet, through the fact that this is a male body, asserts how immaterial this material is.

So while it is the male body within the female covering, is it in some sense the body? Here I think I am truly limited to my personal experience. Many cross-dressers have asserted the sensuality of the nylons, the joyful constriction of corsets, etc. All I can say is that this has not been my experience. Rather for me, it is my subjectivity, and I think I can say very much my mind, responding to the appearance of my male body in female clothing. Thus for me this is almost a defining element of the mind/body dichotomy. While it is important to me that it is my body within, the experience is very much scopophilia: it is looking at my body within the dress that appeals to me. It is seeing my body within. And even when there is no mirror around it is the sense of being seen, the Bishop Berkeleys around me who I perceive perceiving. And of being "scene." The female attire is very much the Derridean supplement, the thing written on top that is both obviously superfluous and also absolutely intrinsic. The drag queen is thus a graphological experience.

The last paragraph is in the present tense. When it was first written, it was very much in the present, as I was dressing in drag often. After a bicycle accident, I decided to put my dresses and heels away and I have not appeared in drag for some eight years. Putting the heels in storage was the easy part, as I now have a pronounced limp and walking in running shoes is difficult enough. As for the dresses, the explanation is a bit more complicated. I had always put a time limit on my life as a drag queen. I have had far too many experiences of seeing other drag queens who perhaps did not look like Margaret Thatcher but were at least looking decidedly past their prime. At the point where the wrinkles were overtaking my eyeshadow, it seemed to be appropriate to hang up my nylons. Of course, this is yet another space where the male femaler has a freedom lacking to the real woman. At the point when I felt I could no longer inhabit that come-hither female sexuality, I gave up female representation. This is very different from the story so many women tell of continuing to be a female heterosexual but reaching an age where their role as a female heterosexual object seemed erased.

The double bind of the woman who laments the limitations of the woman-as-object and yet also laments the loss of her own attractions as woman-as-object is but one of the many contradictions encountered by feminism. The various feminist rejections of male femalers, whether transsexual or drag queen, might be seen as another one. The sexist man with no understanding of women is seen by some feminists to be less of a problem than the man who devotes his life to becoming a woman. Or to another part of graphological experience, feminist studies. Part of my choice to discuss male feminism in this chapter is simply that two things that have given me a kick are wearing dresses and studying feminist theory. I also feel, however, that there is something more linking the two than my idea of fun. The connection is often there in fiction and theatre, but usually represented obliquely. Thus in the play *Angels in America*, when Prior's AIDS hallucination dream invades Harper's Valium hallucination dream, he is in drag. There is something about his flagrant eye makeup that connects with Harper's *Feminine Mystique* problems as a repressed housewife.

Yet when considered more directly, drag and feminism are viewed as in opposition. In the conclusion to a 1983 essay on male feminism, Elaine Showalter engaged in a *jeu d'esprit* that she might wish to temper now but that nevertheless gives a good introduction to my point here.

Showalter offered her "dream of the feminist literary conference of the future":

> The diacritical woman rises to speak, but she has no head.
> Holding out the empty sleeves of her fashionable jacket,
> she beckons to the third panelist. He rises swiftly and
> commands the podium. He is forceful; he is articulate; he
> is talking about Heidegger or Derrida or Levi-Strauss or
> Brecht. He is wearing a dress. (132)

The sensibility here was not at all uncommon and it still persists in many quarters. The anger underlying it can be seen in the title of Suzanne Moore's 1988 article: "Getting a Bit of the Other—the Pimps of Postmodernism."

These articles attack the view of the feminine presented by various French theorists: some, but by no means all, male. Jane Gallop captures the sense of the argument in her confrontation with Jean Baudrillard. I shall quote at some length to establish the principles involved in what is rather like a dialectic:

> He does not consider it an insult to say that woman is only
> appearance. Baudrillard is writing against the history of
> writing against appearances. He is for appearances, and
> against profundity, so that when he says that 'woman is
> only appearance' it should be taken as a compliment.
>
> Nonetheless, when I read this passage, as a woman, I feel
> insulted. Baudrillard would have it that my feeling of
> offense is a great error which stems from my inscription
> within the sort of masculinistic essentialist thinking
> which condemns appearances as misleading mediations of
> essences, realities, and truths.
>
> Yet, in considering the passage carefully, I decide that it is
> not what he says about 'woman' that offends me so much
> as what he says about 'women': 'Women would do well,'

he advises, 'to let themselves be seduced by this truth.' It
is the phrase 'would do well' (*feraient bien de*) that irks me.
Although he puts 'insulting' in quotation marks [to call
woman as appearance an '"insulting formula"'] he uses
the word 'truth' (*verité*) straight. He knows the truth—the
profound or hidden truth, I might add—about women,
and women 'would do well to let themselves be seduced'
by the truth he utters. (113-114)

All of us who are somewhere on what might be called the "queer
axis" realize the impossibility of using the word "truth" straight. No
matter how often the truth is let out of the closet it never becomes
straight. But we also know the multiple powers of seduction.

At the end of her piece, Gallop does a more extended turn on Baudrillard's belief in seduction as opposed to feminism. She offers the
alternative of being seduced by feminism, but she does not explain what
she means by feminism in this context. If, as I assume, feminism is
some direct assertion of power by women, it is difficult to see this as
seducing. The most prominent definitions of seduce in the *Oxford English
Dictionary* are based on some version of "to lead astray" or "to tempt,
entice, or beguile to do something wrong, foolish or unintended." It
seems to me that Baudrillard has it right in the implication of seduction
leading to something at least apparently untoward. I doubt that the em-
powering of women should be seen as such a direction.

Instead I would like to try to slip between Gallop and Baudrillard, to
allow the seduction but not be tempted toward that straight truth. One
answer is to follow the suggestions of Butler and play with the seduc-
tions of gender performance and gender performativity. Thus the problem becomes not women as depicted by Gallop, a social fact. Instead
it becomes an opportunity, the possibility of "woman." Like the drag
queen, the male feminist takes on a supplement. One of the obvious
difficulties is that it is more than possible that for the person living as a
woman this supplement can be instead a denial. This is invariably the
argument of those opposed to drag queens but it often works as well for

those opposed to male feminism. The drag queen and the male feminist use attributes associated with women, female sexuality and philosophical and theoretical responses to women in society, often in directions that offend many of those same women.

Jane Gallop seems to me a particularly interesting example for this discussion. Her *Feminist Accused of Sexual Harassment* attempts to trace a feminism that offends many women's view of feminism. She has been attacked for trying to embrace two contradictory positions: the overt one being feminist and the covert one being a powerful academic who uses that power to harass students sexually. But she questions the possibility of a female being in this position. She instead reflects on the "classic case" of sexual harassment that is a male superior harassing a female inferior. She seems unable to accept the possibility that a female professor can take on the supplement of male power and be transformed. She does not accept the variant dangers of the seduction of the female. But the indeterminacy of gender is not a free space. It has limitations and constraints, some of which can be specific to the sex of the person within the gender and some of which are dependent on that sex.

As Grosz most specifically has pointed out, the simple binary of sex and gender has resolutely failed. There is something almost intrinsic to sex. That "almost intrinsic" is my oxymoron, not hers, but it seems a good fit for the problem. It is the reason why Prosser is so assertive about the indeterminacy of gender and yet himself is transsexual. The sex cannot be denied, no matter how much a gender theorist might wish to deny it. So the drag queen and male feminist move into genders that work because of the sex behind the gender. Perhaps the only way a born female can inhabit those genders that way is to somehow move out into the male sex as gender before taking on the female gender. As I look back at that sentence I realize how mind-boggling such a possibility seems. Yet I have at least a glimmer of that process in Mae West. And perhaps this is at least a preliminary description of Jane Gallop's trajectory, although arguably hers might end with a map of infinite detours.

This might seem like just so much dancing, whether by a drag queen or a male feminist. It is possible to trace a series of separations, however. Part of this might be the strategic essentialism to which Diana Fuss refers, but I think the first step is a separation between women as sociological space and the individuals who inhabit that space, and woman as performance and as performativity. The sociological woman thus does not follow that sex/gender dichotomy, but instead is the position of those who live that gender, whether born women or transsexual. Those who are women in that sense have been economically disadvantaged, legally restricted, and medically oppressed. Such processes as affirmative action in the work place and reproductive rights are necessary responses to such oppression.

But there are other parts to the possibility of woman. A group that at times seems highly disadvantaged in such discussions is heterosexual women. A number of recent commentators have been trying to find a way in which the heterosexual woman can overcome the anatomy is destiny arguments of Andrea Dworkin and Catherine Mackinnon and produce the female receiver of the male penis as a viable feminist and, even more, an individual. Camille Paglia's well-known paeans to Madonna are but the most public example of this. The separation of the highly gendered sexuality and theory, from the sociological category can be liberating in exactly this way. The issue need not just be that a man, Baudrillard, inflicts "straight truth" on women in the name of seduction. No one should be allowed to do that. Instead, the multiplicity of appearance, which Baudrillard labels as woman, is a gender production that can be theoretically liberating for anyone. If I allow myself to be seduced by the theories of Derrida, this does not preclude me fighting for the appointment of a woman in my department. I remember many years ago when in discussion Derrida used the word "invagination" in a specifically literary way. Asked about the implications for women of such a usage, he said that it had nothing to do with women, it was just a word. I cannot agree that this is the case, but perhaps it should be. Woman as appearance is a product of the gender traditions of our culture. Woman as seductress is the same. To inhabit the theoretical slipperiness of the endlessly polysemantic is an opportunity for both male and female. To inhabit the sexuality of stockings and a garter belt is similar. To extend Butler's argument about the denaturalization of gender, the stockings and garter belt show that the female sexuality that is the figure for substantiality is just a figure and a signifier in motion.

I must develop here, on closing, my comment at the opening that this is very much a personal essay, even more than usual a product of my own subjectivity. While I cannot subscribe to the claims of abnegation in Leo Bersani's "The Rectum Is Also the Grave," I share his belief that one's own position in sexuality has a significant effect on understanding. As someone who has always been, as the books say, "anal passive," perhaps I am not the best drag queen to consider the possibility of the phallic woman. As I said to one of my classes, "I get fucked, therefore I am." The possibility of this existential ontology is explored in the "... Up the Ass" chapter in this book.

Penetration does not, of course, mean I am a woman. If not the phallic woman, I remain, as the line goes in *Priscilla, Queen of the Desert*, "a cock in a frock on a rock." I am a man who at times has inhabited spaces associated with female sexuality. I would say the same about my ventures into feminist theory. And I always remain responsive to those more experienced, in whatever sense that word might be taken, with écriture féminine, or with lip gloss and eyeliner.

## 9. Love With a Perfect Stranger

Gay men often resent their association with anonymous casual sex, but the simple fact of the matter is that throughout history gay men have had a lot of anonymous casual sex. On the other hand, both the reasons for and the meaning of this fact are constantly under dispute. Janis S. Bohan, in *Psychology and Sexual Orientation*, gives this overview:

> A number of explanations have been offered for
> this pattern of higher rates of sexual behavior and
> nonmonogamy among gay men. Among these are the
> equation of sexuality with masculinity and the need for
> gay men to assert their masculinity in the face of cultural
> assumptions that they are effeminate; the tendency for
> men to separate sex from emotional commitment; norms
> of the gay male community, which stress sexual freedom;
> and the availability of many opportunities for casual sex
> in the gay men's community. (193)

She leaves out what I believe to be the most popular explanation, at least among the more liberal but mainstream observers: ubiquitous homophobia has made it impossible for gay men to have normative coupled relationships and as a result they have been driven to a rather unhealthy form of sexual release without emotional fulfillment. Another possibility, more often mooted in the gay community than outside, is that this is not an assertion of some false masculinity but rather normative behaviour for men. Those who express this attitude might be accused of a lack of "emotional commitment," but their response in turn may be "whatever, Mary." According to them, the repressive attitudes of women make it impossible for heterosexual males to live this life, but since gay men are seeking only other men, they can get the varied pleasures their gender naturally desires. Not surprisingly, Carol Gilligan's *In a Different Voice* presents what has become a classic argument about gender difference as a larger view of that lack of emotion: "Since masculinity is defined through separation while femininity is defined through attachment, male gender identity is threatened by intimacy while female gender identity is threatened by separation. Thus males tend to have difficulty with relationships while females tend to have problems with individuation." (Gilligan as quoted in Friedman 238)

Jeffrey Weeks, in *Sexuality and its Discontents: Meanings, Myths & Modern Sexualities*, offers a cogent summary of this view of maleness:

> The image of male sex as an unbridled almost
> uncontrollable force (a 'volcano,' as Krafft-Ebing
> graphically put it, that 'burns down and lays waste all
> around it; ... an abyss that devours all honour, substance
> and health' [*Psychopathia Sexualis*, 2]) is one that has dominated
> our response to the subject. (81)

Weeks also quotes *The Evolution of Sex* (1889), by Patrick Geddes and J. Arthur Thomson, a very symbolic version of the argument presented by Gilligan. Geddes and Thomson suggest that maleness is marked by the "tendency to dissipate energy (katabolic) and femaleness by the tendency to store up energy (anabolic)." (84) Thus the katabolic and the anabolic are a marriage made in heaven, while two katabolics would produce the disastrous result of constant dissipation. Yet, as Weeks notes, the heavenly pairing of kata- and ana- is a joining of two apparently complementary and yet usually antagonistic elements: "Hence the enduring paradox: heterosexuality is natural yet has to be attained, inevitable but constantly threatened, spontaneous yet in effect to be learnt." (84-85) This leads to the assumption that the social is the compulsory natural unnatural: "Within the general formulation 'sex' versus 'society' two responses have been possible—what we can best term the 'repression model' and the 'liberatory model.'" (98) In the former, sexuality is an evil that must be contained, and in the latter, it is a good that must be allowed expression. Needless to say, arguments in favour of stranger sex tend to follow the liberatory model.

My title for this chapter attempts to see at least the beginnings of a few more nuances. One gay man in his seventies told me of his first sexual awakenings as a teenager. When he went, during the day, to a park near his home he could see that it was a popular "beat," a location where men met for sex. He observed particular areas that were hidden from general view where the bushes had been trampled during sexual encounters. He said to me, "I was overwhelmed to discover these places of love." Many might find it surprising to call this activity "love," but he firmly believed this was the right word. For him, all such moments were expressions of an unnamed community, a multiple version of what so often is called "making love."

Clearly Gilligan's comment about separation versus intimacy would suggest that this man was making impossible emotional claims but he is far from alone. Some of the strongest statements about stranger sex as love come from the most intensely complex and psychoanalytic analyses, such as that provided by William Haver in *The Body of This Death: Historicity and Sociality in the Time of AIDS*. Haver considers what he calls "the sexual nomad":

> "This loving, this love, is therefore, as Lacan says
> somewhere, a 'psychological disaster,' for in the
> anonymous singularity of an absolute promiscuity (which
> is a nonmonogamy even if enacted in the passion of only
> one other) there is that which transgresses the essential
> reserve, or 'armor,' that is the ego. Something more,
> something other than a mere libidinal cathexis (at least in
> its normative psychoanalytical constructions), this loving
> is an existential, rather than psychological, 'loss of self,' a
> ruination, a loving *a corps perdu*." (143-144)

Haver looks to abjection for love, a place many would deem unlikely, but he finds it. At least in gay analysis, stranger sex is not a place to avoid love but rather a place to find a very special form of it. Perhaps it is less about the "perfect stranger" and more about losing the self in a "perfect love."

The adjective "perfect" is partly irony. Those who believe in the couple as ideal see anonymous sex as a constant search for that one man who might "take me away from all this." An entertaining representation of this is found in the play *Torch Song Trilogy*, where the central character performs a monologue about his experience in a sex venue. As he is roughly entered from behind, he chatters about the affection his partner must be delivering through his thrusting penis. Even when the partner shuts him up with a rap on the back of the head, it doesn't convince him that this is not love. An opposite view is provided by the assumption that the more absolute the distance between the partners, the closer to perfection. This is a possible justification for the person who seeks a romantic partner who is racially other, such as the dinge queen. The ultimate encounter would be with the person who is completely alien.

As her title suggests, Sara Ahmed's *Strange Encounters: Embodied Others in Post-Coloniality* is about overcoming the dismissiveness of a pejorative view of the foreign. She asserts, "The alien stranger is hence, not beyond human, but a mechanism *for allowing us to face that which we have already designated as the beyond.*" (3) While her stranger is always racialized, her depiction suits any situation in which the stranger embodies that outside the home, that which is other than the same. This creates an interesting possibility for stranger sex between men, between those who are asserted to be "homo-", the same. Ahmed looks at the apparent reversal when the stranger is not frightening but attractive: "The turn to the stranger as a figure who should be welcomed does question the discourses of 'stranger danger', *but only insofar as it keeps in place the fetishism upon which those discourses rely.*" (4) Thus in gay stranger sex, "stranger danger" is very much a part of the attraction.

Arguably, the bathhouse is exactly a place in which the stranger is fetishized. Some men will go to a bathhouse with a friend, albeit a friend who is left at the entrance and not encountered again until the debriefing after the activities are over. Most prefer, however, to be there at a time when there is no one there who he knows. He wants as much anonymity as possible. Thus one of the unwritten rules in many such sex venues is: No talking allowed. A friend of mine who enjoys his persona of naïveté recounted his first time at the baths. A man came up to him and said, "What do you do?" My friend responded, "I work in accounts at Qantas." The essence of the joke is that my friend assumed that this was in some sense a social encounter, in which occupation or home setting is an unthreatening opening question. Instead, the inquiry was the only one acceptable to many in the baths: what is your sexual interest? More often than not, even this type of question is avoided. An interested glance is followed by an erect penis and then a series of moves as both men find out what will and will not take place. This preserves anonymity and secrecy, but it also purveys an illusion of a lack of any proximity except the physical one, what one sees and what one feels. The stranger can be perfect if he is never other than a stranger. John Hollister captures this in his article "A Highway Rest Area as a Socially Reproducible Site":

> In an activist organization, gayness is an almost asexual
> vocal declaration of one's identity, while in the tearoom it
> is an unspoken—even unspeakable—mutual recognition
> that precedes relatively efficient sexual gratification. In the
> world of gay organizations, where public declarations are
> privileged, fine distinctions between 'gay' and 'bisexual'
> and 'queer' can become major points of contention. In a
> tearoom, such distinctions are absurd except as a possible
> element of participants' fantasies about each other. (64)

Even the term "tea room" seems to fit. Apparently a take on "t-room" or "toilet room," it provides an ironic view of the activities: all fantasies are possible.

If the "tea room" is exactly the opposite of its namesake, the dark room is an enhancement of its usual meaning. This room is not just "dark," it is a place where sight is impossible. This is only one term for the open space without lights in a room at the back of a bathhouse or bar; often called a "back room." Sometimes it is given what might be called a reverse idealization when it is identified as a "dungeon" or some such, but only a few have the sado-masochistic paraphernalia that makes what S/M practitioners would call a dungeon. Instead, these rooms remove sight as well as speech, becoming places where the only communication is through touch. Many tell stories of encounters in such venues where one later discovers—or at least guesses—that a sexual partner was actually an unrecognized friend. Thus not only does the room enable sexuality without any of the interference of appearance and the assumptions of what might make a man's face or body attractive, it also removes the possibility of identity. This enables stranger sex even with those who are not strangers. Anonymity becomes inevitable, a universal condition.

Various factors have made gay sex a secret, something that is almost inherently to be hidden away. The obvious one is homophobia. At its extreme, the revelation of gay sex can mean the deaths of the participants. There are other parts to this, however. One is that the primary object of the scopophilic gaze cannot be seen. In the chapter on the penis, I make a brief comparison between the heterosexual male's attraction to the breast and the homosexual male's attraction to the penis, but they are very different objects. The breast is a secondary sex characteristic while the penis is a primary one. Regardless of the focus on the breast and the sexual stimulation available to both male and female nipples, the breast is not central to what most heterosexuals call "sex," but few homosexual men engage in "sex" without considerable attention to one or more penises. Still, just as there is a tradition of heterosexual males evaluating women by "hooters," "jugs," etc., so does the homosexual male judge the "cock," the "dick." But even if a man is wearing very tight pants, unlike the breast, it is not really available to public judging. Thus the very focus of attention for the gay male is a secret. Something is hidden in the dark and must be found, perhaps visually but often just by touch.

It may be absurd to make stranger sex into something so existential and idealized as does Haver, but the delirium of sex is, as we are so often told, delirious. Many men have talked about the joy that is the ultimate disintegration that can happen during stranger sex. This approximates the fundamental experience Ahmed claims in meeting the stranger: "Such encounters allow the stranger to appear, to take form, *by recuperating all that is unknowable into a figure that we imagine we might face here, now, in the street."* (22) Thus the estranged sexual partner offers Haver's ab-jection but also the equivalent of anal sex, going beyond the sexual as-sociations approved by society. Stranger sex is another form of deviant penetration. Ahmed states, "The analogy between the ideal neighbour-hood and a healthy body serves to define the ideal neighbourhood as fully integrated, homogeneous, and sealed: it is like a body that is fully contained by the skin." (25) The passive partner in anal sex is refusing containment, but so are both partners in stranger sex, no matter what their sexual activity.

Frank Browning's *A Queer Geography: Journeys Toward a Sexual Self* no doubt overstates the case, but his rhapsodies about stranger sex are simply more florid versions of what most gay men have heard and many gay men have felt:

> I go into the darkened corner, find myself wedged
> between bricks and bodies known to me only by the
> touch of skin unseen, and I am grasped in a collective
> disappearance. My knees dissolve and I descend, as in a
> recurring dream of a free-floating, weightless elevator
> moving randomly through the walls of an enormous
> building. Head to breast to navel to groin, and I am
> engorged by the flesh of another's flesh, released from the
> contingent aloneness of my life, all limbs my limbs, all
> heart one heart. (117-118)

Once again, stranger sex takes him beyond his skin:

> As I merge myself into the sweet grip of a dozen others,
> and a dozen dozen of their others, I take myself to
> the biological brink. Not only do I take myself to the
> abyss, but I make my body a conveyance through which
> unknown agents track their way into unknown other
> bodies. I become an altar of secrets: secrets whose
> (microbial) nature I do not know and whose destination

> I cannot specify. I become the abyss of the unknown. For
> that (sublime) reason alone, I, like any abyss, become yet
> more attractive, more alluring to those others drawn to
> the dark secret. I am the escape from the floodlit world of
> *outness*. (118)

Any attempt to make sense of this would somehow make it less sensual, especially in a reaction to the hyperbole (were there really 144 men?). Still, his belief that stranger sex can reach an ultimate secret suggests the ecstatic claims often made. But why the aversion to "outness"?

Stranger sex denies the identity that outness asserts. How can you claim that it is important to identify yourself as "gay" when you are in the middle of an experience that denies any identity beyond being a participating body? Browning's book has a political intent, but it might be viewed as apolitical in presenting an ideal of anonymous orgies. It is revealing to consider Browning's argument in the light of Douglas Sadownick's *Sex Between Men: An Intimate History of the Sex Lives of Gay Men Postwar to Present*. Quite opposite to Browning, Sadownick sees stranger sex as a manifestation of homophobia: "In one way or another, twentieth-century gay culture has been a response to these myths. It had evolved into a world of *doing* more than *being*." (169) In other words, the lack of a homosexual identity necessitates an ardent *practice* of homosexuality.

The truth is no doubt somewhere between Browning and Sadownick, but Sadownick's comment about "doing" is important. Homosexuality is simply sex between two persons of the same gender. Thus two men in a monogamous marriage certainly practice homosexuality. Yet, observers from the most homophobic to the most homosexual identify gay culture with stranger sex. This is perhaps because so much of today's gay culture has no sexuality. What makes Brad Pitt straight and Elton John gay? The primary explanation is simply self-claims about identity. On the other hand, stranger sex is a performance of sexuality. It is not that stranger sex is not social: of course it is. However, unlike marriage, the term "boyfriend," etc., it cannot be just social.

This need for an overt sexuality is never more evident than in one of the classic documents on anonymous gay sex, John Rechy's *The Sexual Outlaw: A Documentary*. The memoir has a lot of Kerouac in its style and could be said to be putting the beat in the beat. Perhaps more than anyone else, Rechy fully idealizes this mode of being: "The promiscuous homosexual is a sexual revolutionary. Each moment of his outlaw existence he confronts repressive laws, repressive 'morality.' Parks, alleys, subway tunnels, garages, streets—these are the battlefields." (28) Rechy shows no attraction to any of the recent normalizations of homosexuality, such as gay marriage. His sexual expression finds its vitality in the rejection of the straight hegemony:

> What creates the sexual outlaw?
> Rage.
> None more easily prosecuted—even so-called liberals
> condone his persecution—his is the only minority
> against whose existence there are laws. (28)

The inaccuracy of the last statement makes it seem that much more visceral. For Rechy, the pursuer of anonymous sex is a hero of epic proportion:

> In this context the sexual outlaw flourishes. The pressures
> produce him, create his defiance. Knowing that each
> second his freedom may be ripped away arbitrarily, he
> lives fully at the brink. Promiscuity is his righteous form
> of revolution.
>
> No stricture—legal, medical, religious—will ever stop
> him. It will only harden his defiance. Neither sinful,
> criminal, nor sick—he knows that to try to force him
> not to be a homosexual is sinful, criminal, and sick—and
> as impossible as forcing a heterosexual not to be a
> heterosexual. (31)

This "sexual outlaw" is clearly engaged in male-male sex. The suggestion here is that to be heterosexual is to be "straight" in all senses of the word, including, presumably, boring monogamy. Regardless of the thousands of singles bars, the many claims about the liberal sexual attitudes of young women and the eternal assumptions of the sexual aggression of all men, no matter what his claimed sexual orientation, the outlaw must be gay. A friend of mine was staying in a hotel at a conference. On her return to her room very late at night, she encountered her boss just leaving his room. His furtive comment was, "Can't sleep. Going for a walk. Bye." She asked me, "Do you think he is gay?" I answered, "No, he is likely just going out to buy sex from a woman." She was shocked. She would not have been shocked at the thought he might be having an affair, but if someone is engaging in stranger sex, the assumption is that he must be gay. In one of the more surprising permutations of our society, the liberal heterosexual views the gay man who has stranger sex as just pursuing his destiny, regardless of why stranger sex must be his destiny. The straight man pursuing stranger sex is almost unimaginable.

An obvious question to ask is how many of the men having anonymous sex see themselves in any sense as Rechy's Robin Hoods of the beat. Gary Dowsett's *Practicing Desire: Homosexual Sex in the Era of AIDS* is one of the best analyses of anonymous sex. It is primarily a sociological account of various men and sex venues in Australia, but the practiced and experienced commentary raises it well above its value as documentation. Dowsett writes of one group:

> Nullangardie's men are certainly 'sexual outlaws,' yet they
> lack John Rechy's (1977) conscious and political pursuit
> of homosex. They do not present a gay liberationist
> determination to flout the sexual order. It is a group of
> working-class men and boys pursuing a tradition of sexual
> activity among themselves, reproducing the framework for
> the sex lives of generations of men in Nullangardie. (108-
> 109)

In other words, this is a culture of sex with strangers, but it is not about the meaning of sex but rather about sex. Anonymous sex with men offers them a form of release they would not find elsewhere.

One of Dowsett's successes is his ability to understand the ways in

which stranger sex is about something more than just availability and
sexual release:

> There is transgression, a little recklessness, real danger,
> the heightened sensation that accompanies risk and
> fear, the pleasures involved and potentially available
> in each encounter. It is the sensation of an affinity
> between sexually aroused men and the capacity of each
> to read arousal in the other and match it. Within this
> choreography of sex it is important to think of casual
> sex in part as a particular sex practice and not just as a
> description of partner choice. (146)

There is clearly a *frisson* produced by offending the hegemonic morality,
but it is difficult to see these actions as ideological in Rechy's sense, still
less as the opposition to oppression claimed by Michael Warner's *The
Trouble with Normal: Sex, Politics, and the Ethics of Queer Life*:

> One could make an antinomian claim to validity on
> behalf of, say, a blow job in a tearoom. Especially if
> the blow job expressed a stigmatized, forbidden, and
> oppressed sexuality, the pleasure of its realization might
> be intensified by a sense of the wrongness of the law that
> banned it, as that law embodied an unjust social order and
> a lifetime of oppressive experience—all swept aside in the
> discovery, through pleasure, that the desire to reject that
> social order was shared with another. (103-104)

Most gay men have friends for whom stranger sex is the sex of choice.
Many such devotees will explain their lifestyle as not wanting to be tied
down or as trying at least to sample the infinite variety that is out there,
but a longer conversation will reveal much more. One friend who has
been doing the beats for thirty years is likely to emphasize stories of not
unusually attractive men or unusually energetic sex, but rather unusual
negotiations in unusual venues. As Dowsett says,

> One should not ignore the recreational aspects of this

kind of sex. The habitué knows that sex is available at any
given moment or place unbeknown to the world at large.
This is also sex as *art*: the art of the perpetual seduction
and pleasuring of men by men. Compared to the veteran
player in any sport, it takes practice, intuition, experience,
and skill to operate on a beat effectively. (147)

The "pleasuring of men by men" implies that stranger sex is a significant part of creating a community of gay men. There are ways in
which gay men provide the ultimate example of male bonding. Theorists such as Eve Kosofsky Sedgwick have discussed the homoeroticism
of the homosocial in heterosexual society. She and others have claimed
that much of homophobia is a panicked denial of this underlying desire.
Carole Pateman's feminist analysis of the social contract, *The Sexual Contract*, comes up with the following theory:

> The story is about heterosexual relations—but it also
> tells of the creation of a fraternity and their contractual
> relations. Relations between members of the fraternity lie
> outside the scope of my present discussion, but, as Marilyn
> Frye has noted, 'there is a sort of "incest taboo" built into
> standard masculinity.' [Frye, *The Politics of Reality*, 143] The
> taboo is necessary; within the bonds of fraternity there is
> always a temptation to make the relation more than that of
> fellowship. But if members of the brotherhood extended
> their contracts, if they contracted for sexual use of bodies
> among themselves, the competition could shake the
> foundations of the original contract. From the standpoint
> of contract, the prohibition against this particular exercise
> of the law of male sex-right is purely arbitrary, and the
> fervour with which it is maintained by men themselves
> is incomprehensible. The story of the original creation of
> modern patriarchy helps lessen the incomprehension.
> (192-193)

Thus there are many ways in which gay men assert the healthiness of their exploration of this eroticism. While some gay men lament that gay culture is just male bonding with sex added, others extol it for exactly the same reasons. Gay sports leagues often emphasize this and many gay bars make team sport an explicit theme. The homophobic jokes about male touching in rugby and American football become labels of pride.

The gay male obsession with the body beautiful is another element visible everywhere but often lamented as superficial and limited. The attraction becomes less uniform in the realm of stranger sex. Advertisements for bathhouses inevitably feature muscular young men, as do their floats in Gay Pride parades. Anyone who has ever been to a bathhouse can attest to a time when he was rejected in favour of someone else with a better, younger, body. However, there are a number of instances where this is not the case. Whatever the reason, gay men have "types" who range from Arnold Schwarzenegger to Homer Simpson, with alternatives from Michael Jackson to Humpty Dumpty. Different bathhouses have different emphases and any frequent customer knows not just which one to attend, but also the best time and day for his type to appear. I tend to go in the middle of the afternoon on Saturday or Sunday. This is a time when few of the body-beautiful young men would think of appearing, and there are a number of older men, men I would fantasize as "heterosexual" and married. This is a good time for my interests and it seems a good time for those interested in me.

There is a significant gay contingent who almost stridently reject the body beautiful. There are of course categories such as bears, who create a social and sexual life around their type, in this case large and hairy. There are others, however, who celebrate the body in its greatest variety. This might seem to be simply a gay version of naturists. The latter claim that there is no body too unusual to be allowed out without clothes. The obvious difference is that the heterosexual naturist claims that there is no sexual component to all this unclothed flesh. The gay naturist, who often celebrates the more flamboyant term "naked," instead acclaims the sexual element. A group called Toronto Naked Men always marches in the Toronto Gay Pride Parade and flamboyantly presents a variety of bodies and an unusual variety of genitalia. Besides organizations, there are also independent naked parties, which accept various degrees of sexual touching. The enjoyment of the body in such venues can be quite extravagant. At one party I attended, one man who seemed to have extraordinary control just stood in the corner with erections that came and went like a hydraulic toy. One man playing pool loved to lean over to make a shot, his buttocks spread as widely as possible. Others just chatted as though they were trying to pretend they were somewhere else. This was difficult given that five or six of the hundred or so men were on a constant inspection tour, leaning in to peer as closely as possible at whatever drew their interest. The venue was so much more open than the baths, and yet given that there was no aggressive sexual touching there were different rules, which seemed to accommodate that intense scopophilia.

It is difficult to depict exactly how nakedness, stranger sex, and such unbeautiful bodies link to make a community, but they capture the spectrum of the homoerotics of gay male bonding in a way that other things do not. One link for me, at least in the North American context, is the word "buddy." I had one boyfriend who always used the term during sex. Stan Persky's wonderful memoir of various sexual encounters recalls a Vancouver gay bar in its title, Buddy's. Once I was sucking a man in a bathhouse and when he came he said, "Thanks, buddy." It could be "mate" in Australia, or any similar term. My premise is that it assumes a camaraderie, a link through sex that goes beyond sex. The connection is assumed to be larger than that possible in two genders. It also is larger than that between two people. The imitation of heterosexuality enshrined in the couple ideal of gay marriage is quite different from the experience of these many buddies enjoying stranger sex.

Browning captures the idealized view of ultimate buddy-ness:

> At the crudest level it is the tacit, physical knowledge
> shared by the band of orgiasts, who, as one of their
> members nears climax, lock arms and thighs together
> with him, pressing themselves into a straining web of

muscle and sinew aimed not at their own release but at
propelling him into greater, wilder ejaculatory pleasure.

For many men that is the essential homo-moment, a
merger of self-identities released from the separateness
of difference. Sublimated, socialized, reconfigured as
language and artifice, that self-effacing merger of selves
is a central fount from which modern homosexual
identity flows, articulating a longing for the release from
difference through a bonded union with one's own. (201-
202)

Thus while Browning's argument seems for the most part to be opposed
to identity, here he claims an over-wielding identity that overcomes
separation through sexual release.

The possibilities of stranger sex also move homosexuality beyond
the gay community. The assumption is often made that bathhouses are
full of men in the closet. The closet is usually a pejorative term in the
gay community, but it also can imply masculinity, the "straight-acting"
who is so often claimed to be attractive in his masculinity. As I note in
the chapter on anal sex, in many cultures the penetrator has no sexual
orientation, only a gender. The male enters, whether females or other
males. This reflects the myriad stories of situational homosexuality, in
prisons, in the military, etc. While the penetrated is depicted as weak
and dominated, the penetrator is not gay but rather so testosterone-lad-
en that he must penetrate some orifice, whatever is available. The connection between situational homosexuality and what might be called
normative homosexuality is much more complex than it might seem.
This is one of the reasons why a key venue for stranger sex is the cinema
that plays heterosexual pornography. Who knows who first realized that
a place devoted to individual heterosexual men watching heterosexual
encounters was actually a perfect opportunity to find men interested
in sex with other men? The argument could be that these men are so
aroused by films of men with women that they become available to
men. A friend told me a story of being in such a venue and perform-

ing fellatio on a rather rough-looking young man. In the middle of the encounter, the latter looked at the screen and said, "Look at the gash on her. God, I missed that in prison." Was this man returning to the situational homosexuality he had developed in prison? Was he so newly released he had not yet found any women? Or was he like the men in Dowsett's study, not gay but someone who recognized that male sexuality is the one that is the most readily available?

Most of this book, including this chapter, depicts a North American experience. However, stranger sex is universal, although it takes different forms in different cultures. A significant part of stranger sex is sex tourism. In the popular imagination, this is linked to both pedophilia and western imperialism. It has led to various laws in western nations that punish pedophiles for crimes committed in other countries. I was once sitting in a bar in Sri Lanka, having a conversation with a mixed company of western visitors when a gay friend referred to an encounter the night before with a number of local "boys." The gay members of the group understood this to mean adult sex workers who made significant attempts to appear younger than they were. The heterosexuals were revolted at this admission of pedophile tourism. Once again, stranger sex had different auras in the gay and the straight worlds.

I have never engaged in what might be called sex tourism. I don't see it as inherently any more immoral than any other system in which wealthy westerners travel and buy services from less-advantaged locals. Still, it is not a form of adventure that appeals to me. I have, however, been a tourist interested in things sexual and have often been aided in my explorations by local people who understand what I do not. Still, this book is not about such travel, and I will not make an attempt to repeat the work done well by Dennis Altman in *Global Sex*. Instead, I will look briefly at one society that I know quite well, India.

It is a suitable model because arguably stranger sex is most prevalent in urban cultures that are most heterosexual and most homosocial, as are the cities of India, which seem to be places of ubiquitous "opportunistic" homosexuality. This responds to the individual's degree of same sex attraction, sex drive, and the situation that presents. While homosexual acts remain illegal in India, opportunistic male-male sex has been tacitly accepted. Shivananda Khan refers to this as "masti." "The word is not easily translated, but in a sexual context it means sexual 'playfulness,' and is usually used in the context of sexual play between males. It is not seen as a serious act, because it does not involve a woman. Nor is it really seen as sex. To some extent it is even socially permissible, 'young men letting off steam,' as long as it remains invisible." (32) It does not necessarily disrupt the essence of Indian society, which is heterosexual marriage.

Anyone who has been to India will note how many working-class men are just hanging around wherever you go, and most often with few or no women present. These men recognize that a sexual opportunity is more likely with a man of any class than with any woman except a wife or a prostitute. Thus, as in Dowsett's example, sexual opportunity is perceived as homosexual opportunity. Shivananda Khan refers to "an almost indiscriminate sexual activity by many men without regard to the gender of the sexual partner; where such sexual behaviours are not defined by any form of sexual identity but rather by the concept of availability and discharge...." (4) In my experience, such sexual opportunity is much much broader than that experienced in Canada, the United States, or Australia. In those countries, outside of the beats one must practise a careful gaydar to find an interested man. In India, the interest can begin to seem inevitable. One of the reasons is that homosocial erotics, from touching through longing glances, are a constant throughout society, but so is a general claim that homosexual activity is not just illegal, it is non-existent. Homosocial bonds do not suggest homosexuality to Indians because it is not deemed a possibility. The amazing thing to a non-Indian is that the crime of homosexuality leads not to a lack of homosexual activity but instead ubiquitous homosexuality in a land of complete denial. This is "don't ask, don't tell" with a vengeance.

George Chauncey, in *Gay New York: Gender, Urban Culture, and the Making of the Gay Male World 1890-1940*, depicts a society where homosexuality as an identity was one-sided in sexual terms. The "fairy" was someone who serviced men who claimed to be heterosexual: "One of the reasons fairies were tolerated by tough working-class men and often had remarkably easygoing relations with them was the care they took to confirm rather than question the latter's manliness." (80) One hundred years later, North Americans assume that men who have sex with men cannot be "straight," yet there remain many gay men who look for men who are at least nominally heterosexual. Some just claim it as a challenge: one friend believed the energy of his homosexuality was such that it could make any straight man fall into his arms. Of course, if no identity is acknowledged, there is no reason to assume that homosexual activity denotes homosexuals. Thus every man might be a heterosexual man. Attracting the heterosexual also idealizes the category of the stranger as part of some magical universal of male sexuality. The desire is not to convert a straight man into a homosexual partner but rather to draw his body into the world of gay comrades. In chapter seven I referred to Walt Whitman and Edward Carpenter, the most famous of the many nineteenth-century authors who idealized an eroticized male friendship. While Whitman avoided any overt comment on sexual expression, the symbolism of the sprouting reed in *Leaves of Grass* leaves little to the imagination. Carpenter was still more explicit. In both cases the goal is a male who recognizes the erotics of comradeship, something that is presented as if not universal, at least generally available. Today many would present the same ethos in stranger sex, as does Browning: "Our camaraderie at its best becomes a zone of trust, a fraternal fellowship from which we both look outward to touch the lives of others among whom we also find and extend fulfillment." (188)

My own experience is limited. I have had sex many times in bathhouses. My first sex with a man was in a non-gay steambath thirty-five years ago. Still, my sexual encounters with strangers outside such more-or-less sanctioned venues have been rare. My usual experience has been cruising in bars or elsewhere, leading to conversations, discussions, and sexual relations, often as not at a later time. In other words, my life has been not unlike that of many heterosexuals. I have never found the first sexual encounter to be very fulfilling. My best sex has always been after the relationship has had at least a few weeks to develop an understanding of mutual needs and desires. I could be deluding myself, but I don't think my lack of sex in parks and toilets is a fear of legal implications. I have often thought it would have been a good thing for my character had I been caught in the Toronto bathhouse raids in the early 1980s. It would have given me some credibility, but it also would have given me first-hand knowledge of the suppression of homosexuality, something with which I have had only cursory contact. I have never suffered the many repercussions of anti-sodomy laws, whether in Canada or elsewhere. On the other hand, while I have nothing against the idea of public sex, neither do I feel any need to pursue it. For me, it looks uncomfortable in a variety of ways, quite unlike the beds and showers available in the bathhouses. Similarly, while I find public decency laws offensive, I don't feel a large need to oppose them by my actions as I primarily find them simply illogical. Public decency laws seem inevitably to be about social propriety rather than some actual harm of the sort offered by smoking in a public room, verbal abuse, or even playing baseball in a crowded park. For the most part, public sex affects others only as an unattractive sight, like a Fortrel leisure suit or televised snooker.

Yet, every gay man recognizes the role of public sex—or at least anonymous sex—in our culture. The most monogamous gay man with the most limited sexual palate knows that stranger sex is somehow a part of who he is. I think that my periodic ventures to the baths are just a means of finding sex when I am in a period without a male sexual companion. Still, I am quite willing to admit that there must be a particular *frisson* that draws me there. I have tried personal ads, online dating, and chat rooms, but I have found them less successful. In my experience, few of the people who respond actually want to cut to the chase. It could be just my own limitations, but my experience consists of many phone calls followed by coffee, followed by dinner and then, in most instances, "I'll see ya when I see ya." Yet my own claim here, that I am just making a choice for efficiency's sake, could easily be interpreted in a different direction. I might enjoy most the sexual relationship produced by long-term intimacy, but I don't seem to prefer the casual intimacy of chat rooms and phone conversations. If I can't get capital-I Intimacy, then I choose to move directly to strangers.

An important part of stranger sex is prostitution. In the heterosexual world prostitution is usually seen primarily as a desperation move by a woman driven by poverty and/or addiction. The "john" is identified as lonely, sleazy, or perverted. That the label "john" is pejorative is indicated by the fact that while I have known many men who have paid for sex from men and have done so myself a number of times, I have met only two men who have admitted that they hired women for sex. While masculinity is emphasized in both the gay and the straight world, in the straight world one evaluation of masculinity is the ability to convince women to have sex. It is not that this is not the case in the gay world, but rather that it is not so simplistic. Similarly, the ideal object of the sexual urge is not so unitary. Many gay men admit to a variety of alternative sexual interests, both in activity and in object, and it is generally accepted that the more specific you get the more likely that you will need to pay. My own experience of prostitution is ambivalent. I have used gay "escort" advertisements to find a sex worker. At first I was surprised at the quality of person available, but then realized this no doubt simply reflected my own prejudice. Instead I found that I could depend on meeting a pleasant man with whom to spend time, but that sexual satisfaction could be a bit arbitrary. In other words, I was paying for the same category I could find in the baths. Still, I have continued to pay from time to time, primarily because it is one more sexual experience that consistently gives me pleasure, if not something that could be called fulfillment.

I am using an arguably narrow definition of prostitution. If a young man goes out with an old troll who has a Mercedes-Benz and pays for the young man's expensive lifestyle, it might seem to be prostitution to some, but it is more a continuation of a model familiar in both gay and straight worlds. On the other hand, the teenage hustler who stands on a corner in boys' town is certainly engaged in classic prostitution, although his clients and procedures are again more similar to those of a woman working the streets. While the method of contact for the male sex worker advertising online or in newspapers is the same as for a female, the role in the community is very different.

I realize that I might be falling into the common gay delusion of equality. Gay men often claim that in heterosexuality, patriarchy inevitably leaves women oppressed. They are sexual objects rather than subjects with free choices. Sexual performance is oriented to pleasing the man rather than both partners. One need not have too many gay experiences to realize that all sexual relationships are imbalanced. Still, my encounters with male sex workers have been quite different from those described to me by female sex workers. I don't feel an unusual power over the man nor do I find him to have an unusual neediness. It is similar to stranger sex with the exception that I pay for the service. It seems to me the equivalent of a friend doing some house repair for which you pay him. The payment does not create what might be the expected hierarchy.

Many gay men with a significant and respectable profile have been paid for sex, but one of the most interesting in the Canadian context is Gerald Hannon. He is best known as a part-time university lecturer who lost his job because of assumptions that he approved of certain aspects of pedophilia, as suggested by an article he wrote for the magazine *The Body Politic*. He is also the recipient of many journalism awards. As well, he has acknowledged his own sex work and is a classic example of the social acceptance of prostitution in the gay community. One might expect a female prostitute who is similarly fiftyish to be downtrodden and a social reject, whereas Hannon is neither. He himself has noted that his success as a sex worker shows the openness of gay society, a world in which the older man is often an attraction, especially if willing and able to play a "Daddy" role. As well, however, Hannon himself, both in his writing and in his public profile, is clear that he sees his role as a sex worker as both part of gay liberation and also about sexual liberation in the sense depicted by Rechy.

The elements of the gay community that seem the most transgressive are also part of its capitalist economy. The role of prostitution in stranger sex is an example, but so is the bathhouse. Historically stranger sex among men was largely outside the cash economy, with a few ancillary exceptions such as bribes for policemen. Today the bathhouses and advertisements for "escorts" and "massages" are no doubt a small part of what is sometimes called the "pink dollar," but their tentacles can reach quite widely, particularly through the Internet. Yet most of us constantly believe, in a way not too unlike Rechy, that our sexuality is not compliant with the capitalist or any other system, yet is somehow profoundly transgressive. As Dowsett says, "It must be remembered that gay sex is perverse; gay sex is different." (37) Elizabeth Wilson asks the inevitable question "Is Transgression Transgressive?" and responds,

> the term transgression in a sexual context implies not only
> shock but—perhaps most strongly—forbidden pleasures.
> So the transgressor, getting under the skin of mainstream
> society, claims not only to expose the falsity of the society
> that is shocked, but also claims access to some kind of
> intensity of experience from which the mainstream of
> society is cut off. (111)

Warner elevates transgression through a note on Erving Goffman's categories of "stigmaphiles" and "stigmaphobes." The religious right has claimed that gay men pursue deviance for the sake of deviance, but Warner goes further: "The stigmaphile space is where we find a commonality with those who suffer from stigma, and in this alternative realm learn to value the very things the rest of the world despises—not just because the world despises them, but because the world's pseudo-morality is a phobic and inauthentic way of life." (43)

The view of stranger sex as both ultimately transgressive and also identifiably gay has been met by the AIDS epidemic. AIDS is not a gay disease; the experience of the world demonstrates this. However, it entered the consciousness of North America and of much of the world, as "GRID": gay-related immune deficiency. To many on the Christian right, it seemed God's punishment for stranger sex. Others with no religious axe to grind, such as playwright and gay activist Larry Kramer, believed that its origin or meaning was irrelevant: the only practical response was to reject stranger sex. Gabriel Rotello's *Sexual Ecology: AIDS and the Destiny of Gay Men* would maintain that avoiding promiscuity is simply a practical response to an epidemic, but there is a moral tone in the language he uses: "Among a dedicated and significant core of urban gay men, the spiraling escalation of the seventies had produced a culture of unprecedented sexual extremism." (64) He disdains the libertarian and innovative nature of stranger sex and is particularly sneering when it comes to the acceptance of certain health risks:

> Multipartner anal sex was encouraged, celebrated,
> considered a central component of liberation. Core group
> behavior in baths and sex clubs was deemed by many
> the quintessence of freedom. Versatility was declared
> a political imperative. Analingus was pronounced the
> champagne of gay sex, a palpable gesture of revolution.
> STDs were to be worn like badges of honor, antibiotics to
> be taken with pride. (89)

Many consider this sort of reaction to be internalized homophobia: the gay man opposed to stranger sex is opposed to gay sex. The response of the gay community in general was to move to concepts such as "safe sex" or, more accurately, "safer sex," or, more accurately still, "negotiated risk." "Negotiated risk" means that sex with strangers is still acceptable for gay men. Perhaps it is even necessary for many men. The danger is met by an ardent drive to participate. Still, like all extreme sports, participants need to know what they are doing.

If Rechy's memoir makes him the Kerouac of stranger sex, Warner, with his various polemics and analyses, is the Lenin. Warner's faith in the importance of stranger sex, as depicted in his book *Publics and Counterpublics*, is almost unbounded. Part of Warner's argument is that stranger

sex is a reversal of the assumptions of public and private, which he artic-
ulates as homophobic: "Same-sex persons kissing, embracing, or holding hands in public view commonly excite disgust even to the point of
violence, whereas mixed-sex persons doing the same things are invisibly
ordinary, even applauded." (24) Warner does not wish to convince the
world that public displays of affection should be *public* for both straight
and gay. Rather, he believes that a gay—or rather "queer"—presentation of the private in the public creates a new public force in opposition
to the hegemony: "It is often thought, especially by outsiders, that the
public display of private matters is a debased narcissism, a collapse of de-
corum, expressivity gone amok, the erosion of any distinction between
public and private. But in a counterpublic setting, such display often has
the aim of transformation." (62) While he does not use the term "stranger
sex," he comes close to it in his claim for what constitutes "a public."
"A public is a relation among strangers." (74) As in Sadownick's comment
about "doing," Warner presents stranger sex as a creation of identity
not through being but rather through acting: "A public, however, unites
strangers through participation alone, at least in theory. Strangers come
into relationship by its means, though the resulting social relationship
might be peculiarly indirect and unspecifiable." (75)

I have made a variety of assertions here about stranger sex, from
claims in praise of its abjection to claims in praise of its expression
of masculinity, from claims of its ultimate anonymous individuality to
claims of its ultimate collectivity. The one element that is reasonably
consistent, even if one includes the institution of the bathhouse, is that
it takes place outside of the normal boundaries of organized gay life. As
Dowsett and others observe, it of course has its systems, as do all human
interactions, but it retains the patina of freedom. In *The Trouble with Normal*,
Warner claims:

> Strangers have an ability to represent a world of others
> in a way that sustained intimacy cannot, although of
> course these are not exclusive options in gay and lesbian
> culture. This pleasure, a direct cathexis of the publicness

of sexual culture, is by and large unavailable in dominant
culture, simply because heterosexual belonging is already
mediated by nearly every institution of culture. (179)

Thus I circle back to Ahmed. Stranger sex is not the ultimate abandoning
of couple fulfillment but rather the hope, illusory though it might be,
of an ultimate connection with the human world that can never be
known.

## 10. Being Out: The Closet with the Revolving Door

As I write this I am in St. John's, Newfoundland, where I spend my summers. It is a small city, around 120,000 people, with a small gay community. There are a number of highly visible people in the city who are known to be gay, but none has ever appeared in the Pride parade, which is lucky to get one hundred people. There is no bar that is overtly gay, although a couple have predominantly gay clientele. Last week I went with my two-year-old daughter to get some milk from the local grocery. Only when I returned home did I realize I had been wearing a T-shirt that celebrates the "La Vie en Rose" conference and features about one hundred words that run together, including "fag," "sodomite," and "queer." I cannot say that the middle-aged woman at the counter had any unusual response. I have no idea whether she read any of these words. Was I coming out to her?

Another story, same spot, this morning. This time outside the store. I was walking without my daughter, no identifying insignia on my chest, when one of two young men sitting on a step yelled, "Nice purse, fag-got." Given my urban neighbourhood, that it was nine a.m., and given that he was already drinking a beer, one can come to all kinds of assumptions about his character and the homophobia of "his kind." Given that I was carrying a case of beer, one can guess why his attention was drawn to my accoutrements. And there is no question I was carrying a leather bag that could accurately be called "a purse." But was there something else? Was there something in my walk or appearance that made him "read" me, in the sense I explore in the chapter on *The Crying Game*? Should I have walked up to him and said, "Yes I am" to strike a blow for gay liberation—and receive whatever blows he drunkenly decided to strike?

There are many different parts to the process of the closet but they all assume, at least at some level, that some identity can be revealed. Among the many popular culture examples, performers from Elton John through George Michael assert how improved their lives have been since they revealed their homosexuality. Biographies of past figures from Liberace to Rock Hudson state how tortured they were about not being able to admit their sexual orientation. Lord Alfred Douglas wrote, "I am the love that dare not speak its name" ("Two Loves") but not a few wits, among them the American conservative Pat Buchanan, have now called it "the love that won't shut up."

The importance of coming out goes well beyond the celebrity bio. Karla Jay and Allen Young published a number of books in the 1970s about being "out." In one, *After You're Out: Personal Experiences of Gay Men and Lesbian Women*, Young offers a summary of the reasons for being out:

> First of all, identifying ourselves as gay is truthful, and
> brings with it the righteousness of spirit that comes with
> the truth.... Second, saying 'I am gay!' has the important
> element of *self-definition* to it. It is not the negative definition
> of others (homo, lezzie, queer, pansy, fruit) but a positive
> term we can call our own.... Third, the affirmation of gay
> identity allows us to get together and achieve unity with
> others of like identity. (27-28)

This was published in 1975 and it is no doubt a part of its period. Elsewhere in the article, Young states that he felt guilty because "I failed to denounce my straight friends for their straightness and their marriages." (29) In other words, not only was it necessary to be "out," it was necessary to denounce those who were not out, including those who had nothing to be out about. The guilt seems based on the assumption that such a denunciation would have left him guiltless. Today, the comfort of that oppositional dichotomy is gone for most of us. It is difficult to see any gay men today saying that. It has been a long time since I heard someone disparagingly refer to "breeders." Many of our more radical contingent might "denounce my gay friends for their gay marriages," but that is another story. Still, the essence of Young's argument about being out continues today, enshrined in the words he italicizes. One comes out because it is "truthful," because it offers "self-definition," and because it provides an opportunity for "unity" among homosexuals. Young's piece also assumes a binary, defined by that closet door. The person behind it is a liar who lacks self and is isolated. The person in front of it has a true self in a world of solidarity.

Some ten years ago, a gay student of mine said of another student, "He's not gay." I replied, "Yes, he's gay. You just don't like him." Part of this is just a question of being on the team. If I don't like him, I don't want him on my side. There is also an element here, however, of some larger perspective on what it means to be "truly" gay. In *A Social History of Truth: Civility and Science in Seventeenth-Century England*, Steve Shapin considers how truth was ascertained in that era: "Veracity was understood to be underwritten by *virtue*. Gentlemen insisted upon the truthfulness of their relations as a mark of their condition and their honor." (410) Today most would consider this ideal of the gentleman to be hopelessly out of date: "A popular response is that we now live in a 'postvirtuous' culture. Modernity guarantees knowledge not by reference to virtue but to *expertise*." (412) One could easily say that to claim to be gay is to claim a certain sexual expertise, but I think in the gay community it also is an assertion of virtue. By coming out of the closet, you show that you are a good person, a truth-speaker. In a strangely circular argument, to say "I am gay" is an inevitably true statement and so anyone who says it can now be depended upon to tell the truth. Thus when my student saw a deceitful person saying, "I am gay," he knew the person must not be gay or the whole system would break down: one could no longer depend on the virtue of all homosexuals. Given that the term "queer" was first applied to homosexuals on the grounds that we are crooked and false, we seem to have come a long way.

Of course one of the assumptions of this system of truth is that "the homosexual" is itself a truth. The chicken cannot be a chicken if there is no such thing as a chicken. Ian Hacking, in "Making Up People," ruminates on the process:

> Suppose there is some truth in the labeling theory of the
> modern homosexual. It cannot be the whole truth, and

this is for several reasons, including one that is future-directed and one that is past-directed. The future-directed fact is that after the institutionalization of the homosexual person in law and official morality, the people involved had a life of their own, individually and collectively. As gay liberation has amply proved, that life was no simple product of the labeling.

The past-directed fact is that the labeling did not occur in a social vacuum, in which those identified as homosexual people passively accepted the format. There was a complex social life that is only now revealing itself in the annals of academic social history. (83-84)

Thus for the purposes of the argument here, while I do not claim a "whole truth" for being out, I must assume that there is such a thing today as a "homosexual," regardless of the many arguments, such as Foucault's, that such an identity is questionable. Another past-directed element that may be presumed here is that there is a possible "homosexual" throughout human history; he doesn't just appear out of the blue when it is finally possible for him to be out as a label in the late nineteenth century. A future-directed element is that this label will continue for at least some time, in spite of the arguments presented by various critics, such as Bert Archer in *The End of Gay (and the Death of Heterosexuality)*, that identity by sexual orientation is not long for this world.

This of course presumes that as well as there being a "homosexual," there is a coherent and always existent truth of self in anyone who is in that category. Jonathan Dollimore, in *Sex, Literature and Censorship*, describes becoming gay at the age of twenty-eight: "In other words, I didn't fit a classic coming-out narrative: I had not at last become the person I had always really been. On the contrary, almost overnight, so to speak, I had become a different person. This wasn't so much a self-discovery as a bewilderingly radical transformation of the self." (15) One could argue that this still might suit the closet metaphor: once you realize you are gay, whenever and however that happens, at that point you must come out. According to this process, the issue is not the emphatic truth of the homosexual identity, something that must not be kept in the closet, but rather the truth of homophobia, something that must be fought by as many claims of homosexuality as possible. It is the equivalent of the familiar story where some obvious flamer is attacked at a bus stop, believed by the attackers to be alone, the only apparent pervert, when the little old lady standing there yells, "I'm gay too," and one by one the crowd presents the thugs with an overwhelming homosexual presence. The event probably never happened, but the story's ubiquity suggests how attractive is such a narrative of the power of coming out.

The importance of this assumption arises in many contexts. In the introduction to my book *Pink Snow: Homotextual Possibilities in Canadian Fiction*, I explore many inflections of homotextuality, which often comes down to assumptions as to who is homosexual and who is not. There, in an extensive examination of Eve Kosofsky Sedgwick's *The Epistemology of the Closet*, I note that she seems to acclaim the closet as an "essential metaphor of the homosexuality that is either 'kept in' or 'let out,' like some particularly active garment..." She presents it as the key to the secrets of many texts. Her interpretation seems to be one more attempt to deconstruct the aporia contemporary literary critics so often seek:

> 'Closetedness' itself is a performance initiated as such by
> the speech act of a silence—not a particular silence, but
> a silence that accrues particularity by fits and starts, in
> relation to the discourse that surrounds and differentially
> constitutes it. (3)

The analysis of the closeted text is specifically literary, but it has a much wider cultural implication, such as in my use of that figure, that the beer drinker might have "read" me. I wish to be read by other gay men, but do not always wish to be so legible to heterosexuals, especially drunken homophobes. Yet that silence of "particularity" suggests that the gay man is "differentially constituted" whether or not he chooses to mark that constitution publicly. Perhaps he might just as well come out.

Mark Blasius, in "An Ethos of Lesbian and Gay Existence," senten-
tiously delineates his ontology of the gay community:

> I begin by arguing that lesbian and gay existence should
> be conceived as an ethos rather than as a sexual preference
> or orientation, as a lifestyle, or primarily in collectivist
> terms, as a subculture, or even as a community. While
> lesbian and gay existence may include some elements of
> these conceptualizations, 'ethos' is a more encompassing
> formulation, better suited for understanding lesbian
> and gay existence politically. I argue that the key to
> understanding ethos is through the lesbian and gay
> conceptualization of 'coming out,' understood as a process
> of becoming in which the individual enters into a field of
> relationships that constitute lesbian and gay community.
> Through this process, the individual participates in a
> collective problematization of self, of types of normativity,
> and of what counts as truth. It is in the relationship that
> the individual creates with her- or himself and with
> others in this practice of the self that is called coming out
> that an ethos emerges. (143)

Most analyses suggest that the importance of the collectivity formed
by Blasius's "ethos" is primarily as a collection of fulfilled individuals.
The American National Coming Out Day was established after the
March on Washington for Lesbian and Gay Rights on October 11, 1987.
One of the organizers was a psychologist, Rob Eichberg, founder of
the self-actualization workshops known as "The Experience." His
book is constantly recommended by gay and lesbian groups. I have
found citations in documents from schools, religious organizations,
community groups, and therapist after therapist. Clearly, Eichberg has
an understanding of the process that appeals to those in the helping
professions who are dealing with people in the closet. The title of his
book, Coming Out: An Act of Love, suggests the tenor of his claims. One might
compare this to the motto of a group such as Queer Nation: "We're Here.

We're Queer. And We're Not Going Shopping." The latter is making an oppositional claim of identity, which seems more of an "ethos" than that described by Blasius, but no doubt such a group is much more narrow in its membership than the homo-inclusive community conceptualized by Blasius. To be "queer" is to be as the derivation suggests, warped, not normal. To be "queer" is to be feared.

According to Eichberg, the "out" person is not frightening, but rather an object of affection. To take this a step further, the self-actualizing approach believes that the closeted gay person cannot be loved because he is not a whole person (a position quite similar to most self-help doctrines, which assume something of "damage," "wound," "trauma" or even just inadequacy). To come out is an "act of love" because it enables the person to love and to be loved. This is not simply a sexual or romantic love, for which there might be a simple logic: you must come out in order to find a same-sex lover. Instead it refers to all love. Your mother might claim, "I love you no matter what you are," but Eichberg's position is that she cannot fully love you because you cannot fully love her until you come out. For Eichberg, "being out" is precisely the term because you cannot *be*, in that full ontology of "be-ing," unless you are out. Thus National Coming Out Day is an annual festival akin to a national birthday. As you might join with others on the fourth of July to celebrate *being* American, you join other gay people to celebrate *being* out. In this case, however, it seems less about being a part of a collectivity, in the sense of an association that surpasses the value of its participants, than it is about being part of a collective celebration of a true individuality.

Throughout this book, it would be tempting to return to Freud again and again. I am trying to avoid too many arbitrary references, but being out, especially in the context of Eichberg's argument, leads to a tangent that seems quite telling. In *Beyond the Pleasure Principle*, Freud goes further than simply identification of the "sex drive." He sees the sex drive as rather a "life drive." In other words, his implicit claim that healthy sex is inevitably heterosexual reproductive sex becomes explicit. When he introduces what is "beyond the pleasure principle," the desire for death, he suggests it is a regressive desire for stasis, to become that unique thing one once was. This is in tension with the progressive desire for reproduction, to produce something new and potentially better than that which already is.

In a therapeutic context, Freud was careful to limit his denigration of homosexuality. He believed it to be a pathology, but also one that did not limit great success and even reasonable psychological health in other aspects of self. Still, his association of homosexuality with melancholia and his emphasis on the links between sexual desire and reproduction seem to place homosexuality in opposition to the pleasure principle. Homosexuals are often attacked for being too intent on pleasure, but Freud's equation suggests the opposite. However, Freud's view is quite different from that of the outing therapists. They see coming out as "an act of love" but even more an act of life. It combines progress and stasis. On the one hand, it is progressive because it moves the person into a new realm, one of full identity. It produces the healthy gay man. On the other hand, it is, like Freud's death drive, the movement towards the past, towards that unique self long lost to a heterosexual socialization. Theoretically anyone might become "homosexual." The only requirement is that the person must identify with those that have same-sex desires. Even actually having sex with another man is not required. Thus someone who sees his gay identity as socially constructed rather than an essence of self could come out. However, my admittedly limited perusal of self-help books on the topic of coming out suggests that few even mention the possibility of anything other than a true, consistent, and potentially coherent identity, homosexual since birth, no matter how repressed. Thus coming out is not becoming something new but rather a return to a stasis previously unacknowledged. The narrative presented by Dollimore is so alien to this mindset that it would be beyond comprehension. According to the coming-out books, one leaves the closet not to enter a new existence but to acknowledge an old essence.

While coming out is individual, perhaps absurdly so, "being out" is a collectivity in many ways, given the number of enterprises that are directly associated with those who are openly gay and lesbian. An obvious example is all the community groups that use "out" in the title, from the segment of Alcoholics Anonymous called "Out and Sober" to the adventurers club called "Out and Out." One of the most prominent magazines in the culture is simply named *Out*. Early in its existence, *Out* offered subscriptions in a plain brown wrapper. The practical explanation, of course, is that it was an ideal magazine for someone preparing to come out but not yet ready. The irony of this closeting wrapper is, however, obvious.

There are many aspects of gay culture that depend on "outness." Catherine Nash's "Siting Lesbians: Urban Spaces and Sexuality" considers the importance of openly lesbian businesses in a community. The common term "gay ghetto" has resonances that those who employ it often forget. While the historical ghetto was created to keep Jews within, it also, like any enclave, left non-Jews outside. It is but one of many examples where restrictions lead to an ironic support: all who are so restricted in place are yet comforted by the knowledge that all in that place are one with them. Thus in major North American cities, small gay ghettos existed long before there was any concept of being out. Those who lived there, worked there, played there, knew they were in a strange porous place of visibility/invisibility. While many straight people passed through without even noticing they were in a special land of sexual orientation, the gay population and most of the straight residents knew exactly where they were and functioned accordingly.

One aspect of truth and authority is the ideal of "Pride Day." In a typical opposition, one cannot be ashamed for being gay if one marches in a parade labeled as "pride." In most cities, the parade centres on the gay ghetto and thus it becomes the geographic heartland of being out. This seems similar to the medieval fair as depicted by Stallybrass and White. They assert that the medieval fair was "a site of pleasure" and also "a commercial event." (30) No matter how disreputable, it had a commercial value, but as its apparent negative qualities were more contained, the commercial value became more powerful. Thus many argue that the commercialization of the gay ghetto and of Pride Day is problematic, as they lose their sense of opposition to the straight world. Yet as Stallybrass and White state of the fair:

> However, such oppositional splitting into incompatibles
> required much conceptual (and material) labour. The fair
> as a site of hybridization epistemologically undermined
> the separation of the economic from 'play' and the clean
> from the dirty. As a result the emergent middle classes
> worried away at it, particularly striving to separate and
> consolidate the binaries which the fair so mischievously
> attempted to intermix and confuse. (31)

The bourgeois gay life, in which to be out seems to have little negative effect, seems to follow exactly this model. Thus the boundaries are emphatically defined so all know where the gay area is and yet the boundaries are also blurred because the social and commercial activities are so similar within and without. Both those within and without try to create new separations from the dirty as they seek restrictions on the amount of nudity of Pride Day, the implications of overt leather wear, and any open displays of sexuality.

Many gay people are uncomfortable with such elements of Pride Day, which to them seem too out. Whenever I said something a bit too overt about gay sex in mixed company, one boyfriend of mine revealingly would say, "Not in front of the neighbours." As I mention in the "Stranger" chapter, while almost all gay people accept forms of sexual practice that most straight people find off-putting, such as the baths, few of them wish such practice to be part of the gay profile "outed" to outsiders. A straight woman friend of mine was visiting Toronto on Pride Day, and walking back to her hotel late at night, she encountered two men fucking in a well-lit public passageway near the subway. She described herself as "shocked," but did not seem offended. I think I was offended. While I would find such practice erotic in the baths, or even perhaps in the bushes in a dimly lit park, in such a bright setting visible to anyone, underneath Toronto's landmark hotel, it went beyond my boundaries of "out."

But now that I think of it, even in bright sunlight I might have found this acceptable within the boundaries of the ghetto. In *A Queer Geography: Journeys Toward a Sexual Self*, Frank Browning tellingly observes:

> More than any genuine ethnic group, gay people owe
> their existence *as a separate people* to geography. Original
> as homosexual desire may be to human beings, the
> arrival of gay people as a coherent social presence and
> political force owes everything to the transformations
> of modern urban geography. (2)

Whenever there are complaints about certain performances or signs within the ghetto having too much nudity or too overt sexual references, someone answers, "They know where they are." Of course, the problem is usually a display of penises. While the terminology in descriptions is often genderless, as in Browning's "gay people," the culture is highly masculinized. Apologies to the lesbians who are residents, business owners, and activists, but, with very few exceptions, gay ghettos today are as they have been since their beginnings, marked by gay males. Some of the reasons for this are obvious. One that follows the observation about the increased commercialization of gay culture is that males have a much higher disposable income. This is especially true of gay males, who seldom have custody of children, unlike lesbians, who often have children. Another consideration, however, is the unusually public tradition of gay men, as noted in the "Stranger" chapter. To consider the environment that I know best, the Church and Wellesley district of Toronto, there are many restaurants with very public eating areas. These provide an opportunity to see and be seen, but they also require that the individual be out of the closet. This might seem unnecessary, in that many heterosexuals eat there, although usually only in association with gay friends. However, the assumption is that any male who eats there is gay. Someone in the closet is not likely to enjoy the implications.

Yet there is no obvious implication about sexual practice. Presumably many of the men in these restaurants lead quite celibate lives. This is in contrast with the bathhouses, where there are "out" people as well as many who are closeted. In spite of the fact you can often see men in the baths chatting over a coffee, there is a general understanding that no talking is expected beyond that necessary to decide on sexual activity. It is an optimum place for those in the closet to find sex. You might be recognized by someone from your Bible studies group, but if you never acknowledge that you saw him, you will both be, if not comfortable, perhaps satisfied. This is one of the reasons the typical bathhouse is itself in the closet. In Toronto, most are near but not within the gay ghetto. It must seem surprising to many outsiders that few have signs outside the building or even a minimal marker on the door itself. This might be explained as a reflection of the history of harassment by police. However, presumably no one believes that the police are under any delusion as to where bathhouses are. Similarly, the gay community is very happy to discuss "the tubs" and has no doubt about locations. The bathhouses are in the closet to assure those in the closet that they can have sex in secure premises and remain in the closet.

It would be tempting to over-rate the symbolic import of these hidden dens of opportunity. Still, the fact that the place most identifiable as a place of same-sex activity is also the least identifiable is suggestive. Being out might appear to be a comment on sexual activity, but it is only minimally so. Those in the baths might fear coming out, but they may also have no interest in it. Many no doubt want heterosexual privilege, although there could be some who simply do not want to assume a sexual identity. Browning observes: "Like many homosexual men, I cherish and am aroused by the curtains of secrecy that surround sex.... The easy vernacular of *outness*, however, leaves no room for shrouded, furtive, disguised sex." (117)

Browning's comment might just be a desire for some association of the perverse with sexuality, something Freud noted to be a part of all sexuality. As Freud said, arousal for one person is often associated with something that another would see as disgusting. Coming close to the boundary between the two is exciting to most humans. But perhaps there is something particular for gay men. The history of homophobia and the various forms of isolation experienced by gay men have meant that almost all gay sex has been in the hegemonic category of disgust. Thus a homosexual knows that his sex must be between two men, but he recognizes at the same time—or even before—that his sex must be hidden. As I explore in the chapter "The Homo####ual Child," this is a lesson learned at his mother's knee. Thus no matter how out the gay man is, there will be a residual recognition of sex as an activity not too far from a dark and scary closet. Where the wild things are?

To come out, to be "gay," is at least to some degree to accept the choice of sexual object as a definition of self. It is interesting therefore to note those who have come out as gay, only to come out later as an S/M practitioner, or as a transsexual, and no longer to be as invested in the gay identity activities to which they had been committed previously. The transsexual decides that "gay" is simply a misrecognition of self, but the S/M practitioner has decided that "gay" is insufficient to identify a person who feels a primary identity not through sexual object but through sexual aim. Then there are the aberrations such as the Republican Party gay caucus, Log Cabin Republicans, who conservatives reject because Republicans can't be homosexuals and who gays reject because homosexuals can't be Republicans. Clearly, personal recognition and declamation of sexual object is the beginning of being out, but it is never that simple.

In my own life, I call myself "out" as a gay man in the face of many contradictions. While publicly gay, in newspapers, my writing, and my employment, I am often privately in the closet, as with my neighbours, and in my decision to live with a woman and have a daughter and son. We probably seem the portrait of heterosexuality. In the world of the Internet, of course, I am only a Google away from being outed by anyone. Recently, a neighbour went from being friendly to being wary. I mentioned this to my partner and she said, "She Googled." Still, the "partial closet" is inevitable for all of us. Some might try to be "out" in all contexts, such as the playwright Tony Kushner, but without some constant visible denotation, this is not possible. Perhaps self-outing should be a religious ritual, so every two hours each person could say "I'm gay" to a stranger. Ridiculous as this might seem, all possible alternatives are problematic. The assumption that all gay people should in some sense "look gay" could lead only to the reaffirmation of stereotypes, or more likely a ubiquity of rainbow buttons, the elective labeling to replace the pejorative one so often forced on deviants. In many contexts, any overt label would be life-threatening. It is difficult to think of an appropriate analogy, but perhaps the Sikh turban is one. One might think that any North American would recognize the religious identity of a person wearing a turban, but in the paranoia following 9/11, various instances when Sikhs were mistaken as Muslims show that this is not the case. A number of commentators have noted how fatiguing it is for gay activists who feel the need to assert a gay identity in every new venue on every new occasion. Think of your primary "hidden" identity markers, those of you who are, say, "closet" bowlers or bassoonists (both true of me to the surprise of many), and think of the need to ensure verbally and visually that everyone you meet knows of this identity. We have seen the closet and it is us.

But both that closet and that "us" are highly variable markers. Regardless of the growing acceptance of homosexuality in North American culture, there are many for whom coming out might be liberating but it can also be dangerous. I have never been, for any reason, in that state bordering on suicide so common for men feeling unstoppable pressure to reveal their homosexuality. Although I had been married to a woman, I was single when I came out and my parents were dead. Thus two of the major problems in the coming-out narrative, spouse and family of origin, were not an issue. I had two children, which created my primary difficulties in my day-to-day life. One of them became involved with a rather rough crowd and when I said I would pick her up at a certain building, her "friend" said, "Don't. They kill fags there." Pleasant. On the other hand, my ex-wife was quite supportive. In the present climate, coming out was arguably a good career move for an English professor.

I became most aware of the other side of coming out when I joined a group called the Gay Fathers. Most of the men were in occupations that precluded coming out. A suburban accountant believed he would lose half his practice if all his golfing and barbecuing buddies knew he was gay. While I had expected the discussions at the Gay Fathers to be mainly about dealing with children, in most cases it was about dealing with the absence thereof. A number of men were prevented by their ex-wives from even seeing their children. They could, of course, pursue legal redress, but some felt this would only add to their pain. In some cases there were also religious issues. I was surprised to find how many of those associated with explicitly gay-positive religions or parishes of the more moderate established religions came from explicitly homophobic religious backgrounds, usually cultures in which their ex-wives had become even more enmeshed after they came out. After being rejected by the Church of the Latter Day Saints or orthodox Judaism, these men felt even more need to find a venue in which they could practice their religion and be out. In many cases, however, their joy at sexual acceptance was somewhat in conflict with the liturgical liberalism. They were somewhat like Log Cabin Christians.

Presumably we all need to belong somewhere, but these men seemed to feel it even more strongly. I found a surprising insight into their situation in Sara Ahmed's *Strange Encounters: Embodied Others in Post-Coloniality*. She writes, "The analogy between the ideal neighbourhood and a healthy body serves to define the ideal neighbourhood as fully integrated, homogeneous, and sealed: it is like a body that is fully contained by the skin." (25) For me, having developed a liberal and rather undefined social life, alongside a liberal and often overtly progressive occupation, my difference was confusing but not a threat. Of course, all of us in the Gay Fathers were privileged to avoid many of the world's limitations. We were all North American, predominantly middle class and mainly white. Still, the other members seemed to have needs that I seldom felt. I have usually identified more with Jamake Highwater's sentiments, as expressed in the revealingly titled *The Mythology of Transgression: Homosexuality as Metaphor*: "Yet, for me, being 'left out' has always been a luxury, because it allowed me to evade the rules governing conformity." (10) Thus for me acknowledging that difference that I had always felt, that had left me "out" in Highwater's sense, through coming out, was as liberating as the books told me it should be. The men from the Gay Fathers had been living in that "ideal neighbourhood" and had been taught that the "different" was a disease invading that fully contained body. They were being invaded by themselves and needed a new neighbourhood. For them, "outside" had been a threat, but now they were being forced to be out.

Are there ways in which I behave either as a repressed homosexual the more I am within the closet or as a more functional person the more I am "out"? I find a few beginning answers in the process of identification. In her very useful book, *Identification Papers*, Diana Fuss reflects on Lacan's comments on "Identification with the object of love." Fuss continues, "Identification, in other words, invokes phantoms. By incorporating the spectral remains of the dearly departed love-object, the subject vampiristically comes to life." (1) This is that first process of identification, the one that gives rise to assumptions about homosexual melancholia, in which the homosexual makes the error of seeing the same as the love object instead of seeing the other as the love object. As Fuss states:

> Freud distinguishes identification (the wish to be the
> other) from sexual object-choice (the wish to have the
> other). For Freud, desire for one sex is always secured
> through identification with the other sex; to desire and to
> identify with the same person at the same time is, in this
> model, a theoretical impossibility. (11)

Still, as Lacan shows, there is often more similarity than difference between desire for and desire to be. Thus the subject begins to identify the self through this identification. As Lacan states, every process of recognition is a misrecognition in which the subject mistakes that which is other for the self and that which is self for the other.

Most of us—a first person plural by which I think I mean gay intellectuals—see a homosexual identity as too simple and would be more
comfortable with a homosexual identification. This would be defined
both by desire for men and by, if not a desire to be definitively "gay,"
at least a desire for a misrecognition with other gay males that leads
to that unity for which Young, Blasius, and so many others hope. For
many of us, this unity is not just a political gesture. It goes beyond what
Freud saw as the voluntary associations of identification through which
one participates in an identity group. The feminist philosopher Lorraine Code maintains that a woman's understanding of herself is always
shaped by stereotypes of what that self could be:

> ... a principal requirement of epistemically responsible
> knowing centres about the need to become aware of the
> extent to which stereotypes govern perception and shape
> alleged knowledge (both one's own, and those of other
> members of one's epistemic community). It is part of
> responsible epistemic practice to work towards freeing
> cognitive activity from such constraining influences: this
> is an indispensable first step in the project of developing
> an epistemological approach that can maintain continuity
> with experience. (190)

Those of us who are self-consciously gay, and especially those of us
who work in gay studies, wish to recognize such stereotypes and deal
with the ambivalence that they reflect. While we realize they inevitably
shape our views and actions, we hope that our "experience" will offer at
least some "freeing" from the stereotypes at the same time as we must
live within them. Coming out of the closet is both a stereotype and a
liberation.

In trying to work through various aspects of the subject in *The Sublime
Object of Ideology*, Slavoj Žižek turns to certain foundation texts, one of
which is *Das Capital*. Marx attempts to understand commodity as:

> This *inversion* through which what is sensible and concrete

> counts only as a phenomenal form of what is abstract and
> universal, contrary to the real state of things where the
> abstract and the universal count only as a property of the
> concrete.... (32)

I use this passage in an attempt to find Code's "epistemically responsible
knowing centre." It seems to me that there is a constant assertion in the
gay community that there is a gay identity which must be true, self-
defined, and united, but this is actually a commodity that gains value
through being abstract and universal. This gives it the power that Hacking
describes. In the context I am discussing here, it is a commodity chosen
by some men who sense, who find "sensible" and "concrete," sexual
desire for other men. Among these men are those who feel no desire for
a female sex object, and also many men who feel desire for many other
objects. Among these men who identify with the word "gay" as opposed
to other sexual identities are no doubt many whose primary sexual
object could provide them with an identity that is far more dangerously
hidden than "homosexual." S/M is one, but it is still less prohibited than
others. From my studies, there is no reason to assume homosexuals have
more "perversions" than heterosexuals but neither is there any reason
to assume they have significantly fewer. Thus if homosexuals are one to
ten percent of the population they are probably also one to ten percent
of pedophiles, one to ten percent of necrophiles, one to ten percent of
those attracted to bestiality, and so on.

For these men, coming out as gay is a mark that is potentially pejorative, but it could seem to preclude the dangers of a still more damning
label. But what of those for whom "straight" is dangerous? I am particularly interested in the role of the closet in my social experiences with
people of different genders. My own practice has been bisexual. I have
experienced many taboos, based on both homosexual and heterosexual
panic. One example of the latter happened when a female undergraduate student told me that she slept with her male tutorial leader. Given
that he was a teaching assistant in a different department and given that
my student felt in no sense misused, I saw no need to divulge this infor-

mation to anyone. But I mentioned it in passing, without any suggestion of the student's identity, to a colleague. She suggested that I should be more careful about engaging in such a dangerously intimate conversation with a student who already has experience of crossing the professor/student boundary. I replied that I have often had such discussions in the past and never had any trouble. She said, "But back then you were known to be gay, now you are living with a woman." Rather shocked, I said, "You mean I had a free pass that I have now lost?" "Exactly." This seems to me the beginning of heterosexual panic. At least mine.

A friend once said to me, "No one would ever accuse you of being in the closet." My female partner has said, "How could anyone accuse you of being in the closet?" There are many aspects of my performance that reflect this. A gay friend wrote me an email when he saw a book that published an earlier version of the "Dragging Feminism?" chapter. He wrote, "I am holding a book in my hands that has a photograph of Terry Goldie. In a dress." He and I have not discussed his email, other than to repeat it as a good story, but I presume he has never been photographed in a dress. If he has ever done drag, he has never told me. But his sexual orientation is public and consistent, with his prominent participation in gay activism going back twenty years. He seldom does anything that screams "OUT," but his life is so consistently out that there can be no question of the possibility of being in. Yet even in his case, no matter how many times or how consistently he comes out, there are times and places when he goes back in, as do we all. Mariana Valverde said that there is no such thing as a bisexual. According to her analysis someone whose sexual practice is bisexual instead switches periodically between the homosexual and the heterosexual identities. Each time I exhibit any type of "couple" gesture with my girlfriend, I seem to be once more shutting the closet door simply by opening the heterosexual freeway.

I often think there is no answer. Many years ago one of my students gave a quite intelligent and useful presentation on the homoerotic. Another student, someone who took the expression "openly gay" to all possible extremes, said, "He's never sucked cock in his life." So is my role here, as someone caught in that revolving door, forever to reply to that long-gone student that "yes I have, and often," like some gay ancient mariner? A number of friends, gay and straight, have questioned my openness in including a chapter on anal eroticism. Is it necessary to be much more public on all aspects of my sexual practice than I would be if there were no reason to question me as "gay"? Very few of us know anything about the sexual practice of our friends, but we are quite comfortable in delineating others as "straight" or "gay." When was the last time you were at a cocktail party where someone said, "Oh yes, my uncle Fred lives with a woman but he likes it up the ass."

The only role I can find is one in which I verbally open the door as often as possible. Rather than comforting myself with the term "bisexual," I continue to call myself gay, as a statement of "self-identification," of "unity," and even, contrary though it might seem, of "truth." This is a word that resonates in this context. Lacan's "Seminar on the Purloined Letter" seems to suggest that truth is found by the analyst simply through the rational power of that analysis. In Freud's account of his first psychoanalysis, "truth" is known by the analysand herself, but she does not recognize it as truth until the analyst engages this knowledge in a way that allows the analysand to label it as truth. In the world of the gay—not the homosexual but the "gay"—the truth is singular: gay.

This seems remarkably similar to the account of truth in J.M. Coetzee's novel, *Waiting for the Barbarians*. When the colonel claims that he is able to judge when a prisoner is telling the truth, the magistrate, caught by his liberal humanism, is amazed and impressed. While he clearly finds the colonel to be a vile agent of the worst elements of the oppressive state, he cannot help but be fascinated by this possibility. But then the colonel tells him that the truth is what arises after torture, when he finally hears what he had wanted to hear. Thus "truth" is identified by the torturer, in a fashion not unlike Freud's account of the beginnings of psychoanalysis, with his hands pressing on Elizabeth R's forehead. One friend told me of growing up sissy and heterosexual. He made an attempt to be gay ,but found it does not suit his sexual practice. He returned to being heterosexual. In other words, he talks like a duck, he walks like a duck, yet he finds he is a rooster. This is no doubt not the end of the story. Anyone who manifests as many gay signifiers as he does will be outed constantly. His claims that he is not gay will just lead to him being labeled as closeted, as someone unable to deal with that larger and inevitable truth.

So many theorists, from Foucault to Lacan, have noted that truth has little social or psychological value outside of authority. Few wish to assert a "truth" that offers no power, no authorization to do something. Thus there must be positive attributes to this claim or it would not be made. In this context, moreover, there can be no authority if the truth loses its possibility. In an episode of *Desperate Housewives*, a man beats up a gardener because he believes his wife is having an affair with him. The gardener reveals, "I'm gay." In the narrative of the popular soap opera, this means the affair could not have happened. If, however, "gay" does not have a unitary truth, then there is no authority to this statement and the plotline becomes lost.

And yet I personally attempt to continue that sense of truth by labeling myself gay in spite of my personal circumstances, because I find my object of desire has not wavered, although the object of my love seems to contradict that. So I resort to that last refuge of scoundrels, irony. I gave my female partner a T-shirt that I bought in our local home of the "out," Toronto's gay ghetto. The T-shirt reads, "I'm not gay, but my boyfriend is."

# Works Cited

Abramovitch, Henry. "Images of the 'Father' in Psychology and Religion." *The Role of the Father in Child Development*. Third Edition. Ed. Michael E. Lamb. New York: John Wiley & Sons, 1997. 19-32.

Ahmed, Sara. *Strange Encounters: Embodied Others in Post-Coloniality*. London: Routledge, 2000.

Altman, Dennis. *Global Sex*. Chicago: University of Chicago Press, 2001.

Archer, Bert. *The End of Gay: (And the Death of Heterosexuality)*. Toronto: Doubleday, 1999.

Barret, Robert L. and Bryan E. Robinson. *Gay Fathers: Encouraging the Hearts of Gay Dads and Their Families*. San Francisco: Jossey-Bass, 2000.

Behar, Ruth. *The Vulnerable Observer: Anthropology that Breaks Your Heart*. Boston: Beacon Press, 1996.

Bergling, Tim. *Sissyphobia: Gay Men and Effeminate Behavior*. New York: Harrington Press, 2001.

Bersani, Leo. "Is the Rectum a Grave?" *AIDS: Cultural Analysis/Cultural Activism*. Ed. Douglas Crimp. Cambridge, Mass: MIT Press, 1988. 197-222.

Bigner, Jerry J. and Frederick W. Bozett. "Parenting by Gay Fathers." *Homosexuality and Family Relations*. Ed. Frederick W. Bozett and Marvin B. Sussman. New York: Haworth Press, 1989. 155-175.

Bigner, Jerry J. and R. Brooke Jacobsen. "Parenting Behaviors of Homosexual and Heterosexual Fathers." *Homosexuality and the Family*. Ed. Frederick W. Bozett. New York: The Haworth Press, 1989. 173-186.

Bigner, Jerry J. and R. Brooke Jacobsen. "The Value of Children to Gay and Heterosexual Fathers." *Homosexuality and the Family*. Ed. Frederick W. Bozett. New York: The Haworth Press, 1989. 163-172.

Biller, Henry B. and Jon Lopez Kimpton. "The Father and the School-Aged Child." *The Role of the Father in Child Development*. Third Edition. Ed. Michael E. Lamb. New York: John Wiley & Sons, 1997. 143-161.

Blasius, Mark. "An Ethos of Lesbian and Gay Existence." *Sexual Identities, Queer Politics*. Ed. Mark Blasius. Princeton: Princeton University Press, 2001. 143-177.

Blum, Deborah. *Sex on the Brain: The Biological Differences between Men and Women*. New York: Viking, 1997.

Bly, Robert. *Iron John: A Book About Men.* Reading, Mass.: Addison-Wesley Publishing, 1990.

Bogaert, Anthony F. and Scott Hershberger. "The Relation Between Sexual Orientation and Penile Size." *Archives of Sexual Behavior* 28.3 (1999): 213-221.

Bohan, Janis S. *Psychology and Sexual Orientation: Coming to Terms.* New York: Routledge, 1996.

Boscagli, Maurizia. *Eye on the Flesh: Fashions of Masculinity in the Early Twentieth Century.* Boulder: Westview Press, 1996.

Bozett, Frederick W. "Children of Gay Fathers." *Gay and Lesbian Parents.* Ed. Frederick W. Bozett. New York: Praeger, 1987. 39-57.

Bozett, Frederick W. "Gay Fathers." *Gay and Lesbian Parents.* Ed. Frederick W. Bozett. New York: Praeger, 1987. 3-22.

Bozett, Frederick W. "Gay Fathers: A Review of the Literature." *Homosexuality and the Family.* Ed. Frederick W. Bozett. New York: The Haworth Press, 1989. 137-162.

Bristow, Joseph and Angelia R. Wilson. "Introduction." *Activating Theory: Lesbian, Gay, Bisexual Politics.* Ed. Joseph Bristow and Angelia R. Wilson. London: Lawrence & Wishart, 1993. 1-15.

Brodzinsky, David M.; Daniel W. Smith and Anne B. Brodzinsky. *Children's Adjustment to Adoption: Developmental and Clinical Issues.* Thousand Oaks, Calif.: Sage, 1998.

Brott, Armin A. *The Single Father: A Dad's Guide to Parenting Without a Partner.* New York: Abbeville Press, 1999.

Browning, Frank. *A Queer Geography: Journeys Toward a Sexual Self.* New York: Farrar, Straus and Giroux, 1996.

Bruner, Jerome. "The Autobiographical Process." *The Culture of Autobiography: Constructions of Self-Representation.* Ed. Robert Folkenflik. Stanford: Stanford University Press, 1993. 38-56.

Burton, Anna. "The Meaning of Perineal Activity to Women: An Inner Sphinx." *Journal of the American Psychoanalytic Association* 44 Suppl (1996): 241-59.

Butler, Judith. *Bodies That Matter: On the Discursive Limits of Sex.* New York: Routledge, 1993.

———. "Critically Queer," *Gay and Lesbian Quarterly* 1. 1993: 17-32.

———. *Excitable Speech: A Politics of the Performative.* New York: Routledge, 1997.

———. *Gender Trouble: Feminism and the Subversion of Identity.* New York: Routledge, 1990.

Castle, Terry. *The Apparitional Lesbian: Female Homosexuality and Modern Culture.* New York: Columbia University Press, 1993.

Chauncey, George. *Gay New York: Gender, Urban Culture, and the Making of the Gay Male World 1890-1940.* New York: Basic Books, 1994.

Clatts, Michael C. "Ethnographic Observations of Men Who Have Sex with Men in Public: Toward an Ecology of Sexual Action." *Public Sex/Gay Space.* Ed. William L. Leap. New York: Columbia University Press, 1999. 141-155.

Code, Lorraine. "Experience, Knowledge and Responsibility." *Feminist Perspectives in Philosophy.* Ed. Morwenna Griffiths and Margaret Whitford. Bloomington: Indiana University Press, 1988. 187-204.

Coetzee, J. M. *Waiting for the Barbarians.* Harmondsworth: Penguin, 1980.

Cole, Robert A. "Promising to Be a Man: Promise Keepers and the Organizational Constitution of Masculinity." *The Promise Keepers: Essays on Masculinity and Christianity.* Ed. Diane S. Claussen. Jefferson, N.C.: McFarland & Co., 2000. 113-132.

Cooper, Carolyn. *Noises in the Blood: Orality, Gender, and the "Vulgar" Body of Jamaican Popular Culture.* Durham: Duke University Press, 1995.

Corbett, Ken. "Homosexual Boyhood: Notes on Girlyboys." *Sissies and Tomboys: Gender Nonconformity and Homosexual Childhood.* Ed. Matthew Rottnek. New York: New York University Press, 1999. 107-139.

Crozier, Lorna. "Overture." *Angels of Flesh, Angels of Silence.* Toronto: McClelland and Stewart, 1988. 75.

Cummings, E. Mark and Anne Watson O'Reilly. "Fathers in Family Context: Effects of Marital Quality on Child Adjustment." *The Role of the Father in Child Development.* Third Edition. Ed. Michael E. Lamb. New York: John Wiley & Sons, 1997. 49-65.

Dalziell, Rosamund. *Shameful Autobiographies: Shame in Contemporary Australian Autobiographies and Culture.* Melbourne: Melbourne University Press, 1999.

Davidson, Arnold I. *The Emergence of Sexuality: Historical Epistemology and the Formation of Concepts.* Cambridge: Harvard University Press, 2001.

Dean, Tim. *Beyond Sexuality.* Chicago: University of Chicago Press, 2000.

Deleuze, Gilles. "Bergson's Conception of Difference." Trans. Melissa McMahon. *The New Bergson.* Ed. John Mullarkey. Manchester: Manchester University Press, 1999. 42-65.

D'Emilio, John. *Sexual Politics: Sexual Communities: The Making of a Homosexual Community in the United States 1940-1970.* Chicago: University of Chicago Press, 1998.

Dimen, Muriel. "On 'Our Nature': Prolegomenon to a Relational Theory of Sexuality." *Disorienting Sexuality: Psychoanalytic Reappraisals of Sexual Identities.* Ed. Thomas Domenici, Ronnie C. Lesser, and Adrienne Harris. New York: Routledge, 1995. 129-152.

Dollimore, Jonathan. *Sex, Literature and Censorship.* Cambridge: Polity Press, 2001.

Domenici, Thomas. "Exploding the Myth of Sexual Psychopathology: A Deconstruction of Fairbairn's Anti-Homosexual Theory." *Disorienting Sexuality: Psychoanalytic Reappraisals of Sexual Identities.* Ed. Thomas Domenici, Ronnie C. Lesser, and Adrienne Harris. New York: Routledge, 1995. 33-63.

Douglas, Mary. *Purity and Danger: An Analysis of Concepts of Pollution and Taboo.* London: Routledge and Kegan Paul, 1966.

Dowsett, Gary W. *Practicing Desire: Homosexual Sex in the Era of AIDS.* Stanford: Stanford University Press, 1996.

Du Plessis, Michael. "Blatantly Bisexual: Or, Unthinking Queer Theory." *RePresenting Bisexualities: Subjects and Cultures of Fluid Desire.* Ed. Donald E. Hall and Maria Pramaggiore. New York: New York University Press, 1996. 19-54.

Eichberg, Robert. *Coming Out: An Act of Love.* New York: Plume, 1991

Ekins, Richard. *Male Femaling: A Grounded Approach to Cross-Dressing and Sex-Changing.* New York: Routledge, 1997.

Fausto-Sterling, Anne. *Sexing the Body: Gender Politics and the Construction of Sexuality.* New York: Basic Books, 2000.

Frank, Robert. *The Involved Father: Family-Tested Solutions for Getting Dads to Participate More in the Daily Lives of Their Children.* New York: Golden Books, 1999.

Freud, Sigmund. *The Standard Edition of the Complete Psychological Works of Sigmund Freud.* Translated from the German under the general editorship of James Strachey, in collaboration with Anna Freud, assisted by Alix Strachey and Alan Tyson. London: The Hogarth Press and the Institute of Psychoanalysis, 1953-74.

Friedman, David M. *A Mind of Its Own: A Cultural History of the Penis.* New York: The Free Press, 2001.

Friedman, Richard C. *Male Homosexuality: A Contemporary Psychoanalytic Perspective.* New Haven: Yale University Press, 1988.

Frommer, Martin Stephen. "Offending Gender: Being and Wanting in Male Same-Sex Desire." *Studies in Gender and Sexuality* 1:2(2000): 191-206.

Fuss, Diana. *Identification Papers: Readings on Psychoanalysis, Sexuality, and Culture.* New York: Routledge, 1995.

Gage, Simon, Lisa Richards and Howard Wilmot. *Queer.* New York: Thunder's Mouth Press, 2002.

Gallop, Jane. *Thinking Through the Body.* New York: Columbia University Press, 1988.

Garber, Marjorie. *Vested Interests: Cross-dressing & Cultural Anxiety.* New York: Harper Collins, 1992.

Gay, Peter. *The Tender Passion.* New York: Oxford University Press, 1986.

Gill, Libby. *Stay-At-Home Dads: The Essential Guide to Creating the New Family.* New York: Plume, 2001.

Gilligan, Carol. *In a Different Voice.* Boston: Harvard University Press, 1982

Goldie, Terry, ed. *In a Queer Country: Gay & Lesbian Studies in the Canadian Context.* Vancouver: Arsenal Pulp Press, 2001.

———. *Pink Snow: Homotextual Possibilities in Canadian Fiction.* Peterborough: Broadview, 2003.

Green, Richard. *The "Sissy Boy Syndrome" and the Development of Homosexuality.* New Haven: Yale University Press, 1987.

Grosz, Elizabeth. *Space, Time and Perversion: Essays on the Politics of Bodies.* New York: Routledge, 1995.

———. *Volatile Bodies: Toward a Corporeal Feminism.* Bloomington: Indiana University Press, 1994.

Gull, Richard. "The Anti-Metaphysics Game: A Wittgensteinian Reading of *The Crying Game." Film and Knowledge: Essays on the Integration of Images and Ideas.* Ed. Kevin L. Stoehr. Jefferson, N.C.: McFarland & Co., 2002. 81-94.

Gunderson, Bjørn Helge, Per Steinar Melås and Jens E. Skår. "Sexual Behavior of Preschool Children: Teachers' Observations." *Childhood and Sex: New Findings, New Perspectives.* Ed. Larry L. Constantine and Floyd M. Martinson. Boston: Little Brown, 1981. 45-61.

Hacking, Ian. "Making Up People." *Forms of Desire: Sexual Orientation and the Social Constructionist Controversy.* Ed. Edward Stein. New York: Routledge, 1992. 69-88. [Originally in Thomas Heller, Morton Sosna and David Wellbery, eds. *Reconstructing Individualism: Autonomy, Individuality and the Self in Western Thought.* Stanford: Stanford University Press, 1986]

Hall, Donald E. "BI-ntroduction II: Epistemologies of the Fence." *RePresenting Bisexualities: Subjects and Cultures of Fluid Desire.* Ed. Donald E. Hall and Maria Pramaggiore. New York: New York University Press, 1996. 8-16.

Hamming, Jeanne E. "Dildonics, Dykes and the Detachable Masculine." *European Journal of Women's Studies*. 8.3 (2001): 329-341.

Harding, Jennifer. *Sex Acts: Practices of Femininity and Masculinity*. London: Sage, 1998.

Haver, William. *The Body of This Death: Historicity and Sociality in the Time of AIDS*. Stanford: Stanford University Press, 1996.

Hemmings, Claire. *Bisexual Spaces: A Geography of Sexuality and Gender*. New York: Routledge, 2002.

Hemmings, Claire. "Resituating the Bisexual Body: From Identity to Difference." *Activating Theory: Lesbian, Gay, Bisexual Politics*. Ed. Joseph Bristow and Anglia R. Wilson. London: Lawrence & Wishart, 1993. 118-138.

Hewlett, Barry S. "Introduction." *Father-Child Relations: Cultural and Biosocial Contexts*. New York: Aldine de Gruyter, 1992. xi-xix.

Highwater, Jamake. *The Mythology of Transgression: Homosexuality as Metaphor*. New York: Oxford University Press, 1997.

Hollister, John. "A Highway Rest Area as a Socially Reproducible Site." *Public Sex/Gay Space*. Ed. William L. Leap. New York: Columbia University Press, 1999. 55-70.

Howe, David. *Patterns of Adoption: Nature, Nurture and Psychosocial Development*. Oxford: Blackwell Science, 1998.

Humphreys, Laud. "Tearoom Trade: Impersonal Sex in Public Places." *Public Sex/ Gay Space*. Ed. William L. Leap. New York: Columbia University Press, 1999. 29-54. [Originally in *Tearoom Trade: Impersonal Sex in Public Places*. Chicago: Aldine, 1970. Second edition 1975]

Ingram, Gordon Brent. "Redesigning Wreck: Beach Meets Forest as Location of Male Homoerotic Culture & Placemaking in Pacific Canada." *In a Queer Country: Gay & Lesbian Studies in the Canadian Context*. Ed. Terry Goldie. Vancouver: Arsenal Pulp Press, 2001. 188-208.

Ingram, Michael. "Participating Victims: A Study of Sexual Offenses with Boys." *Childhood and Sex: New Findings, New Perspectives*. Ed. Larry L. Constantine and Floyd M. Martinson. Boston: Little Brown, 1981. 177-187.

Jay, Karla and Allen Young, eds. *After You're Out: Personal Experiences of Gay Men and Lesbian Women*. New York: Links, 1975.

Johnson, Bret K. *Coming Out Every Day: A Gay, Bisexual and Questioning Man's Guide*. New York: New Harbinger, 1997.

Kalamka, Juba. "How Can I Be Down? A bisexual black man's take on 'the down low'." *Colorlines* 7:4 (Winter 2004-2005) http://www.arc.org/C_Lines/CLArchive/story7_4_02.html.

Kaplan, Louise J. *Female Perversions: The Temptations of Emma Bovary.* New York: Doubleday, 1991.

Kennedy, Sheldon (with James Grainger). *Why I Didn't Say Anything: The Sheldon Kennedy Story.* Toronto: Insomniac Press, 2006.

Khan, Shivananda, *Making Visible the Invisible: Sexuality and Sexual Health in South Asia: A Focus on Male to Male Sexual Behaviours.* London: The Naz Foundation, [1996] .

Kincaid, James. R. *Child-Loving: The Erotic Child and Victorian Culture.* London: Routledge, 1992.

King, Michael. *Splendours of Civilisation: The John Money Collection at the Eastern Southland Gallery.* Dunedin, New Zealand: Eastern Southland Gallery in association with Longacre Press, 2006.

King Missile. "Detachable Penis." *www.anysonglyrics.com/lyrics/k/kingmissile/detachablepenis.htm.*

Kipnis, Kenneth and Milton Diamond. "Pediatric Ethics and the Surgical Assignment of Sex." *The Journal of Clinical Ethics,* 9.4 (Winter 1998): 398-410.

Klein, Fritz. *The Bisexual Option.* Second Edition. Binghamton, NY: Haworth Press, 1993.

Krisel, William. "Regarding 'The Relation Between Sexual Orientation and Penile Size,' by A. F. Bogaert, and S. Hershberger (*Archives of Sexual Behavior* 28.3 [1999]: 213-221) *Archives of Sexual Behavior* 29.3 (2000): 303-304.

Kulick, Don. "The Gender of Brazilian Transgendered Prostitutes." *The Masculinity Studies Reader.* Ed. Rachel Adams and David Savran. Oxford: Blackwell, 2002. 389-407. [Originally in *American Anthropologist* 99/3 (1997), 574-84.]

Kus, Robert J. Review of *The "Sissy boy syndrome" and the Development of Homosexuality.* Richard Green. Yale University Press, 1987. *Homosexuality and the Family.* Ed. Frederick W. Bozett. New York: The Haworth Press, 1989. 187-189.

Labonté, Richard and Schimel, Lawrence, eds. *First Person Queer: Who we are (so far).* Vancouver: Arsenal Pulp Press, 2007.

Lacan, Jacques. *The Four Fundamental Concepts of Psychoanalysis.* Ed. Jacques-Alain Miller. Trans. Alan Sheridan. New York: Norton, 1998.

——. "Seminar on *The Purloined Letter.*" Trans. Jeffrey Mehlman. *Yale French Studies,* no. 48, 1972. 38-72.

Lamb, Michael E. "The Development of Father-Infant Relationships." *The Role of the Father in Child Development*. Third Edition. Ed. Michael E. Lamb. New York: John Wiley & Sons, 1997. 104-120.

———. "Fathers and Child Development: An Introductory Overview and Guide." *The Role of the Father in Child Development*. Third Edition. Ed. Michael E. Lamb. New York: John Wiley & Sons, 1997. 1-18.

Lane, Christopher. "'Living Well Is the Best Revenge': Outing, Privacy, and Psychoanalysis." *Public Sex/Gay Space*. Ed. William L. Leap. New York: Columbia University Press, 1999. 247-283.

Lane, Christopher. "Queer, Query? Identity, Opacity, and the Elaboration of Desire." Paper presented at the Queer Sites conference, University of Toronto, May 1993.

Langfeldt, Thore. "Childhood Masturbation: Individual and Social Organization." *Childhood and Sex: New Findings, New Perspectives*. Ed. Larry L. Constantine and Floyd M. Martinson. Boston: Little Brown, 1981. 63-72.

———. "Processes in Sexual Development." *Childhood and Sex: New Findings, New Perspectives*. Ed. Larry L. Constantine and Floyd M. Martinson. Boston: Little Brown, 1981. 37-44.

Lassell, Michael. "Boys Don't Do That." *Sissies and Tomboys: Gender Nonconformity and Homosexual Childhood*. Ed. Matthew Rottnek. New York: New York University Press, 1999. 245-262.

Latour, Bruno. *Pandora's Hope: Essays on the Reality of Science Studies*. Cambridge, Mass: Harvard University Press, 1999.

Laws, D. Richard. "Penile Plethysmography: Will We Ever Get It Right?" *Sexual Deviance: Issues and Controversies*. Ed. Tony Ward, D. Richard Laws, and Stephen M. Hudson. Thousand Oaks, Calif.: Sage Publications, 2003. 82-102.

Leap, William L. "Introduction." *Public Sex/Gay Space*. Ed. William L. Leap. New York: Columbia University Press, 1999. 1-21.

Lecker, Robert. *Dr. Delicious: Memoirs of a Life in CanLit*. Montreal: Véhicule Press, 2006.

Lesser, Ronnie C. "Objectivity as Masquerade." *Disorienting Sexuality: Psychoanalytic Reappraisals of Sexual Identities*. Ed. Thomas Domenici, Adrienne Harris, and Ronnie C. Lesser. New York: Routledge, 1995. 83-96.

Levinas, Emmanuel. *Entre Nous: On Thinking-of-the-Other*. Trans. Michael B. Smith and Barbara Harshav. New York: Columbia University Press, 1998.

———. *Time and the Other (and additional essays)*, Trans. Richard A. Cohen. Pittsburgh: Duquesne University Press, 1987.

Loftus, Brian. "Biopia: Bisexuality and the Crisis of Visibility in a Queer Symbolic." *RePresenting Bisexualities: Subjects and Cultures of Fluid Desire*. Ed. Donald E. Hall and Maria Pramaggiore. New York: New York University Press, 1996. 207-233.

Lurie, Susan. "Performativity in Disguise: Ideology and the Denaturalization of Identity in Theory and *The Crying Game*." *The Velvet Light Trap* 43 (1999). 51-62.

Martinson, Floyd M. "Childhood and the Institutionalization of Sexuality." *Childhood and Sex: New Findings, New Perspectives*. Ed. Larry L. Constantine and Floyd M. Martinson. Boston: Little Brown, 1981. 265-278.

———. "Eroticism in Infancy and Childhood." *Childhood and Sex: New Findings, New Perspectives*. Ed. Larry L. Constantine and Floyd M. Martinson. Boston: Little Brown, 1981. 23-35.

Marx, Karl. *The Eighteenth Brumaire of Louis Bonaparte* (1852). *Karl Marx, Frederick Engels: Collected Works*. New York: International Publishers, 1979. Vol. 11 103-197.

Masters, William H., Virginia E. Johnson and Robert C. Kolodny. *Masters and Johnson on Sex and Human Loving*. Boston: Little, Brown, 1985.

Matteson, David R. "The Heterosexually Married Gay and Lesbian Parent." *Gay and Lesbian Parents*. Ed. Fredrick W. Bozett. New York: Praeger, 1987. 138-161.

McGee, Patrick. *Cinema, Theory, and Political Responsibility in Contemporary Culture*. Cambridge: Cambridge University Press, 1997.

Mead, Margaret. *Male and Female: A Study of the Sexes in a Changing World*. New York: William Morrow, 1949.

Meyer-Bahlburg, Heino F. L., Cyrtis Dolezal, and David E. Sandberg. "The Association of Sexual Behavior with Externalizing Behaviors in a Community Sample of Prepubertal Children." *Childhood Sexuality: Normal Sexual Behavior and Development*. Ed. Theo Sandfort and Jany Rademakers. New York: Haworth Press, 2000. 67-79. [Published as *Journal of Psychology and Human Sexuality* 12.1/2 (2000)]

Midgley, Mary. "On Not Being Afraid of Natural Sex Differences." *Feminist Perspectives in Philosophy*. Ed. Morwenna Griffiths and Margaret Whitford. London: Macmillan, 1988. 29-41.

Millett, Gregorio, David Malebranche, Byron Mason, and Pilgrim Spikes, "Focusing 'Down Low': Bisexual Black Men, HIV Risk and Heterosexual Transmission." *Journal of the National Medical Association*. 97:7 (July 2005): 52S-59S.

Minter, Shannon. "Diagnosis and Treatment of Gender Identity Disorder in Children." *Sissies and Tomboys: Gender Nonconformity and Homosexual Childhood*. Ed. Matthew Rottnek. New York: New York University Press, 1999. 9-33.

Moore, Suzanne. "Getting a Bit of the Other—the Pimps of Postmodernism." *Male Order: Unwrapping Masculinity.* Ed. Jonathan Rutherford and Rowena Chapman. London: Lawrence and Wishart, 1988. 165-192.

Money, John. *Gay, Straight and In-Between: The Sexology of Erotic Orientation.* New York: Oxford University Press, 1988.

———. *Gendermaps: Social Constructionism, Feminism, and Sexosophical History.* New York: Continuum, 1995

———. *Venuses Penuses: Sexology, Sexosophy and Exigency Theory.* Amherst, NY: Prometheus Books, 1986.

———. *Unspeakable Monsters in All Our Lives.* Amherst, NY: Prometheus Books, 1999.

Morin, Jack. *Anal Pleasure & Health: A Guide for Men and Women.* San Francisco: Down There Press, 1998.

Morris, Alex. "The Cuddle Puddle of Stuyvesant High School," *New York Magazine* (Feb. 6, 2006) http://newyorkmetro.com/news/features/15589/index.html.

Morrisroe, Patricia. *Mapplethorpe: A Biography.* New York: Random House, 1995.

Muñoz, José Esteban. *Disidentifications: Queers of Color and the Performance of Politics.* Minneapolis: University of Minnesota Press, 1999.

Murphy, Peter F. *Studs, Tools and the Family Jewels: Metaphors Men Live By.* Madison: University of Wisconsin Press, 2001.

Murphy, Timothy. *Gay Ethics: Controversies in Outing, Civil Rights and Sexual Science.* New York: Haworth, 1995.

Murray, Stephen O. *Homosexualities.* Chicago, U of Chicago Press, 2000.

Nash, Catherine. "Siting Lesbians: Urban Spaces and Sexuality." *In a Queer Country: Gay & Lesbian Studies in the Canadian Context.* Ed. Terry Goldie. Vancouver: Arsenal Pulp, 2001. 235-256.

Norton, Jody. "The Boy Who Grew Up to Be a Woman." *Sissies and Tomboys: Gender Nonconformity and Homosexual Childhood.* Ed. Matthew Rottnek. New York: New York University Press, 1999. 263-273

O'Carroll, Tom. *Paedophilia: The Radical Case.* Boston: Alyson, 1982.

O'Sullivan, Lucia F., Heino F. L. Meyer-Bahlburg, and Gail Wasserman. "Reactions of Inner-City Boys and Their Mothers to Research Interviews About Sex." *Childhood Sexuality: Normal Sexual Behavior and Development.* Ed. Theo Sandfort and Jany Rademakers. New York: Haworth Press, 2000. 81-103. [Published as *Journal of Psychology and Human Sexuality* 12.1/2 (2000)]

Pateman, Carole. *The Sexual Contract*. Cambridge: Polity Press, 1988.

Patterson, Charlotte J. and Raymond W. Chan. "Gay Fathers." *The Role of the Father in Child Development*. Third Edition. Ed. Michael E. Lamb. New York: John Wiley & Sons, 1997. 245-260.

Paz, Octavio. *Conjunctions and Disjunctions*. Trans. Helen R. Lane. New York: Viking, 1974. [Originally *Conjunciones y Disjunciones* (1969).]

Persky, Stan. *Buddy's: Meditations on Desire*. Vancouver: New Star Books, 1989.

Pile, Steve. *The Body and the City: Psychoanalytic Spaces and Subjectivity*. London: Routledge, 1996.

Pleak, Richard R. "Ethical Issues in Diagnosing and Treating Gender-Dysphoric Children and Adolescents." *Sissies and Tomboys: Gender Nonconformity and Homosexual Childhood*. Ed. Matthew Rottnek. New York: New York University Press, 1999. 34-51.

Pleck, Elizabeth H. and Joseph H. "Fatherhood Ideals in the United States: Historical Dimensions." *The Role of the Father in Child Development*. Third Edition. Ed. Michael E. Lamb. New York: John Wiley & Sons, 1997. 33-48.

Possover, M., J. Drahonowski, et al. "Laparoscopic-Assisted Formation of a Colon Neovagina," *Surgical Endoscopy* (2001) 15(6): 623.

Pramaggiore, Maria. "BI-ntroduction I: Epistemologies of the Fence." *RePresenting Bisexualities: Subjects and Cultures of Fluid Desire*. Ed. Donald E. Hall and Maria Pramaggiore. New York: New York University Press, 1996. 1-7.

Probyn, Elspeth. *Outside Belongings*. New York: Routledge, 1996.

Prosser, Jay. *Second Skins: The Body Narratives of Transsexuality*. New York: Columbia University Press, 1998.

———. "Transsexuals and the Transsexologists: Inversion and the Emergence of Transsexual Subjectivity." *Sexology in Culture: Labeling Bodies and Desires*. Ed. Lucy Bland and Laura Doan. Chicago: University of Chicago Press, 1999. 116-131.

Raglan-Sullivan, Ellie. *Jacques Lacan and the Philosophy of Psychoanalysis*. Urbana: University of Illinois, 1987.

Raymond, Janice. *The Transsexual Empire: The Making of the She-Male*. New York: Teachers College Press, 1994. [originally Beacon Press, 1979.]

Rechy, John. *The Sexual Outlaw: A Documentary*. New York: Grove, 1977.

Reid-Pharr, Robert. *Black Gay Man: Essays*. New York: New York University Press, 2001.

Reik, Theodor. *Of Love and Lust: On the Psychoanalysis of Romantic and Sexual Emotions.* New York: Jason Aronson, 1974.

Rogers, J. "Testing For and the Role of Anal and Rectal Sensation." *Baillieres Clinical Gastroenterology* (1992) 6(1): 179-91.

Rorty, Richard. *Essays on Heidegger and Others.* Cambridge: Cambridge University Press, 1991.

Ross, Michael W. "Married Homosexual Men: Prevalence and Background." *Homosexuality and Family Relations.* Ed. Frederick W. Bozett and Marvin B. Sussman. New York: Haworth Press, 1989. 35-57.

Rosser, B.R., B.J. Short, et al. "Anodyspareunia, the Unacknowledged Sexual Dysfunction: a Validation Study of Painful Receptive Anal Intercourse and its Psychosexual Concomitants in homosexual men." *Journal of Sex & Marital Therapy* (1998) 24(4): 281-92.

Rotello, Gabriel. *Sexual Ecology: AIDS and the Destiny of Gay Men.* New York: Dutton, 1997.

Sachs, Benjamin. "Contextual Approaches to the Physiology and Classification of Erectile Function, Erectile Dysfunction and Sexual Arousal." *Neuroscience and Behavioral Reviews* 24 (2000). 541-560.

Sadownick, Douglas. *Sex Between Men: An Intimate History of the Sex Lives of Gay Men Postwar to Present.* San Francisco: HarperSanFrancisco, 1996.

Sandfort, Theo. *Boys on Their Contacts with Men: A Study of Sexually Expressed Friendships.* Elmhurst, NY: Global Academic Publishers, 1987.

Sandfort, Theo G.M. and Peggy T. Cohen-Kettenis. "Sexual Behavior in Dutch and Belgian Children as Observed by Their Mothers." *Childhood Sexuality: Normal Sexual Behavior and Development.* Ed. Theo Sandfort and Jany Rademakers. New York: Haworth Press, 2000, 105-115. [Published as *Journal of Psychology and Human Sexuality* 12.1/2 (2000).]

Savage, Dan. "How to use 'Santorum' in a Sentence." *The Village Voice.* (July 2-8, 2003).

Savin-Williams, Ritch C. "Gay and Lesbian Adolescents." *Homosexuality and Family Relations.* Ed. Frederick W. Bozett and Marvin B. Sussman. New York: Haworth Press, 1989. 197-216.

Sawday, Jonathan. *The Body Emblazoned: Dissection and the Human Body in Renaissance Culture.* London: Routledge, 1995.

Scheman, Naomi. "Queering the Center by Centering the Queer: Reflections on Transsexuals and Secular Jews." *Sissies and Tomboys: Gender Nonconformity and Homosexual Childhood.* Ed. Matthew Rottnek. New York: New York University Press, 1999. 58-103

Schwartz, David. "Current Psychoanalytic Discourses on Sexuality: Tripping Over the Body." *Disorienting Sexuality: Psychoanalytic Reappraisals of Sexual Identities.* Ed. Thomas Domenici, Ronnie C. Lesser, and Adrienne Harris. New York: Routledge, 1995. 115-126.

Schwartz, Joel. *The Sexual Politics of Jean-Jacques Rousseau.* Chicago: University of Chicago Press, 1984.

Sedgwick, Eve Kosofsky. "How to Bring Your Kids Up Gay." *Fear of a Queer Planet: Queer Politics and Social Theory.* Ed. Michael Warner. Minneapolis: University of Minnesota Press, 1993. 69-81.

———. *Epistemology of the Closet.* Berkeley: University of California Press, 1991.

Seidman, Steven. *Difference Troubles: Queering Social Theory and Sexual Politics.* Cambridge: Cambridge University Press, 1997.

Seward, Rudy Ray. "Determinants of Family Culture: Effects on Fatherhood." *Fatherhood and Families in Cultural Context.* Ed. Frederick W. Bozett and Shirley M.H. Hanson. New York: Springer Publishing, 1991. 218-236.

Shapin, Steve. *A Social History of Truth: Civility and Science in Seventeenth-Century England.* Chicago: University of Chicago Press, 1994.

Showalter, Elaine. "Critical Cross-Dressing: Male Feminists and the Woman of the Year." *Men in Feminism.* Ed. Alice Jardine and Paul Smith. New York: Methuen, 1987. 116.

Silverman, Michael I. "Men With Older Brothers More Likely to be Gay: Study Points to Biological Origins of Homosexuality." *ABC News* (June 26, 2006) http://abcnews.go.com/Health/story?id=2120218&page=1.

Somerville, Siobhan B. "Scientific Racism and the Invention of the Homosexual Body." *Sexology in Culture: Labeling Bodies and Desires.* Ed. Lucy Bland and Laura Doan. Chicago: University of Chicago Press, 1998. 60-76.

Stallybrass, Peter and Allon White. *The Politics and Poetics of Transgression.* London: Methuen, 1986.

Stearns, Peter N. "Fatherhood in Historical Perspective: The Role of Social Change." *Fatherhood and Families in Cultural Context.* Ed. Frederick W. Bozett and Shirley M.H. Hanson. New York: Springer Publishing, 1991. 28-52.

Stein, Edward. *The Mismeasure of Desire: The Science, Theory, and Ethics of Sexual Orientation.* New York: Oxford University Press, 1999.

Stokes, Joseph P., Will Damon and David J. McKirnan. "Predictors of Movement Toward Homosexuality: A Longitudinal Study of Bisexual Men." *Journal of Sex Research* 34:34 (1997. 304-312.

Stoller, Robert J. *Sexual Excitement: Dynamics of Erotic Life.* New York: Pantheon, 1979.

Stratton, Jon. *The Desirable Body: Cultural Fetishism and the Erotics of Consumption.* Urbana: University of Illinois, 2001.

Sullivan, Andrew. "Not Dead Yet: An Apology" *The Advocate* (July 5, 2005).

Summit, Roland and JoAnn Kryso. "Sexual Abuse of Children: A Clinical Spectrum." *Childhood and Sex: New Findings, New Perspectives.* Ed. Larry L. Constantine and Floyd M. Martinson. Boston: Little Brown, 1981. 111-127.

Tattleman, Ira. "Speaking to the Gay Bathhouse: Communicating in Sexually Charged Spaces." *Public Sex/Gay Space.* Ed. William L. Leap. New York: Columbia University Press, 1999. 71-94.

Thomas, Calvin. *Male Matters: Masculinity, Anxiety, and the Male Body on the Line.* Urbana: University of Illinois Press, 1996.

———, ed. *Straight with a Twist: Queer Theory and the Subject of Heterosexuality.* Urbana: University of Illinois Press, 2000.

Treichler, Paula A. *How to Have Theory in an Epidemic: Cultural Chronicles of AIDS.* Durham: Duke University Press, 1999.

Ucko, Peter J. "Penis Sheaths: A Comparative Study." *Proceedings of the Royal Anthropological Institute of Great Britain and Ireland.* No 1969 (1969). 24A-67.

Underwood, Steven G. *Gay Men and Anal Eroticism: Tops, Bottoms and Versatiles.* New York: Harrington Park Press, 2003.

Valverde, Mariana. *Sex, Power and Pleasure.* Toronto: Women's Press, 1985.

Van Leer, David. *The Queening of America: Gay Culture in Straight Society.* New York: Routledge, 1995.

Walters, Lynday Henley and Steven F. Chapman. "Changes in Legal Views of Parenthood: Implications for Fathers in Minority Cultures." *Fatherhood and Families in Cultural Context.* Ed. Frederick W. Bozett and Shirley M.H. Hanson. New York: Springer Publishing, 1991. 83-113.

Warner, Michael. *Publics and Counterpublics.* New York: Zone Books, 2002.

———. *The Trouble with Normal: Sex, Politics, and the Ethics of Queer Life*. New York: Free Press, 1999.

Warner, Sylvia Townsend. *T.H. White: A Biography*. London: Jonathan Cape with Chatto & Windus, 1967.

Weeks, Jeffrey. *Sexuality and its Discontents: Meanings, Myths & Modern Sexualities*. New York: Routledge and Kegan Paul, 1985.

Weinberg, Martin S., Colin J. Williams and Douglas W. Pryor. *Dual Attraction: Understanding Bisexuality*. New York: Oxford University Press, 1994.

Williams, Craig A. *Roman Homosexuality: Ideologies of Masculinity in Classical Antiquity*. Oxford: Oxford University Press, 1999.

Williams, Linda. *Hard Core: Power, Pleasure, and the 'Frenzy of the Visible.'* Berkeley: University of California Press, 1989.

Wilson, Elizabeth. "Is Transgression Transgressive?" *Activating Theory: Lesbian, Gay, Bisexual Politics*. Ed. Joseph Bristow and Anglia R. Wilson. London: Lawrence & Wishart, 1994. 107-117.

Wittig, Monique. "The Point of View: Universal or Particular," *Feminist Issues* 5, no. 2 (1983), 62-69.

Wyly, James. *The Phallic Quest: Priapus and Masculine Inflation*. Toronto: Inner City Books, 1989.

Young, Allen. "On Human Identity and Gay Identity: A Liberationist Dilemma." *After You're Out: Personal Experiences of Gay Men and Lesbian Women*. Ed. Karla Jay and Allen Young. New York: Links, 1975. 27-34.

Žižek, Slavoj. *The Sublime Object of Ideology*. London: Verso, 1989.

———. "The Seven Veils of Fantasy." *Key Concepts of Lacanian Psychoanalysis*. Ed. Dany Nobus. New York: Other Press, 1999. 190-218.

**Terry Goldie** is the author of two previous nonfiction
books, and the editor of the anthology *In a Queer Country*
(Arsenal Pulp Press). He is a professor of English at
York University in Toronto, where he teaches Canadian
and postcolonial literature with particular interest in
gay studies and literary theory.